Blood
Orchid

Blood
Orchid

An Unnatural History
of America

Charles Bowden

Random House
New York

Grateful acknowledgment is made to the following for permission
to reprint previously published material:
FARRAR, STRAUS & GIROUX, INC., AND FABER AND FABER, LTD.:
Excerpts from *Nunca Mas: The Report of the Argentine National Commision
on the Disappeared*. Translation copyright © 1986 by Writers and Scholars
International, Ltd. Reprinted by permission of Farrar, Straus & Giroux, Inc.,
and Faber and Faber, Ltd.
IRVING MUSIC, INC.: Excerpt from "Joy to the World" by Hoyt Axton.
Copyright © 1970 by Irving Music, Inc. All rights reserved. International
copyright secured. Reprinted by permission of Irving Music, Inc.
MARY MCGRORY: Excerpts from a Mary McGrory column from
August 3, 1971. Reprinted by permission of Mary McGrory.

Library of Congress Cataloging-in-Publication Data
Bowden, Charles.
Blood orchid: an unnatural history of America/Charles Bowden.—1st ed.
p. cm.
Includes bibliographical references.
ISBN 0-679-43336-8
1. West (U.S.)—Description and travel. 2. Natural history—West (U.S.)
I. Title.
F595.3.B69 1995
978—dc20 94-33306

Manufactured in the United States of America

24689753

First Edition

Book design by Deborah Kerner

It was the time of the preacher
In the year of '01
And just when you think it's all over
It's only begun.
—WILLIE NELSON

For the QUICK. And the DEAD.
And all the lovers of this good and lusty earth.
And the whore with the blue teeth and the lucky coins,
a woman who didn't let the orchids get her down.

Mine heritage *is* unto me *as* a speckled bird, the birds round about *are* against her; come ye, assemble all the beasts of the field, come to devour.

—*Jeremiah, 12:9*

Gold is a wonderful thing! Whoever owns it is lord of all he wants. With gold it is even possible to open for souls the way to paradise!

—*Christopher Columbus, 1503*

At what point shall we expect the approach of danger? By what means shall we fortify against it? Shall we expect some transatlantic military giant, to step the Ocean, and crush us at a blow? Never! All the armies of Europe, Asia and Africa combined, with all the treasury of the earth . . . could not by force, take a drink from the Ohio, or make a track on the Blue Ridge, in a trial of a thousand years. . . . If destruction be our lot, we must ourselves be its author and finisher. As a nation of freemen, we must live through all time, or die by suicide.

—*Abraham Lincoln, 1838*

In living one swims through seas strewn with wrecks, where none go undamaged. It is as bad as going to Congress: none comes back innocent.

—*Ralph Waldo Emerson*

Gold was discovered there, a railroad is built, and the beautiful forests are being swept away, and the virgin lakes & streams robbed of their trout and I am forced to choose this great city, for the final act of my drama and life. I feel like apologizing but on the whole it is the best I can do.

—*General William Tecumseh Sherman, 1888,*
explaining why he retired to New York City
instead of Coeur d'Alene, Idaho

And I say it for myself: the moment I get on one of those sidewalks, I start to fall down.

—*Emiliano Zapata, December 4, 1912*

I shall try to make plain the bloodiness of killing. Too often this has been slurred over. . . .

—*John Baker, 1967*

Phoenix is Thunderbird, Billings muscatel, L.A. white port and tokay ("all the way with tokay"), Seattle Apple Andy, around the reservations muscatel ("mustn't tell").

—*Robert Sundance, 1992, on the*
favorite booze of skid rows in various
western towns

how it came to pass

I am not of sound mind. I cannot seem to stop moving—as I write this I have clocked 7,000 miles by truck in the last thirty days and I am hunkered in a motel room high in the Rocky Mountains and yet no nearer to God. I seek roots, just so long as they can accommodate themselves to around seventy-five miles an hour and no unseemly whining about rest stops or sit-down dinners. I am, I suspect, a basic American, a perpetual violation that loves the land and cannot kick the addiction of velocity. A person fated never to settle yet always seeking the place to settle. Like cocaine-powered athletes, lying presidents, Miss America, and the Internal Revenue Service, I am not a role model. And I am always hungry.

I can only make a stab at writing the truth if I tell others it is fiction—that way nobody gets too upset with me. I can only get started writing if I think it is music—that way I beat back my own cowardice.

I can only write if I don't think at all.

I have changed names and locations at times to protect the guilty. But everything happened as it is reported in this book, including the things scheduled for tomorrow or the day after that.

a walk in the garden

I was always a lover despite the killings and I don't care what anyone says. When I was a boy in a Chicago apartment I wanted to be a farmer—never a cop, never a soldier, never president, always a farmer. I craved to put my hands into the soil and to make things grow. My parents, who had escaped brutal rural poverty, used to shake their heads over my demented ambition. I wound up teaching in a university and when I could not abide this crime against feeling, I wandered into a terrain I still lack a word for. They call it the street but often there is no pavement or any straight lines. But in my heart, I'm still a farmer looking for that good ground where I can make things grow.

I've just finished this book you are holding and I have fled from the work of it and the world of it. I am standing in the courtyard of a sacked hacienda in southern Chihuahua. I am but a few miles from the rancho where Pancho Villa retired after his years of steady killing. He also said he just wanted to farm. The ruined hacienda was built like a fort with a big gate, stout walls, its own granaries, stables, and living quarters, a private chapel safe and sacred within its bowels. No one who lived here ever thought any force could touch its brooding power. Now the roofs have caved in, the rains lick the adobes each year and crumble the soft bricks leaving fabriclike tears in the ramparts. Pigeons roost and shit in the family's former salon. Between 1910 and 1920, haciendas just like this one were gutted all over Mexico and left to die like flopping fish trapped and doomed by a receding flood. They did not see it coming; we never do.

In the center of the courtyard is a stone monument. Once it was topped by an obelisk but someone has smashed the top off and it now lies in the weeds at the base. The inscription is simple: a man's name, his birth date in 1897, his death date in April of 1919, and then a single phrase: CAYO EN LA DEFENSA DE ORDEN. He fell in the defense of order. And he fell just a few days shy of his twenty-second birthday. The world he died defending, a system of huge landholdings, big houses, feudal habits, and mass poverty, was one that had persisted for four hundred years or more. So, quite naturally, he probably thought it would last forever.

I was raised with the same sense of certainty, pride, and passion. My world was based on patriotism, hard work, and love of the land and the flag. I went to church. I never imagined being out of step with my government, my neighbors, or much else. I remember when in the twilight of the Eisenhower years Francis Gary Powers was shot down in his U-2 over the Soviet Union and my government denied that they had been flying spy missions and I believed them absolutely. I was young and foolish, no doubt, but it never occurred to me that my government would lie to me about such a weighty matter. I would like to say that I have changed a great deal since that time but I don't think I have. I am more a scorned lover than a bitter enemy. True, I no longer trust my government, nor any concentration of power, but I still at some level safe from my darkest thoughts believe in the promise of life and especially the promise of life on my native ground.

Which brings me back to the book I have fled, the one I left, as the Mexicans say, *en otro lado,* on the other side. It is my inquiry into what went wrong with my life, my country, and my times. It is a historical work without a footnote, a logical inquiry safe from expository sentences. I did not plan to write it and now that it is in type, I do not really know where it came from. Even the mind of someone who wants to be a farmer is subject to storms. When I was a boy one summer on my uncle's farm, I felt the lust of the July corn and come morning saw it all a dead, green mash from a wall of hail that had swept off the plains. I could tick off all the decisions I made while writing this book but they are really of no matter, save one: I thought it was better to feel what I saw than to weigh and measure and give number to the ferocity of this storm. What is explained can be denied but what is felt cannot be forgotten.

A couple of months ago, while I was deep in the psychosis of writing this book, a friend who had no idea what I was up to, gave me a favorite quotation that ran, "A person's life purpose is nothing more than to rediscover, through the detours of art, or love, or passionate work, those one or two images in the presence of which his heart first opened." Albert Camus wrote that and I believe every word of it. So I went into a strange garden of bloody orchids looking for the hopes that started my life.

And now, I am in this ruined hacienda staring at a memorial to another child of this era of blood and love. Last night, I was in a fancy hotel bar in Hidalgo del Parral, a city of about eighty thousand near the Durango border where Pancho Villa was cut down by assassins July 20, 1923—twenty-two years before my birth. There are few memorials to Villa in his favorite stomping ground of Chihuahua and almost none in the rest of Mexico. He is a man people seem almost afraid to remember. We actually think we get to judge him and decide who he was and whether he was as worthy as we are—tell me now your judgment of a rain forest, a blue whale, a hurricane. So, when I started talking to a table full of prosperous ranchers and businessmen in the bar, I asked them what people today thought of General Francisco Villa. One guy said, "Well, on the one hand, he took money from the rich and gave it to the poor and so some people still think he was okay. On the other hand, he used to bury people in anthills and pour marmalade on their heads." I was struck by the image of Pancho crossing the desert, his saddle bags stuffed with preserves, his bandolier heavy with jellies.

We will probably never find the real Pancho Villa smothered under our lies and myths. (How many people know he did not drink and never smoked and believed he was unfit to be the ruler of Mexico?) But we do know he tried to make a revolution and that when he died, he was trying to forge a communitarian community. And he liked the ladies, lots of the ladies. I suspect he died an optimist, thinking a better world was just over the next hill or year or battle. The boy who died defending his hacienda and order and a world of brutal slavery four hundred years stale probably lacked Villa hopes for a better day. That is why his ancestral hacienda is now a ruin and Villa is still so alive out there in llanos and sierras and desiertos that people fear to mention his name—even though the name he is remembered by was an alias.

I am an optimist myself, despite all the killings and the desert springs with bad water. I wrote this book because I had a simple, straightforward idea—we've been in a long war and we've lost that war and the war has poisoned us and our ground. If we admit these facts, we might be able to survive. If we don't, it really won't matter if we survive because we will be functionally dead. Pick up any newspaper, our obituary is everywhere on the pages. I am a member of the last generation that will ever confuse the idea of progress with the accumulation of more and more material things. I may be of the last generation that will be able to say the word *progress* without a tone of mockery.

Now I dream of the soft touch of women, the songs of birds, the smell of soil crumbling between my fingers, and the brilliant green of plants that I diligently nurture. I am looking for land to buy and I will sow it with deer and wild pigs and birds and cottonwoods and sycamores and build a pond and the ducks will come and fish will rise in the early evening light and take the insects into their jaws. There will be paths through this forest and you and I will lose ourselves in the soft curves and folds of the ground. We will come to the water's edge and lie on the grass and there will be a small, unobtrusive sign that says, THIS IS THE REAL WORLD, MUCHACHOS, AND WE ARE ALL IN IT.—B. TRAVEN. I am not making this up, it will all really happen, it is already happening. Like Villa, I just want to be a farmer. I suspect almost everyone does—Abraham Lincoln with the blood of half a million dripping from his big hands, Sylvia Plath with her head in the oven, both dreaming of the farm.

I don't know what to make of myself. A lot of the time, despite my deepest hungers and best efforts, I see blackness. But I am planting a young oak tree. I really am. It'll be here centuries after I'm gone. Assuming I choose to leave.

Blood
Orchid

T*hey will do anything to reproduce. And they will use the needs of others, the deep appetites they see in all our faces, they will exploit these things to further their own ends. They will take over our ways of loving, they will seize upon our sense of property. They will ruthlessly read our diaries, our secret thoughts, and then make us slaves to our own obsessions.*

Perhaps no clearer example exists than the tactics of the hammer orchid (Drakaea fitzgeraldii) *and its scheme to seduce one particular type of wasp (of the family Thynnidae). Thynnids fall into the trap once they gaze upon the labellum of a hammer orchid.**

---

*The material in this book on the natural history of hammer orchids is derived from Bastiaan Meeuse and Sean Morris, *The Sex Life of Flowers* (New York: Facts On File, 1984), Chapter 5, "The 'Unacceptable' Face of Evolution."

1

They appeared at the time the buffalo went down in the bitter dust with their dark tongues lashing out obscenely for one more taste of the raw, clean breeze in the cold light of morning. Then the black flies soon settled—our hands moving constantly to flick their swollen bodies off our faces, the buzzing crowding our ears—and we went to our knives and had at the hump, the tongue, and the sweet organs. We did not think of what was happening then, we were too happy with the raw liver smeared against our lips to worry about the vanishing hoofprints etched in the light powder and pointing to a country where we could not follow. The blood orchids that came at that time were true to their kind, forms that did not seem to live off the land but instead were sustained by outside forces we could not see and have never understood. Their roots ran down the rough bark of our lives and drank our water, their leaves thrust out into the air of our lives and sucked up all the oxygen and soon our lungs collapsed. The flowers . . . I will get to the flowers in a moment.

(It's afternoon, a storm is whipping off the Rockies onto

*the high plains. The rains, they have not come, so we are
hungry for their fury. The Rocky Flats Arsenal is sizzling a
few miles away, the last refuge for native plants on the entire
Front Range. I am reconnoitering the Flats, and the place
looks as peaceful as a dairy farm. Once they built plutonium
triggers here—imagine that six-shooter, podner—and still
have eleven tons of the stuff stacked up with nowhere for it
to go. The Russkis chickened out, you know, and now refuse delivery. And here we were going to ship it Air Express.
There's a nifty little model shop buried in Rocky Flats where
they made gifts for visiting physicists—lead-lined jockstraps.
Size please, Herr Doktor? God is Lenny Bruce, yes, She is!
I am tired but I will not rest. The orchids never rest, not one
second. They are relentless because they feed on us. But they
have more will, are stronger, can go the distance. I will try
again. I know I must do better. But it is lonely out here. And
besides if I am not careful they will put me in the crazy
place. Or drug me. To be fair, the drugs have gotten quite
good, excellent really. On the street the heroin is so solid
that folks have taken to snorting it rather than shooting up.
The coke is a powder so white the Aryan Brotherhood is
said to be in awe of its purity. And the marijuana now has
a THC factor equal to the lift load of a moon shot. So don't
you believe people when they make blanket statements
denouncing technology, no siree!! The doctors, bless them,
hand out pills like candy to keep strange thoughts from our
minds. I am certain these fine chemicals are working. More
people in this country are wrestling with dim memories of
incest than with blood orchids—a fact. So I must not take
cheap shots at the drugs, especially the legal ones that never
make anyone happy but do at least dim the lights. Pretty
soon, there will just be me and the Prozac eaters.)*

It all happened so very fast, although it took a long

time for the roots like snakes to dig into our lives and take our measure and find us wanting. The long caval-cade of buffalo, dark forms swinging into the sun and going over one hill too many, and then the bones white on the ground, skulls formed in a circle like a last prayer, the medicine wheel and yet the patient seemed to keep dying . . . the towns springing up with the smell of raw lumber, the streets annoyingly straight, the young whores with colors on their faces and a weariness in their ancient eyes as they peered out the frosted panes at the stillness of a winter night, the snows, big, crippling snows, choking the passes, whipping our faces on the plains and winter-kill elk lying among the aspen with their legs stuck up like saplings toward the steel sky . . . the purr of the elec-tric train at the Black Mesa and the pleasure in firing clip after clip into its robot soul *(pen an essay: call it some-thing about mountains and the correct thinking, all of it in that vogue mode, pensive, the voice alto contralto)*, the lips gleaming as she leans across the hard wooden table, her large breasts sagging and fumes of whiskey pour off her invitation face *(the red-faced warbler at the lip of the spring, poor thing will never make a calendar page: not enough flash, you know. Bye, bye, birdie)*. Drunken Indi-ans sleeping like ghosts in the alley—careful where you step! Sundance is raving through the night as his body eats his body *(the white medicine men call this condition cancer: Sundance and I never say this word out loud)* and I go downstairs in the purring elevator and the casino is nothing but whirs and bells and the click of bones on the green felt as we struggle to win what we always lose again anyway. His grandmothers wielded scalping knives at Little Bighorn *(Custer, bless his soul, scribbling that message: "Come on. Big Village. Be Quick. Bring packs.*

Hurry."), they saw the arrival of the blood orchids, Sundance gets to be part of the ending. *(Big interesting clouds rising again and again, like giant mushrooms, they say, and everyone looks up out of pride and patriotism and envy)....*

Fine sepia-toned photographs hang on the walls as I softly pad down the hallway on Two Gray Hills Navajo rugs and out the corner of my eye photographs of Jackson Hole, the Sierra Nevada, unnamed peaks slide by looking just the way they are said to have looked one fine day a century ago when the earth seemed fresh and the blood orchids were a rumor and a very small one at that....

(Okay, I'll calm down. No need for the jacket and the two dull-witted attendants. I was born two or three weeks before Hiroshima and I believed. Hell, I still believe in one sense: I'm not confident I would have made a better decision than they did. Here, I'll show you with a quote from the official report on the genesis of just one orchid, the atomic bomb: "created not by the devilish inspiration of some warped genius but by the arduous labor of thousands of normal men and women working for the safety of their country." But I know. It has played out. I know. And this has to matter or it really all has been for nothing. I know. You know. We know.)

The roots getting thicker by the year, at first fine lines like lace on the bark of our lives, the skin of our life, the hopes of our life, and then coarsening as more and more wealth and power and energy surges through and at first the roots begin to look like snakes, then like cables and later like giant aqueducts, the hidden heart pounding to the beat of explosives, this massive web becomes fat and arrogant and when the ax sinks in there is nothing but

blood, geysers of blood, thick, sticky, virulent. CAU-
TION: Do not dab it against your tongue. The lab report
is never returned to us, we can only guess. But clearly bad
blood.

The bloom is more fearsome. The flower huge and it is
artfully constructed so that we see what we wish to
see—a woman lush and lying on silk with her legs spread
and that beckoning smile on her smooth face, the hair is
black, the hair is blond, the hair is long and a tassel
caresses a nipple, the hair is short, the skull is shaved and
oiled, whatever we wish: or the man is armed, grim looking, a carbine in his hand, blue clothes, olive-drab
clothes, mottled clothes of camouflage, he sings "She
Wore a Yellow Ribbon," he sings. "Over There," he sings
"Lili Marlene," he sings "Purple Haze," and smoke curls
from his Springfield as he lights up his pipe and the
smoke curls from his M-16 as he lights up that joint and
beckons, beckons and we go with Ahab and feel the cold
skin and sharp barnacles of that big white whale that
swims forever in the book none of us can ever seem to
finish *(ah, the shame, the shame we bear over the classics)*
and the blood orchids in flower can never be resisted, the
allure of the colors, the narcotic effect of the pollen, the
giant size of the bloom, the power of the growth with
rank green leaves shooting up and blocking the very sun
from our eyes and the thing comes from nowhere and
seems to bring everything with it, a complete self-
contained organism, and when it does not flower, it simply clones itself and replicates like a berserk cell in a petri
dish and blood orchids appear everywhere. And then the
water goes bad or goes away and the air goes bad and
will not move and the earth, the very dirt, mutinies with
odd chemicals from some alchemy we cannot compre-

hend, and the game beats away and forsakes us. And still we get no reports, they are kept a secret from us. For our own good. And the worse thing—we seldom will say this, even to ourselves, no, no, almost never will we say this—is that we become dependent on these blooms, on these huge plants, on the enormity of them and we turn our eyes toward the blood orchids and away from the land and we will say this is necessary, *essential*. We dress for success. Our women fall in love with the blue clothes, the olive clothes, the mottled clothes and eventually they demand to wear them also. Our children love everything about the orchids and soon they play with miniature versions and invent games around this new culture in our midst.

Bang! You're dead!

We get regular weather reports—it is hot, it is cold—and then suddenly for five years it is very hot and then for the best part of four decades it is cold, endlessly, bone-chilling cold, and yet the orchids thrive and prosper. They seem immune to what makes us sweat, to what makes us shiver. And suddenly the weather breaks—snap! just like that—and our entire garden seems altered. There is word—whispered at first, then said out loud—that the orchids are ill, that they are dying, or simply that their time is over, a finished thing, and we cannot face these reports and a great fear fills our bodies and we worry about the orchids. We glance back over our shoulders at the land and what we see makes us fear even more and our stomachs tighten and our bowels go loose . . . for the soil is bubbling and burning, the waters come off the mountains like lava, the snows blister our fingers if we touch the searing flakes, the trees yellow and sicken and forget to flower, the buffalo cannot be seen *(they say they*

*are hiding, they say they will never come back to us, they
say . . .),* the fish float past our blinking eyes and they are
belly-up with a sweet stench rising off them, the skies are
empty of birds and dead clots of feathers lie at our feet,
and many die of strange diseases, and we grow afraid to
touch each other, we fight our instincts, we do not trust
the food in the kettle, we fear the woman lying wet by
our side, we see the man smiling in the bar as a death
threat, and the big blooms keep beckoning, the colors
intense, the scent of the flower overwhelming to our frail
senses and we do what we have become and we do what
little we still know how to do and we mount the flower
where she waits and we fuck and we fuck and we fuck
. . . fuck . . . fuck. . . .

*(Once, I knew a woman with tattoos. The serpents and
flowers scrolling across her body were part of her secret self
and they could not be seen or even guessed when she was
clothed. She dressed very well in expensive sweaters and
skirts because her work was professional and demanded
such costumes. She had a very nice smile and a wonderful
wit and could not speak without an emphasis that implied
exclamation points, and yet this last fact did not annoy me.
Her diet was very careful, she kept a keen eye for all threats
to her body be they chemicals or fats or forms of flesh that
clogged arteries and stilled the heart. She liked to ride
motorcycles and served meals on expensive black china. But
she did not do this often since, like so many interesting
women of my time, she resented the act of cooking. She
wrote notes using purple ink and cut things out and glued
them on each page. She did not wish to have children either,
and this, like the hostility to cooking, was not unusual. I am
used to knowing women who are survivors of some dark
time I will never know or imagine.*

*Her ex-husband once tried to kill her. He chased her
through the house waving a shotgun. He had often beaten
her but the shotgun was a new tactic and this moment permanently terrified her. She changed states, jobs, for all I
know, even her name, in order to distance herself from the
night when she faced the possibility of being murdered. She
also never trusted her heart again. This also is not unusual.
She had grown very adjusted to being maimed in this area.*

*If I mentioned the orchids, she scorned me, just cut me
dead. You see, she wanted to be happy.)*

The blood orchids remain to be dealt with, the roots
thick, the blood sticky.

But lower your voice, do not repeat this. It is dangerous
talk. The cold spell is over, this is admitted, however
grudgingly. The time of the blood orchids may be passing.
But bend your head, we must whisper. . . . We shall overcome, all we are saying is give peace a chance, Johnny
came marching home again, make love not war, old soldiers never die, never, never die. Make the world safe
for . . . They are handing out condoms in the garden, they
say it will be all right.

The word is out: We Have Won. Time to savor the victory. Walk the metes and bounds of our ground. Careful,
don't trip over those huge roots, watch yourself by the
flower. They predict a spring this year for the first time in
decades. But they warn us it will not be easy . . . because
of our habit, our jones. Something is happening but
you. . . . They say the blood orchids cannot be removed.
They say we have grown dependent upon them. And if
we ask a question they drown us out with bugles.

We have won.

Now enjoy, my child.

(It is 1527 and Wayna Ahapaq, the head of the Inca

empire, takes his rest in Quito. He has just swallowed Ecuador and pauses before chomping on a chunk of Colombia. He is around fifty, fit as a fiddle, and two Spanish captives are being hauled over his empire's 14,000 miles of paved road for his personal examination. He must wonder, just who are these ugly pale guys? He never finds out. Smallpox beats the Spaniards to his door and in a month or two or three about half of his twenty million subjects die. And Wayna Ahapaq is one of the newly minted dead folks. Having lived in that splendid isolation called the Western Hemisphere, he and his fellow citizens have no immunity—and at the moment he falls about one out of every five human beings on earth is what the newcomers decide to call Indians. Biological warfare, an early test case. A few years later, Francisco Pizarro hops ashore with a few desperadoes and some horses and finishes the job we now call the conquest. Toward the end of the sixteenth century, an Indian noble named Pachakuti Yamki tries to make sense out of this rather dark moment. In his account, he has Wayna Ahapaq busy issuing new laws and taxes as he slumbers at Quito with his war machine at idle. Then the news comes to him that a plague has broken out at the capital, Cuzco. At midnight Wayna Ahapaq turns his face toward the sea and looks upon a million people whom he does not know. And he realizes they are the living souls about to die. And then the next day at dinner time a messenger arrives wearing a black cloak. He kisses the ruler and gives him a small locked box and a key. The boss man tells the messenger to open the box, but the visitor says, nope, he can't do that, the Creator has ordered that only Wayna Ahapaq has that responsibility. When Wayna Ahapaq turns the key and lifts the lid things flutter out like butterflies. Within two days, his chief general is dead, along with many of the best officers. The Inca understands. He orders a stone house built, enters it and dies. I like this story because Wayna Ahapaq has his vision of a million living souls, takes the key, and opens the box. He refuses to be a victim, he assumes responsibility. True, he dies. But he refuses to be a victim, and victims can never fix anything because they cannot fight. And of course, the game is not yet over. Most of the people in Peru still speak the language of the Inca, and the ground is not yet safe for those who feel that they conquered it, blood is flowing from a Shining Path. For centuries, many people have faced manifestations of the blood orchids, they have seen strange clouds, felt something seize their bodies they did not fully understand, died painful and surprising deaths. Felt the heel on their necks. And not given in or up. I am not so crazy as I may seem. I have a lineage and I can hear it whispering in my ear. True, I lack a vision of Eden or a belief in such a place. But I have an unending appetite for personal power, for the right to decide my fate. And this sets me at odds with my government, my time, and what all of us have decided is our place—stand over there and wait until your number is called.)

Ah, but there is so much to mention. There is this huge inventory to go over. We must make sure all the china remains, that no linen has been stolen, that our house is in order. Let us begin: The whale dives, sounding deep but never surfaces. Then there are the pockmarked hills where God buried bodies we call ore, the toxic rivers, the strangled rivers, the clean, scientifically leveled fields gleaming with white salts and gone sterile as mules, mountains of empty bottles of Mad Dog 20/20, the holes punched for oil, the roar over our heads as the new silver birds fly by, the waters no one will ever drink again from the Río Puerco *(such a name)*, the best movie of all—

"Apocalypse Then, Now & Forever." Twenty pounds of barbed wire wrapped around your skull. Who do you love?

It is very simple plot. We had to kill the thing we love to prove our love. Lonesome Love, might make a mini-series. *(I read it in a poem: "Take any streetful of people buying clothes and groceries, cheering a hero or throwing confetti and blowing tin horns . . . tell me if the lovers are losers . . . tell me if any get more than the lovers . . . in the dust . . . in the cool tombs."—Carl Sandburg, "Cool Tombs," 1918)* We had to sacrifice our women to prove our love—so many one-breasted ones now ambling around as testimony to our adoration. Kill the thing we love. That is our central legend, our key holy story, the tale in our sacred books. From the halls of Montezuma . . . it has been a long haul, brothers and sisters. We should rest now down by the river. But please do not drink the water. Let's make it linear, our favorite plotting device: We came, we saw, we were conquered. Julius would understand, he has been waiting for us to get the joke. Or let's skip the A+B+C and go into the swirl of things: his name is Sundance, he is Lakota, there is a huge stock of *Hustler* magazines by his bed on L.A.'s skid row and he is a very large man, but he keeps muttering about this thing in his bones. The essential story line is in the bones. It is always is, it is that deep, that basic. Robert Sundance lived our lives before we did. He pioneered our world in special laboratories we called Indian reservations. Long ago, when we still believed in the future, in progress, in hard work, nuclear families, nuclear bombs, and big turkeys at Thanksgiving, he and his friends were drugged, unemployed, and unemployable. They were bored, violent, and almost invisible. They beat their women, abandoned their children, roamed around wreaking havoc. They were us before we even had a clue what we would become. He lived in the West, he served in those wars, he sucked down that air, he drank the water, he is a blood, he is a half-breed, he is dying of cancer, and he can feel the roots of the blood orchids ensnaring him and taking him down. This makes him very angry—but it is too late. Sundance is raving now, it is deep into the night and the pain comes on strong. He is babbling something about scalping knives, the strange curve of the blades. He has killed the thing he loved and now must pay the blood price. His entire story starts and ends with the blood orchids but he is reluctant to admit this fact. We all are. Come here, lie by my side, I will kill you . . . two stretches for manslaughter, yet he survived so that he could live and suffer and pay that blood price.

(I must be responsible. I am closing in on fifty, I've been around several of those city blocks and have been sternly advised about my conduct by the officers—they were just trying to help, they told me so. I am of the belief that our efforts to protect ourselves and our ground and our rivers and our seas have taken a toll. This volume is suggestive of that blood price. Ah, there, a thesis sentence for the boys and girls in the seminar. Of course, my judgment is seriously impaired. I have lived with war every day of my life. And expect to continue this pace. I could as a child look into the faces of my parents and sense what the world of peace must have been like to feel and touch and know. But this thing they could neither keep for themselves nor give to me. Hence, these words as the storm sweeps closer, coming off the Rocky Mountains, several miles from the edge of the Rocky Flats Arsenal where the plutonium will chew the

ground for the next couple of hundred thousand years.
What the hell, a trade-off.)

Should we run through some other kind of inventory to
make it all safe and clear and untrue? Bases, forts, tests,
proving grounds, arsenals, airfields (how light and flut-
tery that phrase seems), war games, wars, gunnery ranges,
research centers, underground sites, aboveground sites,
MOAs, silos, Star Wars, MAD, Dugway, Los Alamos. And
in the name of our Lord and Savior, Trinity. And most
important, No Trespass, the Prohibited Area, and the
very favorite posting of the garden: National Security.

We have achieved our Historical Absolute like good
Doktor Hegel promised us so long ago. We have made
our entire nation into a reservation with a population
unemployed or underemployed, and our merchants eager
to supply us with a lot to drink or snort or dose ourselves
with. We display a frisky penchant for violence, enjoy an
abandonment of everyone by everyone, stare at a future
as blank as the president's ass and a past increasingly lost
in the fogs that flood our brains. As our bodies become
emaciated, our government fattens on our plight and
grows larger. They are going to send us to school—
apparently forever—so that we can do little jobs around
the rez. There seems no end to the work they see for us
and they promise that each and every one of us will have
six or seven careers in our twinkling lifetimes. There has
been some grumbling about the pay, however, and
increasingly folks in our cities prefer self-employment—
whether with muskets or syringes. There is bold talk that
free trade is good for us—free love is no longer permitted,
it seems we have diseases—and will make us stronger
and quicker and more productive. We are going to get
national health care, so don't be scared of the rashes, pus-

tules, tumors, genital sores, and erratic heartbeat. We're going to be one big tribe, the rainbow tribe it's rumored (they're working out the reading list this very moment) and at the end of the rainbow, by God, there is pot. We have nothing to do and we know it, so we spend our time doing what little is left to do: we wait. Or look backward.

(There is an artist who is going to place one thousand cast-bronze buffalo on 370 acres of Wyoming. All he requires is 450 tons of bronze and $45 million. He will mount the metal herd on swivels and when the wind comes up its force will rush through tubes in the cold, dead beasts and they will moan. The buffalo will stretch over a half mile and form the shape of, what else, a buffalo. The artist desires that his work be visible from the moon. The site the artist has selected is the only known home of the desert yellowhead, a plant no one seemed to notice until 1990. Perhaps metal yellowheads can be added to the plan. The state endorses this work of art. They say it will be good for tourism. I am not making this up. No one can make up much of anything anymore. The artist says the site is "empty desert." Besides he explains, "The only way we know the beauty of things is through art.")

We have 105 million cows, tens of thousands of nuclear warheads, 435 representatives, 100 senators, one president for vice, one president for other matters, and liposuction machines. We outnumber spotted owls, buffalo, elk, deer, antelope, wolves, sea turtles, pupfish, and blue whales. Microorganisms outnumber us, but we do not like to think of that fact. We have the best orchid garden on the surface of the earth, and the only one that is still intact. And we love to work in our garden. We won't give up this horticulture, we don't know how.

We now hold many meetings; we wish, we say, to know the meaning of things. We yearn to drive down the information highway. Everyone is gearing up for this journey. Only no one is willing to go out at night anymore.

Female Thynnids prosper by parasitizing the larvae of Scarabacid beetles, and the particular beetles favored as prey live by being root parasites. To find them, the females have to dig and since they spent their time digging, they lost the ability to fly. Indeed, they have lost their wings, a sacrifice which makes it easier for the females to tunnel under the earth. The hammer orchid lives high above them in the trees but somehow has become conscious of their strange ways.

Since the female Thynnids cannot fly, they cannot search the forest above them for food. This problem they solve by sucking fluids from the beetles that are their victims. That leaves the great subject of mating. Most wasps of this type have a culture in which the males are the active *parties in mating. Usually, a female just plants herself in an easily reached location, releases a pheromone, and lets time solve her problem. Possibly, it is an intoxicating situation.*

2

The magic numbers are nine and four. He cannot say why this is so. As he leans against the craps table his big body is poised, the long gray ponytail trails down his back, and he thinks nine and four. He wears new running shoes, Levi's, a floral cowboy shirt, and a serious face. This is serious business, this gambling, and he must see if the table is warm. Then there is what he calls "the bone thing." The doctors, they say his body is riddled with cancer, that his bones weep with these dangerous cells, and when two weeks ago he stumbled and had to go on crutches, the men of medicine nodded knowingly and said it was the bone going in the ankle, the final movement of the cancer as his sturdy joints crumbled into dust. He will have nothing to do with this bone thing. It is not a matter to consider at this table, besides he must see if the table is warm.

He rolls the dice, wins, and turns to me with silent satisfaction.

"This table," he says very evenly, "is warm."

We are in downtown Las Vegas and the casino sign blazing against the wall boasts LUCK AVAILABLE.

He is very alert to warmth. The poker machines vary

*greatly. Some are hot, some are cold. The numbers vary
also, and today the numbers are nine and four. These things
come to the mind if the mind is open.*

*"Ah," he says to me, "the buffalo are there now, four hun-
dred of them. And soon they will have a thousand. And my
brother, he is bringing some in also."*

*Hot, cold, nine, four, buffalo. It is the way of power. He
is a Lakota and these are the things he says as the red dice
tumble down the green table in the tired casino.*

Last night, I dreamt the hours away and in my dream
I romped with Sioux Indians. In this dream the houses
were all small (four rooms—a kitchen, living room, and
two bedrooms—always four rooms), the wind a moan,
and the lights in the kitchens were too bright and hurt my
eyes. People sat around in these kitchens and smoked. A
woman with long hair, a thin body, and good breasts
unrolled a medicine bundle on the Formica table. No
explanation was ever offered of where the thing came
from or who it had belonged to. She merely said, "These
things may interest you." Inside the old and stained rag
wrappings were a hash pipe, a stolen credit card, a .45
automatic, and the lid off a Sterno can. I think I woke up
early so I could end this dream.

I took reassurance from the hardwood floors of the
house nestled above Los Angeles, where I was staying.
When I was a child, we had a privy, a pump, a wood
stove, and hardwood floors. Cold floors remind me of
some ground zero. These floors and this house belonged
to someone else—everything seemed to belong to other
people then. I was broke, several thousand dollars below
water and the debt was growing, a wave getting higher
and higher at my back, and soon—God, I hoped it would
be soon—the wave would crash down over me, take me

under and cleanse me through some kind of economic death. Or any other form of death. I cannot recover from that Baptist Sunday school, I want to get through the eye of that needle and reach the Promised Land. I could not pay the bills of life any longer—the mortgages, the rents, the taxes, the utilities. Instead I kept spending. Yet, the hardwood floors gave comfort, so cool under my bare feet in a house where no one else was yet awake. Outside gray light was seeping, the air was moist and heavy, and I sat out there and smoked and let my mind rattle about.

I had come to Los Angeles looking for sign. Recently, I had made $40,000 and spent $50,000. I am now saving to buy an AK-47. True, some of this money went for what my critics called wine, women, and song, but the bulk of it disappeared into an effort to save a forest. The particular forest had been selected at random one fine fall day as I drank a beer on the back porch and looked up at a mountain. The bottle was dark Mexican beer, the air was frisky with mosquitoes, and at that exact moment I had suddenly realized that I wanted something concrete, something where there would be a one-to-one experience, a dollar in here and dollars worth of result out there. A Mexican sat across from me drinking my beer, I had a case in the kitchen, and his feet were brown and seemed barely protected by the flimsy sandals he had made. He said, "Do you have any other pussy?"—referring to the woman scurrying about the house. And I said nothing. That is when I decided to spend all my money to save this forest. I wanted to know what would happen if one did not ask for something, did not seek foundation money, did not go to meetings, did not . . . go through the motions. Just had an idea, acted on it, and spent the money.

Now I have spent all the money, and more, gutted every bit of savings. This has changed me. I have dug the gun out of the closet again, an old .45 automatic from World War I that my father had boosted from his time in the service and that I had boosted when he died. I oiled it up, loaded the clip, and shoved it under the truck seat on the driver's side where, as I watched the L.A. dawn that morning, it rested right next to the machete I always carry. At the same time as I mounted my arsenal in the truck, I placed a teddy bear on my bed. You want reasons? So do I.

For months I have done nothing but drive, three, four thousand miles a month. I explain this motion as an economic necessity. This is a lie—God, I have got to stop lying, but the lying seems to make everything easier for everyone. The travel is for some kind of need that money cannot answer. How could money help me?—I give it all away. At present I am shedding about one or two thousand dollars a month. None of the money I give away is tax deductible. I have gotten it into my head that if the government will sanction my giving, then I am giving to a cause or place or thing that is either ineffectual, malignant, or the enemy. So I do not give to such places. I have no health insurance, I have no savings, I have no job, I have no money. My child support runs $600 a month, the wave is getting larger behind my back. I will see what will happen. That is my advantage: something will happen. I have done my damnedest to make sure of this fact. I live in a world and time where all is limbo. I am no longer of this world and time: I have lit some kind of fuse. True, I drink cheap wine. But I eat good meat. There is an expression for my condition: The wolf is at the door. But I want the wolf at the door. I am tired of living in a world without wolves.

On the way to L.A., I pulled into a truck stop in Arizona and I ordered the chicken fried steak because it was cheap. The waitress was one of those women we call mousy—small boned, scant flesh, tight constricted face, a pinched life. She'd worked for fifteen years for Westinghouse Air Brake back in Pennsylvania and waited bar at the Slovenian hall on the side. Then she'd been laid off and gotten a year or so of unemployment. She'd used up every dime and minute of that unemployment. She said, "I figured I deserved it, that I'd earned some kind of vacation." When the money ended, she drifted down to Florida where there were sun and rumors of an economy. She could only find the sun and wound up taking care of a forty-year-old man who, as the doctors say, had the mind of a child. His folks paid her wage, and the guy, while a bit simple, could eat, dress, talk, do most of the things Americans are asked to do. She fucked him, taught him about sex, and then his folks took notice and said, hey, why don't you two get married and we'll leave you all the money if you'll take care of him for the rest of his life. It was tempting, truly tempting. But she hit the road, and here she was in Arizona waiting tables until she saves up enough for good tires so she can press on. She needs a clutch too. As she told me all this she kept saying like the downbeat from a drummer, "You know, dontcha?"— saying it just like that, as a kind of punctuation. Christ, she didn't want much and she wanted me to know that. Back in her Westinghouse days, "I had a nice place, dontcha know?, I mean I'd have people over and set a good table with linen, nice china, a roast. A washer and dryer too. Look at me now, I don't know, dontcha know? I mean look at me. I never saw this happening to me, I never saw myself this way, I paid bills, I wasn't . . . dontcha know? But what do I do, well, I just keep chipping along, chipping along, that's the way I see it, I don't look right or left, I just keep chipping along, right? Maybe I'll go back to the idiot in Florida, I mean he was okay. He's got this thing where he can get a little rough, but I can handle him. What else I got? Where am I supposed to go? I'd leave here tomorrow if my car was fixed, dontcha know?"

And she asked me how my steak was and I said fine.

I think I have a prayer because of Columbus. If he had not sailed, if we had not raped and sacked this New World, I would be finished and so would you. The Admiral, he is out there on the deck of his ridiculous little ship, the green Atlantic spitting spray into his mad eyes, and he is looking, looking for what we are. He is the Great Captain of biodiversity, of the food chain, of modern ecology, of the double helix. *(The Great Captain loves to rave, don't we all? And here he is in the year of Our Lord 1503, sputtering another pearl of wisdom: "Gold is a wonderful thing! Whoever owns it is lord of all he wants. With gold it is even possible to open for souls the way to paradise!")* He has brought us together. He, and those who followed in his wake, collide with a legion of new species, with thousands of new databases that other humans have cobbled together, and though he will largely misunderstand these things or denounce them or seek to slay them, they will have their way with him and his kind. Oddly enough, we will later see him in two ways that ignore his real achievement: one as the great mariner, the exemplar of the rational European mind that does not think the earth is flat, that navigates strange waters, keeps written records, casts light where there had once been darkness. Or at times we will see him as a mystic, a religious fanatic, a final sputtering of a distasteful world we label medieval. These interpretations will not do. I see him as a funnel and through this funnel the New World pours into my genes and becomes, perhaps, the saving remnant. For what this discovered hemisphere gave us is a chance to recover the irrational, the illogical, and the powerful. The forests that overwhelm us, the mountains that dwarf us, the forces that crush us. Here the drums were not yet stilled. Here God still lived, though at times God drank copious goblets of blood, or was a stone, or a buffalo skull, or a mountain. Here we could glimpse what it meant to not be disturbed by our own smell or by our hunger for each other's bodies.

Here . . .

I speak for the mongrel, the mestizo, the half-breed, the bastard, the alley cat, the cur, the hybrid, the mule, the whore, the unforeseen strain that pounds against all the safe and disgusting doors. I speak for vitality, rough edges, torn fences, broken walls, wild rivers, sweat-soaked sheets. Who would want a world left mumbling to itself, a perfect garden with the dreaded outside, the fabled Other held at bay and the neat rows of cultures and genes safe behind some hedgerow? I dread a world that is all Iceland, the people fair, their genealogies stretching back in a dull column for a millennium, their folkways and mores and lifeways and deathways all smug and pointless. I speak for graffiti. Look there is Christopher, watch the son-of-a-bitch, watch'm, he's got a spray can of paint and look what he's writing on that temple wall. . . .

We waste too much time on arguments about nothing. It happened, we are what became of it. There is no Eden to save, not now, not in 1492. True, we could have done better—but then everything is like a love affair, everything could have been done better. But the mess we lament, that is the thing that a part of me celebrates. The strange mongrel mixture of races, ideas, seeds, spores, viruses, bacteria. Ways of making love.

By 1492, Europe was a death house with a dead God and legions of dead souls. The Mongols had been beaten back, so too the Moors. The cathedrals were huge and yet empty, dull sanctuaries bereft of magic. No one could remember the Druids and we all had serious doubts about the women. It seems the priests told us they were unclean. The landmass we call Europe had been butchered, all the forests made groves, all the meadows made fields, all the ground made tame. A place used up. All the signs of decadence were present and this failure of the heart was seen as innovation. A new burst was occurring in writing, in painting, in machines. The things scholars for the coming centuries would celebrate and call a rebirth, these things were actually signs of a vast dying of the spirit. Of this I am convinced because five centuries later I live at a similar moment in the history of my breed. We too live in a dead culture with dead gods and yet we are flailing outward into space, the depths of the seas, the secret crevices of the earth, the once sacrosanct gardens of our cells. We are mining the double helix, poking about in the strange codes of life itself. We sail on our own clumsy caravels and galleons just as Christopher himself once did. But, getting back to 1492, I shudder to think what would have happened to Europeans if they had not found, murdered, fucked, and become mired in the cultures of the New World. I fear they would have been lost forever and taken everyone and everything down with them. They were heading down that metal highway that leads to the kingdom of the cyborgs. What the jungles and plains and mountains and deserts and forests of the New World accomplished is this: they permanently poisoned the faith of Europeans in rationality. They brought back the night.

I realize that some will disagree with me on this. The general belief is that the people of the New World went down, and their ideas went down with them. We pay odd clerks called ethnographers to gather scraps of what we consider this vanished lore. We are fools, of course.

There are other matters. The radio this morning announced that condors are going back into the mountains, birds baked in some laboratory and brought forth to the skies without the memory of a mother. They will find our kills. But the wolf can hardly be located except in zoos. This is of small note to most of us. Also, the air is heavy with dangerous gases. This is true everywhere now. And the sun shines too fiercely because of new holes in the sky. Many of us will die of cancers because of this sun. They keep doing polls that discover no one any longer believes in the future. Except me.

I have visited the future. She lives a mile or two away in a cheap cathouse. No one likes her and hardly ever will a customer take her upstairs. This is odd—most of my life has been spent in an America that loved fucking the future. The past was largely forgotten, the present given scant attention because no one had any time, but the future—that was the territory for hope and dreams and love. Perhaps the problem lies in her face—it is of indeterminate origin, in some light looking white, in others brown or yellow or black. The color of her eyes shifts also, as does the size of her breasts, the fineness or coarseness of her hair. The guys tell me that she doesn't look European, you know, and they don't want to fuck a future that doesn't look like them. She has very little to do and if you ask her she'll say she is a surplus human being, a soul no one needs in the urgent business of producing thing. She is too poor to buy much so the stores don't give a damn about her. She, being the future, has had six or seven jobs but they all seem to have been in cathouses just like the one where she now lives. She says her work bores her but it pays some bills. She is very lean, not frail, but streamlined. One night she laughed and said she was the ultimate model of the consumer society, a creature totally consuming herself. At night she keeps candles burning, one a green wax Buddha, another a glass jar with a decal of the Virgin of Guadalupe, and the yellow glow glistens off the faces on the walls, masks from Africa, Borneo, Mexico, Mardi Gras, Oktoberfest, the Inaugural Ball, and so forth. She never explains the masks to me, nor does she ever wear one. Every flat surface in her room is covered with dolls, hundreds of dolls. When she goes away, she covers their heads with little paper bags so they will not witness her departure and weep. The future is usually alone and the future is lonely. She walks around almost invisible to us and no one loves her. True, there are rare moments when she is glimpsed briefly and then suddenly people throng her and try to stone her to death. They leave her mangled and cold on the ground and walk off with their true lovers, the past that never happened. I have found her with her breasts slit, her face scarred, the painted nails on her hands broken. I cradle her in my arms and take her back to the cathouse where she waits and waits for someone . . . to love the future or at least accept her. She is actually quite intelligent and sometimes at night when I am up in her room she will pound me for hours with statistics on resource depletion, global ennui, malnutrition, pollution, population explosions, infant mortality, suicide rates, the strength of the mark against the pound, the yen against the dollar. What is the Polish per capita production of carbon, she will ask, and then she will make a sound like a giggle. She is lovely then, her face aglow with feeling, and all her dolls watch her with quiet pride. Somehow she can measure how many children on earth have too many toys and not enough love. She never does drugs, not a single line. She tells me everything will be fine once I understand . . . the future. That she will not be threatening, harsh perhaps, but not threatening. She will be gentle with me the first few times and then I will remember who I am and my body will sing and I will go forward and not care whether I live or die or whether I get cold or hot or whether I will feel hunger. There will be work, the future promises, an abundance of work. She makes me coffee and the cup is always chipped but clean. She whispers to me that there are no secrets, that I can see everything just as clearly as she can, that all I must learn to do is look. And feel. She presses her breasts against me when she tells me these things and softly sings and I am learning to love her.

Time is of the essence, of this there can be no question, and so I get in the machine and the Bronco dives down the freeway ramp at 105 mph. The driver is the perfect antidote to me. He is precise, he is good with tools, he can fix things, he has a memory like the Library of Congress. And, praise the Lord, he knows the freeways of Los Angeles.

He comes to me with ideas. Wildlife is his passion and he wants to save animals. It can be late at night and he suddenly will have this new idea. He can get the grizzly bears, don't ask how, he says. They are slated for destruction and he can get them. We will put one in the back of a U-Haul truck, he will drive, and I will ride in back with a syringe. If the bear begins to stir, I am to give it a shot, okay? We will release the animal in the mountains where it will be safe. We will restore the bear to its former range. What do I think, he asks?

I realize I am supposed to say that this is an insane idea. But if I do that, then I will not be here, I will be somewhere else. And I want to be here, or at least get closer to wherever this place is.

So I hesitate, but we keep talking.

On the radio this morning a woman announcer with a friendly voice said a newborn baby had been discovered in a Pennsylvania sewer pipe. And that a politician would appear for the prosecution in Los Angeles County Superior Court in the case of the bondholders against a once leading businessman. This last little item had brought me hurling across the Mojave Desert and deep into the canyons of Los Angeles. I felt sure the session in court would provide another clue for me about the future. If my culture is basically sound, the words spoken in court will merely shed light on a crime. If my culture is basically unsound, the words spoken in court will teach me how my society is fundamentally nonfunctional. I tend to the latter position. Which leaves me in a kind of lurch, since I am totally a product of my culture. I cannot survive without a bottle of ketchup or decent, tasteless American cooking.

This is the third day, and still he will not leave the table. He senses it is getting warmer. Hot, cold, nine, four. An old man and his wife lean against the rail, and take in the action. The old man's face is florid from the drinking, and he wears a windbreaker and a white polo shirt. On his finger is the ring of his lodge. He throws a couple of hundred-dollar bills on the felt, get his chips, tosses out bets, and rolls the dice.

Robert Sundance watches, his head barely nodding. Suddenly, bets spew from his big hands and he covers six different positions. "He is warm," he says of the old man.

The old man throws the dice hard, shouts, and wins again. He throws a couple more hundred-dollar bills down and eats up more action. His wife is perfectly calm, her face powdered and lightly rouged, and nothing betrays her feelings except for a gentle tug she makes on the old man's elbow. This gesture he ignores. He is a sultan and at this moment in this universe, the dice belong to him. He keeps winning. The house changes croupiers, and the new one has a shaved head, hooded eyes with bags under them, a three-piece gray suit, and a row of black onyx rings on his fingers. His mouth is like a crack tracing across a concrete floor. But he cannot change the table, it is still warm.

Sundance is the student now. He says, "When I had the dice, I could do nothing. But he is warm, he is doing very good. I will make money with him."

Never once in all the days we spend in the casino does he mention the word gambling. It is not a concept. There are these temperatures to check, hot and cold. The numbers are nine and four. He can see them in his mind.

The way to place a wager is very simple.

"You must see the number in your mind before the dice are rolled," Robert Sundance explains.

I am in the court an hour early. It is on the thirteenth floor but the room is numbered 123. The walls comfort me with rich woods and a large metal seal of the state of California that quietly says, EUREKA. Yellow signs above the jury box warn WATCH YOUR STEP and the judge sits as calm as God above the throng of defendants that parades through. They are the residue of the long nights. Two Chicanos are up for three counts of grand theft auto. (Their lawyer in a cheap tan sport coat and black loafers zips through the arraignment in less than sixty seconds and then hands them a card and says, "You can usually reach me in the afternoons.") There are faceless black men facing years and years for things discussed as statute numbers by the court. A plain white woman with russet hair, her jacket a dark blue that says LA COUNTY JAIL, bows meekly toward the bench. Another black man dressed in prison yellows is shackled by the legs and with his arms manacled behind his back. He cannot focus his eyes. The judge looks down from his bench and with a soft whack of the gavel, the case is continued. The shackled man swiftly disappears through a side door, as have so many others before him. The light is very bright in this ante-chamber and cold pours from the plain walls and I suspect instantly kills the soul. The corridors are probably endless, and those who go through the door surely never return. They are rolled like dice and spend the rest of their days and nights in arduous vision quests.

It was a courtroom just like this one that Rupert McLaughlin entered two decades ago. It was a room like this that Robert Sundance left. I never knew Rupert McLaughlin. I met Robert Sundance one fine April day. He was dying, but he had come to Phoenix to make it official. I was staying in a cheap motel with two beds, a television, and an open bottle of wine. My head was full of wolves then—I had tracked them in the government offices, in the mesas of New Mexico, in the Sierra Madre, in the cages of Arizona. They howled constantly (these were the juicy nights of spring) and I could feel their hot breath against my neck. This was remarkable to me since they had all been officially slaughtered four decades before in order to make the earth ready for our rapture. Sometimes I could smell their doglike odor on the night winds.

Sundance was a very large man of sixty-four, well fleshed and over six feet tall. The tip of one finger was missing, his hair hung in a long silver ponytail, and a tattoo peeked from his forearm and said MOTHER. His body was laced with the broad white trails left by knife wounds. And his skin was very fair, as light as fine porcelain, and his eyes were blue. He was a Hunkpapa Sioux, as was Sitting Bull. Rupert McLaughlin was a descendant of James McLaughlin, the man who in 1890 sent the Indian police to arrest Sitting Bull. The Indian police slaughtered the old medicine man. As a boy on the Sioux reservation, things had been very hard for Rupert Mc-Laughlin because of his ancestor. As a young man after World War II, he had gathered with friends in the grove of trees where Sitting Bull was buried and there they had long and pleasant drunks as the Dakota winds rustled the leaves. But the earlier human being was replaced by a man who called himself Robert Sundance. Perhaps Sundance emerged from his mother's side of the family, for she was descended from Mad Bear, a chief who fought at Little Big Horn, a chief who, when all the wars had finally been lost, led his band into a remote part of the reservation, a bleak slab that became known as Mad Bear country. By the time I met him, Sundance had not had a drink in over a decade and led an alcohol treatment movement in Los Angeles. His journey had taken him to prison twice, to many jails, and to a glittering trail of empty liquor bottles. He had sought power in tokay, muscatel, port, shellac, Sterno, whiskey, and beer. He had survived delirium tremens two or three hundred times. "They come," he advised, "when you are suddenly cut off. They last five days. Always five days."

He had discovered his new problem just a few days before in his room on L.A.'s skid row and now he was in Phoenix visiting the Indian hospital. There was something wrong in his hips, in his lower body, and he was not used to his body failing him. The doctors had shot Sundance full of something—barium? I cannot recall—and he could not sleep. So that night we talked.

He told me of the Montana prison riot of 1957. He was thirty years old then, doing time for manslaughter, when the cages in Deer Lodge erupted in rage. He took charge of protecting the guards. "Some of the prisoners," he said in a soft, lilting voice, "wanted to kill them. I could understand this because the guards had treated us bad. Some of the guys would come crawling at night, they wanted a guard so bad. But this made no sense. I could not let them have the guards. They were our only assets."

His voice was barely audible in my dimly lit room. I think he marveled that I had a corkscrew for the bottle of wine. In his earlier days, he was more of a twist-off cap kind of guy. He was supposed to be dying, the city around us seemed to be dying, in fact everything seemed to be dying. My room was furnished very cheaply with an old sofa, a fragile coffee table, a Formica kitchen table. No one could stay in this room very long and retain any dreams of success in life. The counter in the kitchenette recorded the fingerprints of hundreds of salesmen who always had the door slammed in their faces. This particular night there were plenty of new kills out on the land

offering up fine carrion—it was a time when one knew
one thing had ended and yet nothing new had begun. The
wolves were gone, the skies all but empty of condors.
Sundance's voice droned on oblivious to these facts. They
did not matter to him. His vision quest had taken him
into a far country, one that could never be tracked with
a ledger book or audited by a federal official. Sundance
seemed immune to the prevailing American climate of
failure. He seemed not to be wasting away but storming
ahead. It was just that now he was storming ahead with
a body that was in revolt. And this grim little detail he
could not accept. He told me that the doctors said there
was something wrong in his bones. He would say this as
if it were a marvelous claim, a bizarre statement to make
about his body, which had endured hunger, cold, prison,
bronc busting, beatings, booze, and hundreds of rounds
with the dt's.

He told me of whores he had known in his rambling
days, how in every tank town in the West he had gone to
the whores and how in each town he would find the very
same ones.

"They must move them," he thought.

*Once, Robert Sundance loved this casino. That was back
in the days when the casino was called Sundance. A good
name, he believes. In those days, the management offered to
comp him a two-week stay. He asked if he could bring a
woman and they said that was fine. He then asked if he
could bring two women and they asked why?*

He told them, "I'll burn one out in a week."

*This memory comes to him as he sits and probes the feel
of a video poker machine. The machine, he senses, is warm.*

At a few minutes before ten o'clock, Charlie Keating
sweeps into the court with three well-scrubbed aides and

his attorney. I have not seen him in two years, since the day he held a press conference to denounce the federal seizure of his company. He had looked very angry then as he told an anecdote of Abraham Lincoln's, the tale of a man tarred and feathered and ridden out of town on a rail who said he would have declined all the fun except for the honor. His hands had shaken under the podium. But this morning in Los Angeles, he is very relaxed and incredibly fit for a man in his late sixties. I had thought he would be broken by now, perhaps dead. They had put him in jail, they had shackled him, they had shown him their power. But somehow, no one could drive that wooden stake into his heart.

He does not seem to recognize me, there have been so many of my kind prying into his life. He is here for a nuisance suit, a mere matter of a quarter billion dollars of unsecured bonds that went bad. Across the aisle glares a row of old people, part of an army of twenty-odd-thousand bondholders who lost their savings in Charlie's schemes. Or seventeen thousand bondholders—the numbers, all the numbers in money matters these days keep shifting. There seems no solid ground, no exact accounting of individual objects or actions. We now live in a Big Picture World, one that only entertains the collapse of entire empires, the global rot of a unitary economy, the death of the entire atmosphere, the crash of whole oceans, the poisoning of all the food at the local grocery store. Everything is part of a pattern, and the pattern is part of a conspiracy, and the conspiracy is promoted by invisible forces and there is nothing anyone can do. Except sue.

Because of this befuddling complexity, I think all forms of guns should be totally legal (even though in our present state of mind they are all inadequate to the dreams of people) because such weapons still give folks something concrete to do. True, the fine days are long gone when one could draw down on a single person, pull the trigger, and right some wrong. Now no one can imagine any useful act that does not entail changing entire systems and the systems are so huge that no one can even describe them. I am the person hopelessly out of touch in such a time and place. Perhaps I lack the mind to deal with abstractions or with conspiratorial realities and so fall back on simple, naive notions. I still carry that gun in the truck. But then I still plant trees. I feel a deep kindredness of the spirit with Charlie because, like Stonewall Jackson, another believer in the power of will, he never for a single instant in his life doubted that his actions could make a difference. He never believed a system could stop him, not even today as he sits stuck in a courtroom while rows of bondholders try to burn holes in his body with their bitter eyes. And truly, they fail to invade his calm. One of his legs splays out from his seat, the smiles come easily to his narrow face. He is a man who can handle the heat, handle the cold, and handle the federal government. In Los Angeles, there are two and a half floors of government employees devoted to one single task: putting Charlie Keating in prison. He turns to his secretary and chats, flashing a smile.

In many ways, Keating gives me hope. He is one of the few figures of this particular moment who refuses to quit. After the bond suit, he will face a racketeering suit. After the racketeering suit, there are plans for him to face a criminal suit. And then there are other suits. He lives in fine hotels now and no one knows how he pays for them. He lives in a multimillion-dollar home and no one knows how he keeps it. He orders hundred-and-fifty-dollar bottles of champagne with his lunch. I have drunk champagne with him, his thin lips pursed over the glass, his long fingers holding the delicate stem. Champagne is very important to him and it reassures Charlie Keating. He is part of a problem called the savings-and-loan crisis, and the experts now say this problem will cost the federal government hundreds of billions of dollars. It is interesting to look at a man responsible for something that requires such a row of zeros. His hand lies flat on the defense table, the fingers extended and still. His lips often look like a straight line etched above his chin, and his eyes are very quick.

Like Sundance, he was in the Navy in World War II. Like Sundance, he came from a home without money. Like Sundance, he takes up space, his body seems to demand space. Like Sundance, he has been in jail, the very same Los Angeles jail. In fact, Sundance has told me that the word on skid row is that Charlie did his time okay, that he could handle it. Keating once told me that his biggest regret was that he had not fired enough people. This claim has always stuck in my mind because it seemed like a sensible regret to me, but whenever I have told others, they have seized upon it as final and absolute proof of his truly evil nature. Keating has a lot of rough edges and strange byways. He is not apparently keen on whores—he heads the leading antipornography organization in the United States. He has given at least a million dollars to Mother Teresa. He has given over a million dollars to five United States senators and in a moment, one of these recipients of his largess will walk into this room.

Charlie is part of something in this nation that is very old. Not as ancient as the Sioux, but still very old.

Keating's world began about the time the buffalo died. Sundance does not know of the buffalo firsthand, but when he was a boy, the elders told him of those days, of the endless strands of dark beasts crossing the plains, of the taste of raw liver from a fresh kill, of the hunt and the danger and the sound of the hooves. The horns could open a man up with a casual toss of the great shaggy head. In those ancient days as the great herds fell dead under the guns of a crazed nation, Charlie's world was born. Out on the plains General Custer camped in splendor, his fine hounds staked nearby, his tent sheltering him from the huge nights. In the cities, men gathered and designed things they called instruments—bonds, stocks, preferred stocks, and so forth—and liberated the arm from toil, took the hand off the plow handle, and taught money to breed more money. They said this enterprise was free. There were accidents, of course, the panic of 1873, and many others have followed with the regularity of heartbeats unto this day. Factories would fall still, men would kill themselves from the shame of losing control of pieces of paper, presidents and congressmen would complain. Women would sell their bodies. Through this century or more, the plains were stilled, the buffalo slain, the bones gathered, ground up, and used for fertilizer. The wind never ceased, not for one moment, and on the plains people staggered around with empty sockets where their eyes once had been.

The Sioux had sensed the true nature of their visitors. In 1857 at a mass gathering of the tribe in the Black Hills they fashioned a simple policy: any Sioux who told whites of gold in the Black Hills would be killed. And this policy held. By 1875, in the boom mining camp of Deadwood, Sioux scalps were going for $300 a throw. The

Lakota knew they had originally taken the land from others. And they knew force of arms was the only way to keep it. So they fought. And sometimes when you hear Sundance raving in the night as this thing in his bones eats at him, you think they're likely to fight forever.

It was at this moment, when defeat devoured one people and victory intoxicated the other, that the saddest ending came. The whites had their visions of quick riches quashed by the regular unfolding of calendar years as they paid off mortgages, strung barbed wire, made deposits at banks, and fell into the boredom of normal living. That is why the eyes in all those old photographs of pioneers look so dull—the gleam of possibility, of hope of the bonanza has been replaced by the grind. What could be—gold in them thar hills—gave way to what is, and what *is* played itself out endlessly and remorselessly. In the paintings of the American West, the ones that capture coming into the country are bewitching and the ones that delineate being in the country are flat and unmoving.

If the whites faced boredom and the wind of the plains, the Lakota and other tribes stared at extinction. A vast euthanasia was designed and duly executed. The head of the U.S. Army, General William Tecumseh Sherman (his name was no accident; his father had deeply admired the man who attempted a federation of American Indians), had a way of putting things plainly. He said, "The process begun in Massachusetts, Pennsylvania and Virginia remains in operation today, and it needs no prophet to foretell the end." One of his subordinates saw it differently. General John Pope filed a report in the summer of 1865 that said: "What the white man does to the Indian is never known. It is only what the Indian does to the white man, (nine times out of ten, in the way of retaliation) which reaches the public. The Indian, in truth, has no longer a country. His lands are everywhere pervaded by white men, his means of subsistence destroyed, and the homes of his tribe violently taken from him. Himself and his family reduced to starvation, or to the necessity of warring to the death upon the white man whose inevitable and destructive progress threatens the total extermination of his race." Sherman himself saw things this way: "We must act with vindictive earnestness against the Sioux," he noted when they had killed eighty-one of his troopers, "even to their extermination, men, women, and children. Nothing else will reach the root of this case." But then the general in the closing days of the Civil War in 1865 had argued that about another 100,000 Southerners needed killing because he suspected they wouldn't "adapt themselves to the new order of things." For the Lakotas he plotted a future where they would be penned on reservations along the Missouri River until that magic moment when they became "civilized or demoralized." The Sioux, like many others, got drunk and stayed that way. Sundance is keen on this point: from 1833 until 1954 an Indian could not legally buy a drink in the United States. And yet the tribes stayed drunk, dead drunk.

They are still at it. Last night in Indian Alley, a few blocks from the courthouse, a man had his throat cut. These things happen, it is part of the medicine. Sundance can leave the bottle alone, but he cannot leave the medicine. For almost thirty years he has lived in a room on skid row, close by Indian Alley. Perhaps he likes to walk over there and see the mural, a crude painting of a brave on the wall, the hair long, a single feather dangling, and floating over it two words, INDIAN POWER. The ground below glistens from broken bottles. I have a photograph of him standing in that exact spot, one taken by a woman named Half Pint. It was snapped on the day he first realized that his body was abandoning him and that he was theoretically dying. When he was a boy on the Sioux reservation, he would hear voices at night, people talking. His elders told him that he was hearing dead people, Indian people from the old wars who still lived on the ground and moved about under the stars.

The medicine is very powerful.

He insists I read the book of his life. He has been toiling over this story, now a manuscript of two hundred pages, for most of his life. The book is full of coups counted against the enemies that darken life on a concrete plain. I flip to a chapter on the time in the early fifties when he managed a hotel on skid row in Los Angeles. Rupert packed the place with Indians and the Indians never paid for their rooms. Young Indian girls would be carried up to the rooms and gang-banged—they had no choice, at their age it was the only way they could obtain liquor. White drunks would pay for a room, fall asleep and then be robbed. In the morning Rupert would wake up and look out into the alley and see white drunks lying there in the sun after being beaten and cleaned out in the hotel. Once, he heard one say as he rubbed his sore head, "I could swear I bought a room last night."

A brother came to stay, got drunk, and went to a room to sleep it off. Rupert needed a bottle and so he told a homosexual who hung around the hotel that if he went into his brother's room he could suck him off. This for fifty cents. The man paid and went in. His brother awoke when he felt someone on him and began to yell and hit. This, of course, did not matter since Rupert already had the fifty cents for a bottle.

I read at the book of his life and then I tell him I am not sure how much the average reader will be able to take of these matters.

He looks at me and is silent. Then he says, "The life was very rough. That is what I want people to know: how rough it is to be a drunk."

The testimony rolls along in that dull tone that is the special property of courtrooms. Here all passions are reduced to the emotional pitch of third-year law students. Here the salt has always lost its savor. It sounds something like this:

And you are a United States Senator from Arizona?

Yes, I am.

And you graduated from the Naval Academy at Annapolis?

Yes.

You were a prisoner of war in Hanoi for how long?

Five and a half years.

The prosecutor is bald, dressed in an ill-fitting blue suit, and carries an aura of certain defeat into whatever battles life offers him. He never moves from behind the podium, his voice falls flat on the floor and lies there in a puddle. He has no confidence and the jury can smell his fear. The senator is short, blocky, and tense. When he answers a question he nods his head much like a robot. John McCain, with a single brief exception, never looks at Keating. And Charlie never stops glaring at McCain. Once he gestures with his hand toward Charlie but refuses to look into the old man's cold eyes.

This is the theater called justice. The jury, a panel of nineteen, is bored. Many are black, all look blue collar. Keating wanted jurors who saw the government as the Man, as the cop at the door, the welfare caseworker sneaking around, as . . . the hateful thing that messed up

Charlie Keating's wonderful business empire. This is either a remarkable act of insight or insanity on his part—after all he is charged with clipping a herd of ordinary folks out of $250 million. Charlie's body almost sprawls out at the defense table. He knows his role as the relaxed man, the innocent man, and most importantly, as the Man. And men do not fear and do not show fear. Ever.

Ah, but Mr. Keating did call you a wimp, did he not, Senator?

Yes, and I resented it.

Somehow the senator's vacations at Keating's home in the Bahamas at Cat Cay do not come up. The $112,000 in contributions, that is mentioned but seems to slip away like a whisper. The senator did nothing wrong. This is a given. He is the product of a certain America where a senator is expected to take his leisure in the mansions of the rich. He intervened for Mr. Keating as a constituent but did nothing inappropriate. The Senate Ethics Committee has already cleared him. He is certified as ethical, which is more than I can say.

Outside in the hall, twenty television and still cameras await the end of the testimony. In the courtroom, three armed sheriff's deputies watch the crowd. The row of a half dozen old people glare at Keating—the bondholders, this case's official mourners. Of course, all could not come here today. One man of eighty-nine went into his bathroom a while back, drew a hot bath, enjoyed the warmth, opened his veins with a blade, and died.

The second act features Stephen Neal, Keating's attorney. He walks McCain through his encounters with Keating, and the senator agrees that he never did anything wrong nor was he asked to do anything wrong—

just possibly inappropriate. A huge aerial photograph of Phoenix is entered into evidence. Nine Keating developments are marked by yellow flags and the picture looks like a medieval pageant with pennants fluttering. Yes, the senator says, Mr. Keating was noted for building very fine homes for his customers. The billions missing from the vault, they are silent here. And what do they matter? They are somewhere out in the world's economy at this moment driving other dark engines into the earth, moving other bodies further down the road. There is no way to object to business as usual unless one objects to business in all instances.

Sundance likes to tell of a fellow Sioux who was a very rough man. He would go into Indian bars and get drunk and when he got drunk he would look for a Crow. He hated Crows because they had guided Custer into Sioux country. If he found one, he began to sing a strange song, like a private chant in Lakota. Then he would almost beat the Crow to death. Charlie sits there relaxed and looks at the senator and seems to want to sing his own special song.

Over $2 billion have slid from his hands and yet he seems to suffer no hangover. He is eager to reach for that bottle again. He does not deny this. And he knows the sick people are not all on skid row, he knows this very well. He has been able to find them everywhere, in every office, in every city and town, and house, some even painted white—the president bagged $100,000 for his election from Charlie and his employees. But Keating is still thirsty even though, they say, the bar is now closed. I do not believe them and neither does Charlie.

We will continue this drinking until that bottle is dead. Or until this bottle kills us.

We are standing in Caesars Palace out on the strip. There is very little action here and the rows of poker machines are lonely. Robert Sundance walks up and down eyeing them. But it is to no avail, this hunting. This palace is cold. A white slave woman comes up and asks him if he wants a drink. He scorns her.

He is still rankled that I questioned the book of his life. Goddamn, he wants them to know, to taste, to feel the life. Nothing must be left out, no night left without vomit, no woman left without being raped, no man left without a knife flashing against his flesh.

I ask him why he thinks he was not killed, why he thinks he survived all those years on the street?

He does not like this question. It implies things he will not consider, things he cannot consider. It is a question from the white world, a question that demands the purpose of things. He is silent for a long moment, and then simply shrugs.

He leans into my face and he says, "These machines are cold."

Around 2:15 in the morning the car left the road, sheared a pole, and came to rest partly crumpled in a ditch. Live wires crackled. The driver lived. The woman died. Rupert McLaughlin, he lived also. He said he was drunk and just along for the ride. The court did not believe him and sent him to Deer Lodge for two years for manslaughter. It was 1957 and he was thirty years old. Charlie Keating was thirty-three that year and just beginning his rise as a Cincinnati lawyer and as fierce fighter against dirty books and magazines.

McLaughlin was tough enough for prison. He had entered World War II at the age of fifteen and survived the Pacific war and the kamikazes. He had fucked thirty-seven Filipina whores, so he recalled. It was all part of a contest—he came in second. He had had a lot to drink also.

The food was bad at Deer Lodge. There was no exercise. Men stayed in their cells for decades and grew very white. (Each morning a woman would come out in the backyard of her home near the prison. McLaughlin could see her clearly through the bars of his cell window. She would raise her dress high over her head. She wore no panties. Every day. He never found out who she was.) The prison had been run in precisely this way by the state of Montana since 1914. And then the convicts rose up, seized control, and Rupert McLaughlin took to protecting the guards, the only chips held by the cons. He survived and finally got out with his time served.

He wandered the West, from one Indian bar to another. There were many adventures, all blurrily recalled. The Indian women would often be raped. If they passed out in the bar, they were raped. If they did not pass out, four men would hold down their arms and legs, and they were raped. It was not an easy life but it was a life. When there was no money, one drank Sterno, called Pinky. McLaughlin and his friends would beg money on the streets, telling passersby they needed funds "to get our friend Pinky out of the can."

("The Sioux are thorough savages," noted Francis Park-man; "neither their manners nor their ideas have been the slightest degree modified by contact with white civilization.")

When drunk, life was better. Not good but better. Things felt better, women looked better, the time passed better. The words people spoke, why they all sounded better with drink. It had been this way for a very long time, since before Rupert McLaughlin was born. There was always the drinking, just as there were no buffalo. It was a fact of this world.

(Neolin the Enlightened is a Delaware who visits with the Master of Life in 1762 and returns with a message: "I hate you to drink as you do, until you lose your reason. . . .")

In 1970, Rupert was in a courtroom in Los Angeles, one just like the one that hosted Charlie Keating's trial. He was charged with public drunkenness. He was guilty of the drunkenness and many other things. As he awaited his moment before the judge, he noticed a bunch of other big Indians going one by one before the bench and softly pleading guilty to the charge of drunkenness. But when his turn came, he refused to plead guilty. He said he was sick, that he needed treatment for his sickness. He said that the jail was a form of slavery, and the slaves were the drunks who did the work of the jail for nothing and were never really free. And he proved right in this last fact: over the course of a decade he spent seven years in jail for his drinking. He began at that time to write writs asserting his position. He began to cause trouble. This is where I grow very fond of him: he caused trouble.

("There are no parts of the great plains," artist George Catlin noted in the 1840s when he stumbled upon the Sioux, "more abundantly stocked with buffaloes and wild horses nor any people so bold in destroying the one for food and appropriating the other to their use.")

And he said his name was not Rupert McLaughlin but was Robert Sundance. He began to break the chain of language that connected him to James McLaughlin, the agent on the reservation in the late nineteenth century who left the highly regarded book entitled *My Friend the Indian*. This friend who sent the Indian police to arrest

Sitting Bull on December 15, 1890, because he had encouraged the first Sioux participation in a new Indian craze, the Ghost Dance, a ceremony that had swept out of Nevada in 1888 promising that the earlier world and holdings of the native people would be returned to them. Sitting Bull, his son, and six other Sioux were killed during the attempted arrest. Fourteen days later a thing called Wounded Knee occurred. Of Sitting Bull himself, McLaughlin later noted, "He made 'good medicine.' "

The court as it happened did not agree with Robert Sundance's notion that he was sick, that the system of busting drunks was a form of slavery to make the jails run more cheaply, and they led him screaming from that courtroom. He wrote up that writ—he wrote up many in between his two or three hundred bouts with the dt's— and when each was denied he wrote up another and another. He refused to give in. On the street, the police would try to kill him. This can happen even in a city of angels. He never left skid row. There was once a tradition of bravado among Plains Indians in which a warrior tied himself to a stake on the field of battle and then drove that stake deep into the earth. This proved a man would not run, not run from anyone or anything. Rupert McLaughlin ran. Robert Sundance drove his stake deep into the black pavement of L.A.'s skid row. Eventually, he dried out but he never left. He had found his world, had his vision, and been given a new name to announce his new power. In 1977, his case was won on appeal and from it flowed detoxification centers and the legal right of a public drunk to treatment for a sickness. He became the Sundance Case and the movie offers flowed toward him.

He tells me this as we sit in a bar. When he speaks he leans toward me, his big head insisting on space and respect. He is still a powerful man and carries this air of menace with him always. He is now working on that book about his life. The movie people seem to be coming back again. He wants the money now. He is going to die. The cancer was in his prostate but by the time he came to the Indian hospital in Phoenix it had moved into the bones. It is just a matter of time, a year, perhaps two. He is thinking of going back to the Sioux land for a ceremony, for the old cure. The money from the book and movie, that is for his family, his brothers and sisters as a small repayment for a lifetime of injuries that he inflicted upon them. He is past needing money. I sip my beer as he talks in that low, flat speech typical of so many American Indians and of the white Americans who seized the plains from them.

"I have been reading these books on eating," he says, "and I think I have not eaten right. I have been eating food that is bad for me and now it does not matter. But I think I may go to Tijuana and look into those clinics, see what they have to say."

It can't hurt, I allow.

He eyes my beer but says nothing. I know he wishes to hurl it against the wall. He wishes to bring back Prohibition. The booze, he believes, is killing his race, and his anger ripples through his body. He is old, that is true, but no one will ever be safe around him until he is dead. If then.

We take a spin around skid row. He points out the park he has had the city put in, he points out the detox center he started. He is a man walking his land and talking his land. The sidewalks are crowded with people sprawled out in the night, shoulder to shoulder, block after block. I had a friend once who as a G.I. liberated a death camp in Nazi Germany. When he entered the first barracks he thought the bunks were empty, and then he noticed they were crowded with skeletal, corpselike bodies. And from these bunks rose a low, almost humming, insect sound, the sound of the inmates trying to say something. That is the sound I hear on L.A.'s skid row as the night comes down. The lights are low, the police station stands almost windowless, a veritable fort. The dark hours can be hard, the killings come more easily with the darkness. There are not many women and the few females out and about look harsh even in the low light. The booze is not good for a woman's face. True, they always have something to sell but in this place payment is not easy to arrange. The courthouse where Charlie fought his war today is only a few blocks away. It always seems that way in the American city, that the worlds are so very close yet never touch. But I think this is ending now, I think they will increasingly touch. Even the lawyers will not be able to keep them separate. It takes force to keep worlds separate, it takes money, it takes energy. America is running out of these things. America is running out of the ability to even think up things. Take skid row. No one can really police it anymore. The night is too powerful, stronger even than the cheap wine.

Two cops ride by on horses. Their badges shine on their blue uniforms and they wear blue cowboy hats. They have no medicine.

The geography can get to be too much. We are eating breakfast, taking a brief rest from the craps table, and he is trying to figure out where an event in his life happened. He remembers he trudged out of Phoenix with a woman, hopped a freight, and in the freight car was a black man and a bunch of stolen auto parts. It was summer and about 120 degrees. They all became very thirsty.

Then the train stopped in a town, men appeared and took

the auto parts. The black man, he remembers, seemed to know them, so it was all of a piece, that part. The men who picked up the stolen auto parts left the three of them with a case of peppermint schnapps. God, that stuff is easy to drink, so sweet and smooth. The three of them drank that case and by God did they get drunk sitting in the switching yard of that town in the heat. Sundance passed out. Then he suddenly awoke, he does not know why, reached out blindly and suddenly felt the black man's hard, erect cock. Goddamn, he thought, he is going to rape my woman. So he rose up and pounded on him a while and then he passed out again. Sundance regrets this act now. The sex, that part, he says, that does not really matter. Still, he did beat the man.

But his actions are not what bothers him at this moment, and morality is not the question. What he wants to know is the name of the town: was it Blythe or Yuma? He knows the train stopped along the Colorado River, he is sure of peppermint schnapps. But the town?

Blythe or Yuma?

In the hall outside the courtroom, the senator faces the bank of television lights. He is not at ease, he clutches his hands together, his Annapolis class ring looming on his finger like a malignant tumor. He has come here to perform his duty as an American citizen, he explains, he has done nothing wrong and he hopes his testimony proves useful to the court. He has been told by the prosecution that it would be useful. Why was he called? someone shouts. He suggests the reporters ask the prosecutors. He thinks that would be a very good question. And then he lurches down the corridor toward the elevators with that machinelike walk that suggests that he is some kind of wind-up toy wound up perhaps by his father the admiral or his grandfather the admiral or perhaps by the all those

Navy officers at Annapolis. No matter. He looks like a man who will never know who he is or care. I suspect, when asked, he will say that he is a United States senator. And of course this is true and good enough for explaining a life on any tombstone.

The prosecutors face the cameras next but they have nothing to say. It would not be appropriate, they suggest.

Neal and Keating then emerge, and Charlie, he looks very fine indeed. He flashes a smile, but he is silent. His attorney explains that he has told his client to let his lawyer do the talking, although, he smiles, he knows his client would like to say some things about today's testimony. Everyone laughs at this last statement. The press feels good, they have seen a defense attorney take over a courtroom, they have seen the government falter. And today, there are few of us who root for government regardless of the facts of the matter. The polls do not reveal this fact but it is in the air in every café, every whiskey bar, every woman's eyes, every blade of grass. We know something has ended in our land, and we know the government does not know this, and that the government is part of what has ended.

I know this. Robert Sundance knows this. Rupert McLaughlin, he never knew it. But then he is dead and gone. He was a drunk and had been drunk a hundred years *(ah, booze, ol' "mini wakan, the water that makes men foolish"),* since Little Bighorn, since the buffalo vanished. He died slowly but in a curious way. Part of the dying was tied into the dt's, I think, into the hundreds of episodes of poisoning his body with booze, taking everything to the edge (about ten percent of the people who have the dt's never have them again—they die), and riding bareback on that herd of nightmares, hoping for the vision. I think the man exploring the dt's was Robert Sundance, not Rupert McLaughlin, and I think he searched such hard, killing ground because for him the only possible ritual remaining, the last and best Sun Dance left, was in a bottle of tokay.

Once the Sun Dance had been the center of the Lakota world. It is June 22, 1881, and Mini-ho-a (Ink Man), a fellow known to us as Captain John Bourke of the U.S. Army, is with eight thousand Sioux around the sacred tree and the sacred buffalo skull. Red Dog, a chief of the Oglala band, is speaking to Ink Man and he says, "My friend, this is the way we have been raised. Do not think us strange. All men are different. Our grandfathers taught us to do this. Write it down straight on the paper."

Ink Man says, "You speak truly. All men are different. This is your religion, the religion of your grandfathers. Our grandfathers used to be like yours hundreds and thousands of years ago, but now we are different. Your religion brought you the buffalo, ours brought us loco-motives and the talking wires."

Then the dance begins as twenty-six men and one woman take up the challenge. The men were laid one-by-one on a bed of sage and then a medicine man bent over each warrior, uttered a prayer, pinched together some flesh below the nipple "while with the right he boldly and coolly, but leisurely cut the quivering form, making an incision under his thumb not less than an inch and a quarter to an inch and half long." Wooden skewers are slipped through the cut, the man is tied to long strands reaching up into the sacred tree, he clasps a flute between his teeth, leans back on his feet so that the skewers tear and tear at his chest, and then, yes then, he begins to dance. When the flesh rips, and he is free, his dance is ended. One man lasted fifteen minutes, another thirty minutes. The woman, Pretty Enemy, had cuts made from her shoulders to her elbows to spare her soft breasts and danced among the men. It ended precisely at 3:05 P.M. Ink Man made careful notes of every aspect and promised to return. But he did not, nor did the Sun Dance last much longer. In 1883, the government in its effort to bring the Lakota into the world of locomotives forbade it. And the Dance went underground.

I think of this as I ride in a car with Sundance. We are in Las Vegas, and he recalls the sirens' call of World War II for him and his brothers. There was a song on the radio after Pearl Harbor about all the great American warriors of the past, including Custer ("Goddamn Custer," Sundance says as the car rolls through traffic, "goddamn Custer. But we didn't know any better then."), and Sundance and his two brothers went to the big show. One brother parachuted behind Japanese lines on Pacific islands. Another took eleven rounds through his body in Europe. Sundance stayed at his gun on the ship as the kamikazes raked the deck. They were ready for war, they were Lakota. They all came back alive but very thirsty.

And I think they all needed the Sun Dance, the test that took them to the edge and restored their faith in the world as they truly knew it, one where there were no guarantees, no sure things, no security, but a sense of flow, and penance. That is part, I believe, of the need for a couple of hundred bouts with the dt's. Sundance had to find that edge so that he could escape being Rupert McLaughlin. Yet the dt's terrified him, the medicine was so powerful, too powerful. Once he was busted right on the edge of the dt's, and the cop putting him in the tank took a good look at him, and sensed what was coming. He went away, came back with a water glass full of vodka, and he said, "Drink this. All of it." And Sundance did, gratefully, in order to spare himself that monstrous five-day ride.

During our time in Las Vegas he tells me of a final bout with the dt's. The visions came in waves. In one, a bunch of Gestapo, all women in black leather, torture him, but in the nick of time, he is saved from dying. When I was a boy, old people told me that if I died in my dreams I would truly die, right then, at that instant. I would never wake up. In dreams and visions we always get a final reprieve from the medicine.

But Sundance disagrees with this because of what happened in this last round of the dt's. It was in '71, he thinks, and he was penning his writs in that jail in Los Angeles. Solitary confinement could not break him from his new legal crusade. "When I take a stand," he snorts as he leans into my face, "I do not back down." This time in the dt's, he was a prisoner in Cuba and the revolutionaries of Castro dragged him from his cell and put him up against a bullet-pocked wall. He heard the comandante calling out the orders, "Ready, aim, fire," and by God, they did just that, and he died. That is, Rupert McLaughlin died. And when he came out of this five-day hell, Rupert McLaughlin was gone and a new man, Robert Sundance, had taken over his booze-blasted body. It took him four more years finally to beat the bottle. But a new man existed and he began to live a new life. This he knows. And nothing can take this knowledge from him. He is now a dance where you dangle from a tree and your flesh tears and you come close to the power and taste it and drink it and make it part of what you are and can be and will be. He is Robert Sundance. He knows.

It is very hard to tell what Charlie knows. I talked with him for hours once, before his fall from grace and endless riches. He was impossible for me to dislike because he was so alive, so alert to the moment. And he was impossible for me to like because he was so empty. His brilliance was in his knowing his emptiness, in sensing it, and acting on it. He made money meaningless by squandering billions. He made power meaningless by creating nothing but buildings that did not matter even to himself, buildings that will tumble down in a few decades and become lots again. He made power meaningless by having no purpose, no target, no mission. He spent those billions and did not even leave us a huge pyramid or a legend of slave labor constructing some bizarre dream. I can never prove it but I sensed he recognized this emptiness and decided to become a Columbus of this void, sailing out where others did not dare go and all he found was more nothing and more nothing. True, like Columbus he left destruction in his wake, but he failed to mate, to mix, to give rise to some new entity or breed. So he left nothing. Such talk as this is, of course, easy to dismiss. We have a vocabulary for getting rid of it. We say free enterprise, capitalism, and if pushed hard, we say God. Charlie loves to talk this way, especially about God.

But we no longer believe our words. We have begun to wonder about the buffalo, the wolf, the condor, and the Saturday night. We have reached a remarkable point for our breed. Our books are full of generations who blew the future. We may be the people who end the future. All the scary headlines may be true, all the lab reports may be bad. There may be no more for us. The big ball of dirt will continue to spin on, the microbes, the plants, the wolves . . . all these may continue. But for ourselves, for our world, for that outlet in which I will plug this electric cord, well, that future may have ended. We may be the real endangered species, the one not recognized and protected by our walls of statute books. And should we choose to go to the bar, and drink, drink very hard, and then sing, well, there may not be enough Crows to go around.

There can be no reality without fantasy. We can never be large enough to touch the solid, feel the living, move with the energy unless we imagine ourselves as more than we can ever really be. Without bullshit we cannot make it to the real shit. And this is what we are losing now, this is what we have lost. We mock those who seek, we mark them as outlaws. Columbus, a fiend or a fool or a mistake. Keating, a crook or a bigot or hypocrite. Sundance, a drunk, or a fabrication—who gave him the right to rename himself? Ernest Hemingway blew his brains out, right? Maybe that is the place to begin, the reviled Hemingway hero, the figure who faces the collapse of democracy and civility during the First World War and retreats into a self where a man takes his own measure by an internal code of conduct—silence, slaughter of large animals, risk, strong drink, but never, never belief. No, never believe again because belief leads to betrayal. That is why the Hemingway hero is capable of a romantic outlook chugging through the green hills of Africa, hooking trout in lonely strands of surviving streams, sipping fine liquor in small foreign bars, and sitting in a sturdy, plain wooden chair. But this same figure is incapable of sentimentality—always death comes to one alone and there is no family around the bedside, there is no bed in fact, there is no future to connect to since the only thing one possesses is this interior code of manliness that must, of course, die with the hero himself. Life becomes a sterile act of defiance and what is defied is sham whether in the guise of communism or capitalism.

The Hemingway hero worked for much of this century and gave us all a language for confronting a world we could not control or bear. Oddly enough, this hero is now attacked for hygienic reasons, for the messy murder of animals, for seeing women as sexual utility devices, for the boozing, for failure to nurture, support, and listen to the wail of the inner child. And so forth. But the real failure of this hero, the reason this model can longer continue, the reason for the increasing lack of belief in this hero, is that the struggle has gotten too vast. Facing down Rotarians and commissars with a manful silence and resolve is not the same as looking into the dying waters of the ocean sea, meeting the hard stare of vanishing species, walking the mountains studded with bleeding stumps. We no longer can go to Big Two Hearted River because the river is either dry or poisoned. And it does not matter if Lady Brett joins us in bed because our lovemaking cannot shelter us from the acid rain beating against the ancient wood shutters that bang and bang in the storm.

Charlie understood this fact even though he scorned the natural world and gives no evidence of reading novels penned by dead men. Sundance also understood this fact. There is a need for a new fantasy, it is not the time for new rules but for breaking rules. We do not need therapy, we need to burn the clinics. We must go out, out into the stench, out in the frightening night on skid row, and hear the locust cries of our future. We need a fantasy that grabs, takes, molds, seizes. We cannot simply suffer in silence, and spare ourselves the risks of joining into the frays of a sham world.

The century ends and what has it produced? A new warrior cult, an old man battling in a courtroom rather than surrender to the mores and rules of a culture he despises. An old man on skid row with a huge knife on his hip, walking through the herds of broken people who would kill him for his shoes.

Medicine, sweet medicine, strong medicine. Loud voices, hands at the throat. Ready, aim, fire. Ink Man, put this down straight on your paper. Lie on that bed of sage, put this bone flute between your teeth. We will utter a soft prayer, lance the flesh, put in the skewers, tie you to the sacred tree.

Goddamn Custer.

The horses are saddled and it is time to ride.

The stack of chips lining the rail is over a foot long now and most are red five-dollar chips. Sundance never seems to tire when he throws the bones. He is placing bets like a machine gun here, there, the hard way. And he keeps winning and winning. The table is warm. Yet he looks the same as when the table is cold. He is not responsible for the table, he is responsible for paying heed to the table, for sensing its warmth or its chill. He stays at the table as long as he can bear the pain. That is the Dance.

He is now up about $500. The chips loom on the rails like a larder of that fabled pemmican to pull him through the winter of the deep snows. But he clearly does not think this way. He continues to pitch out bets like a catapult, flinging chips down the table with abandon. This is not important. He gets the dice, bets heavily, rolls them, and loses.

He turns to me and says, "I did not do well."

He is very content at this moment.

Do not say the word cancer. Do not say the word gam-
bling. Do not ask why a life is spared.

The numbers today are nine and four.

The buffalo are coming back.

The table is.

I never learned what became of the baby found in the
sewer pipe in Pennsylvania. L.A. can be that way, a blur
where the message never catches up with you. I keep regular and tidy notes, and even still, things become a blur
for me. The wolves will be back. I can feel it in my bones.
They are made for the world that is coming, they have
never destroyed their families, they have never abandoned
them, and in their own curious way, I think, they love the
land. They are like God, never quite dead, always linger-
ing under our concrete and steel and cannons, ready to
move back into the light of day. One after another people
who tell me God is dead finally die, but God, well, people
still talk to God. So you see the killing off is not as easy
as we had hoped.

The condor also looks hopeful. I see more carrion just
over the horizon.

Sundance tells me of the buffalo. Back in the Dakotas
where his brother lives one man had some. A bull hooked
him with a horn, laid him open, and he died. He says this
with a kind of silent laugh, as if that is what buffalo do
and that is why buffalo are fine. Besides, he says, they are
coming back. The Sioux are buying hundreds of them and
they are turning them loose.

How will you fence them? I ask.

Ah, the fences are being taken down, the buffalo will
drift just as they did in the past.

I eye my beer and imagine that as he speaks hundreds
of buffalo are coming down chutes off trucks, shaking

those shaggy heads, glaring with beady eyes, and trotting off into the grass, their ridiculously small asses twitching as they disappear into the land. The wind of the plains rakes their hairy hides and there will be no junk bonds issued on the value of their bones and flesh. It is a very small note in the big scheme of things. No one at a government steelcase desk in Washington, D.C., will register this fact in the compilation we call the gross national product. In the nineteenth century, General William Tecumseh Sherman announced that the buffalo had to be slaughtered off the plains because if a bull mated with a domestic cow, the cow would die in calving because the hump of the calf would kill her. I do not know if this fact is true, but it was true for General Sherman and it was true for the tens of millions of buffalo who were cut down in a few short years. And now, apparently, it is no longer true. They are coming back and their horns can still lay us open with a mere toss of their great shaggy heads.

I cannot feel the baby in the sewer in Pennsylvania and I am ashamed of this fact. I cannot feel the billions missing from some giant drawer when I am in the courtroom at Charlie's trial. I can feel a little bit of when Rupert McLaughlin died and Robert Sundance stood up. The buffalo, those I can feel, their hooves slicing my face, pounding me into mush as they race back into the plains. They are a storm in my world and soon, if God is kind, this storm will wash my face with life-giving rain.

Once Robert Sundance played a big poker machine that featured a giant jackpot of something like four thousand dollars. It stood in the front of a casino like the jewel in a crown. He hit big, a full house, and fifteen hundred dollars cascaded out. This machine was very warm. All this happened at about two o'clock in the afternoon.

Robert Sundance knew what to do with his windfall. He put it back in the machine, and stayed there playing until eleven o'clock that night. He wanted to hit the royal flush, the big jackpot.

He lost every cent, he tells me. He thinks he knows what the problem was. He did not keep playing long enough.

I am driving and I am driving too fast. This often happens. In one hour, I will get a ticket for going fourteen miles over the speed limit, but this does not matter now. I try not to pay attention to limits anyway. Speed is part of the price for me and my kind. I also do not wear a seat belt. This is not a rational act, which is why it occurs. I have become skeptical of many rational things including the deductive skills of my own mind. I know medically that Sundance is dying from cancer in his bones but I do not believe this and neither, I think, does he. I know it is safer to wear a seat belt and drive more slowly but I do not think dying on the highway is where the danger lies for me or for others. I do not think any danger lies in dying. The grave is not the terror, it is . . . I am far from Los Angeles, I will not tell you where.

There is a woman riding with me, a woman of the Sioux nation. As we talk, the land flashes past—trees, rock, grass, river, gulch, badlands, goodlands, graves. I am telling her of drunken Indians. Of the boy who hanged himself with the cord from a toaster, of the drunks who lie down in the road and pray for the traffic, of the women who die in the ditch, their bodies slashed with broken beer bottles, their vaginas left a weeping ruin of wounds. I am having my say, pouring out years of hurts, the bleak graves with no grass, the headstones that topple into the dirt an hour after I leave. I have a solution to the big problem: stop drinking.

"Until the Indian people get their shit together about

the booze," I say, "they will not make it. No program will make it, no idea, nothing will make it. I don't care about this liberal shit, I don't care about federal programs, I don't care about some fucking study by some asshole in a university. It's a killing ground out there, and no one will make it, nothing will happen, until the booze is faced and faced down."

And I think while I say this that I am angry now and I want a drink.

She sucks on her cigarette, and a trail of smoke pours from her nostrils, a trail as long as those trekked by the great herds. She is silent for a while, but I am not disturbed. I sense she has deep wells in her body and they are all full of silence.

Then, she speaks: "I know what you are saying but here is what I think. The drinking, it is bad and there has been a lot of drinking. No one who has lived on the rez can doubt the drinking. Shit, man, the drinking is bad. But here is the way I see it. The Indians, they've been drunk a hundred years and that is why they have survived. That is what has saved them. From this, from this shit outside the windshield, from joining up, from learning those jobs, from doing those things, from giving up on what they are and who they are. From becoming citizens, from walking around dead. So I think the drinking has been good—fucking right, I think it has been good. It has been the only thing that has saved them. Maybe, the time has come to end this drunk. Yeah, maybe that's true. But about the drinking, well, I think this hundred-year drunk, this has been the thing that has pulled the Indians through."

I say nothing to her words. They are the story of every survivor and that is why I know they are true. They are

many days and nights in my life that have been consumed
by the bottle and the joint, and in my heart I know that
these days and nights are the only reason that I am still
alive. They are behind all the rooms and jobs and careers I have walked away from. Her words are like a fist
behind my resignations from positions. Until she speaks,
until that instant I had never really sensed what was
behind my failures. And I have never been able to get past
the word failure. And most of my life, like any American,
I have seen myself as a failure, as the person who fucked
up, did not fit in, lacked the strength or fiber or something to take advantage of a situation or offer or, God
forgive me, an opportunity. Everyone I know in this
country is still in high school in a sense, still living that
moment in the counselor's office when the advisor who
represents success (how, I have never quite understood)
stares down at your test scores and announces that you
are not living up to your potential. He told me I must
become a chemical engineer, it was my destiny. So when
the woman speaks, when in a flat, calm voice she flings
words into my face like acid, at that instant I know I
must face what she says. She is right, right despite the
cemeteries full of young men, right despite the alleys
stinking from vomit, right despite the rapes in the back
rooms of all the bars, right despite the incest, homicide,
suicide. Right despite the irritating litter of empty quarts
of beer and broken wine bottles. And since she is right, I
get rid of her fast, drop her off at her destination, refuse
to come in, no, no, no thank you, and race away as fast
as I can go.

The ticket, it was inevitable.

The cop was very kind. He told me where the next
speed traps were for 130 miles. Shit, he said with a smile,

it's Saturday night and man, we've got a problem here with drunken Indians. Two have died in the last month, he continued, and we've got to clean this road up.

I do not argue. I like the ticket. I have earned it. Night is coming down without fair warning, the sky is going blank, the smells start to pour off the land as the heat leaves and the snakes surface for the hunt. I want a drink bad, but I know it is time to stop the drinking. A hundred years is enough. The bottle can sneak up on you as champagne, or whiskey, or bonds, or easy money, or power. I know one thing for certain: the bottle, whatever its contents, can never be love, never be the love of anyone or anything or anyplace. Charlie, hell, he can kill the bottle. He has been convicted now of all those counts in the Los Angeles courtroom and he is appealing the decision. He has been thrown in prison for ten long years. His life now is a bunch of details in a court calendar. The senator, he can have a hit off the bottle too and wobble around being ethical. Rupert McLaughlin can lie in his nameless grave. I can hear hooves pounding around me in the blackness, I catch a whiff off the hairy hides. I want to slaughter one and eat its meat and then, come morning, look up and see a condor slowly circling over the carcass. The wolves will be nosing about the bones also. Sundance, he is sitting by my fire, sipping coffee and waiting for the sweat to begin—there is this thing, you know, in his bones. General Sherman, he's off there lamenting the world he helped create, a world that made him into a statue in New York and shoveled a lot of money his way if he would just keep on saying that the future was coming to the golden lands of America. He's looking back now and letting his guard down and he says, "Nature in her wild majesty has more charms for me than man's most cultured work and I sometimes deplore the early discovery of gold at Coloma, which has revolutionized the Great West, defaced and deformed the Sierra Nevadas, stript the forests from the Rockies, and swept out of existence the millions of buffalo, elk, deer & antelope which only thirty years ago made the plains the paradise of the hunter and the Indian."

Ah, only thirty years ago. I keep forgetting how fast things happen here, why there is always this blur. In the late nineteenth century the whites took the ground in almost the twinkling of an eye and dreamt of various El Dorados and then it was over, just railroads, deeds, streets, and mortgages. Before the average man or woman had a chance to savor the possibility of getting rich, the plains were taken, fenced, sold, and parceled out and one had to face an eternity of day jobs and squalling babies. After that came the next wave, us, dreaming of oil, subdivisions, factories, all manner of stale ideas that reproduced wherever the hell we had fled from. And now we have used up all the air or drugs or whatever it takes to sustain such illusions. We have used up all the space and the land rebels against us and we must construct something that can put a brave face on this event, some new manner or stance so that we can endure the incredibly shrinking and toxic ground under our feet.

All our drunks are ending now.

All my life I have looked for that light at the end of the tunnel. I have prayed that if I looked hard enough, suffered enough, went far enough, I would find something to believe in beyond the stubs in my checkbook. I have never, not for one instant, wanted to succeed. I have wanted to be good and to do good. I have wanted to love and be loved. The drinking, it has been necessary, and I suspect it will never end. Ending the drunk does not mean simply putting down the drink. That would be too easy. It is putting down the reason for the drunk. The hole.

Black, bottomless, a bad wind rising up from its unknown caverns, a stench I have been taught to call a scent, a perfume. The hole, that emptiness within us that we sense but cannot say, cannot acknowledge. Cannot fill. The hole that booze cannot fill, women cannot fill, men cannot fill. Nothing can fill but love, and to love, you must have not just someone but something to love. I am the product of centuries of long flight from that hole, from a pit that began, perhaps, at Jamestown or Plymouth Rock or in a lonely line at Ellis Island—there are so many points of origin, like my nation I am of many bloods. The hole, the fear behind so many fists swinging in the bar on Saturday night. I am ... in a saloon in a town called Chorizo where everyone sells drugs. It is hard to make enough to eat in America's backwaters and so here they move The Product. The night is Saturday, naturally, and the stranger next to me is drunk and leans into my face and says, "You claim to be a reporter but are you?" And I am happy, I have been waiting for this opportunity, waiting through the time when Boomer got drunk and stomped Little Al into the barroom floor, beat the living shit out of a guy he outweighed by a hundred pounds. Boomer is happy now, sitting over there with a smirk and a long neck, his brain still running from a bad tour in Vietnam. And so I lean back into the stranger's face and say, "Are you fucking deaf? I didn't claim to be a reporter, I said I am a reporter." But he backs down, and I am cheated. And I am left with the hole and robbed of a few moments of mayhem in which I could put its blackness out of my mind.

(In 1572, the Spaniards captured Tupac Amaru, the new Inca, the man who led an uprising against what the conquerors had already decided was the course of history. They put his head on a pike in Lima. Years earlier, his father, Manku, had tossed off some advice on how to deal with the new times and the bad winds: "What you can do is give them the outward appearance of complying with their demands. . . . I know that someday . . . they will make you worship what they worship. . . . [R]eveal just what you have to and keep the rest hidden.")

But there are answers, there are points at which we can begin acting. The hole can be filled—we must believe this because if we do not we are not simply finished, no, no, it will be much worse than that. If we do not believe we can fill this hole then we are cursed to remain what we have always been, an empty people. I've got a friend and he is an old man. The old man says that when a horse is gentle broke the horse works with you but when you simply break a horse, you work the horse. He sits in front of his trailer at dusk shooting coyotes that have foolishly forgotten their fear. So I know it will not be easy, the way will not be plain, that there are these . . . conflicts within me. But the horse, she can be gentle broke. And perhaps I can stay my hand when the coyotes wander too close at dusk. My eye is open, I am alert to sign.

We've got to come up with a way to take care of that baby found in a sewer pipe. It's going to be hard, it's going to be bad, there will be killings, I just know there will be. But the long drunk is over. I can hear the pounding of the hooves. They face the storms, you know. They either are not afraid or they know something we have forgotten. They face the storms.

I hear an old song, and I fill this song with new words.

73

My fist knocks on heaven's door. I am ready for the medicine.

Take this bottle from our hands.

We can't use it anymore.

Vegas disappears in the rearview mirror. Robert Sundance is ahead on the money. This is not what concerns him. His question is very simple: Has he taken enough risks? Or has he choked, backed off from the power?

He stops at State Line and senses the craps table there in the casino. He feels that it is warm. He begins to bet—the dice roll, the players shout, the current flows up from the green felt. Ah, he must plunge. The bets grow heavier and so do the winnings. He is now five hundred dollars ahead, his row of chips is grand. And then it turns around on him— this can happen, and the money goes away. He loses every- thing, every last cent.

This fact does not disturb him.

He once told me, "If I leave with money, then when I get home I think I could have bet that money and have been rich. I could have stayed and played and won big. So the money does not feel good if you take it home because you always think of what could have been if you had acted."

Nine.

Four.

Buffalo.

U sually, the mating process proceeds rather simply. The female sits, releases the pheromone into the air, and business proceeds. For copulation to occur the male wasp must be triggered by scent, by sight, and by touch. So the pretty and winged male flies a patrol, he stumbles upon the inviting scent drifting through the air and follows it. The female, to make it all so easy, has climbed up a ways off the ground on, say, a grass stem. Now the male approaches, the female begins to move her jaws in expectation. The male descends, grabs her with his legs. And off they go, like a military aircraft with a deadly missile slung underneath.

3

The apartment on Russian Hill rents for a few boxcars full of money each month and the view vacuums the bay from bridge to bridge. The refrigerator is stocked with champagne and good beers and the cupboard holds a half-empty bottle of vodka. Fresh cut flowers glow in the living room, but I can smell the legions of past drunks in this space. This time San Francisco is on the house for me. There was a period in my life when my only goal was to be in such an apartment in this city and hold a drink in my hand—a martini with an olive just like the ones sketched by the old neon saloon signs that glowed along 79th Street in the Chicago dusk of my childhood. I wanted to enjoy and belong to one of the most beautiful cities on the planet.

Now it is within reach and my hand does not move. I have not had a day off work in years. I am in the eyes of others a human cinder, a burned-out thing that eventually must stop, die, halt. There will be a shudder and then the glow will leave my body and the embers will cool and that will be it. I feel none of this. I am electric with energy and my ambitions keep pushing me into greater arenas of ruin.

I wear a wool sport coat because I know a job will be offered over a fine dinner in a grand hotel and I want to be appropriate. I will refuse the job and greatly regret not getting the money. The job will be one I have dreamt of for years.

In my pocket I carry a quotation, one I can find no place for in the warp of my life, but one that nags at me wherever I go. It is by Loren Eiseley, the scientist who could write readable English and made a hobby out of questioning the floor under his own work. He is dead now and I never knew he existed during his lifetime. An old man gave me one of his books, *The Star Thrower,* and I grudgingly read it. His world was too cold for me, too filled with unnameable terrors and too empty of nameable and quite enjoyable lusts. He is that creature we claim to revere—the stoic, the calm, cold eye, the lofty perspective peering down at the mess and fuss of our little lives. A wannabe Marcus Aurelius penning snippets of wisdom for low-lifes such as myself. I loathe all this bullshit stancing and prefer a greedier connection with the grubbiness of life. I do not want to sit in my perfect study and muse about the things just beyond the clean pane of glass. I want to spit into the face of death and piss into the fires of hell—The Hero With The Giant Bladder. But still Eiseley's words linger in my mind and I suppose I've been cursed a bit by reading that dry book that the old man loaned me.

I make a pot of coffee—the freezer holds a bank of little brown bags with beans from various poverty centers in the third world—and pour a strong cup. I pluck out the quote and try one more time:

Finally, in blundering, good natured confidence, the last land tortoise had fallen victim to the new expressway.

None of his kind any longer came to replace him. A chipmunk that had held out valiantly in a drainpipe on the lawn had been forced to flee the usurping rats that had come with the new supermarket. A parking lot now occupied most of the view from the window. I was a man trapped in the despair once alluded to as the utterly hopeless fear confined to moderns—that no miracles can ever happen.

The coffee fires up my system and I go down into the street, past the doorman who looks askance, past the tourists waiting for a cable car, across Nob Hill and into the Tenderloin. I have avoided this city for twenty years, since the salad days of the late sixties when music and ideas grew like weeds here. Three blocks from my apartment is Fisherman's Wharf and I remember my first visit here in 1965. I was broke, a sodden provincial shuffling past expensive restaurants and living off cans of sardines. I walked everywhere because I had no ticket to ride. I could afford but one drink then in the Buena Vista bar and everyone else had fine clothes.

Most of my money on that ancient occasion had been taken by the police in Tijuana after some kind of contretemps in a brothel.

We are drinking breakfast. Tijuana is warm air and dust and fading paint and the sound of buses with no mufflers. On my shirt is pinned a rosette of a religious order which I must have bought from some charity in the flush hours of the previous night. I still have my tear gas gun, I can feel my wallet in my front pocket. All is in order. We have been here around a day now and have yet to feel the need for a hotel room or a plate of food.

I am sitting at a small table across from my friend. A

woman with brown skin and a green shiny dress is on the floor under the table sucking him off. He picks up his glass, sips, sets it down, and does not spill a drop. It has been this way for a good long while so far as I can tell. We do not have a car. We do not have very many brains, they seem to have vanished into endless hours of drinking. Nor do we have many words left. We have fallen into ourselves and speak not at all, observe even less. I can hear a clinking sound and look over to see a woman stacking and washing glasses at the bar.

I feel very good, a floating sensation, that oceanic thing that comes, they say, when we melt into Nature and find our nature. I look up and notice that the woman is gone. She seems to have disappeared without a trace. And then another woman sits down and begins to caress my friend and kiss his cheek. She smiles a great deal. This is a friendly town, I can tell. They are talking about something—I can see their lips moving but lack the energy to listen. He gives her a twenty-dollar bill, American. And she goes away.

"What's that about?" I muster the energy to ask.

"She's getting change."

After an hour—five minutes? three days?—we both seem to realize she has not come back. At first, we cannot fathom this lapse of good taste. And then my friend gets up and looks around the bar in the whorehouse. Our table is covered with glasses. He picks them up and one by one shatters them against the wall. Then he moves toward the back bar and there are more loud sounds.

(Uuuummmm, it must be around 1965? 1966? I can't help. If you were there and can remember, they say you weren't there. So watch my words. Am I to be trusted? Sundance, he's doing another hard march on the Tokay

Trail. Let see . . . in the sixties he averaged about 250 or 260 days a year in the drunk tank, courtesy of Los Angeles. He'd be so broke he'd have to write letters for other prisoners in order to raise enough money for his postage. But while he is killing time in the tank, I am in Tijuana drunk, and the bar is disintegrating around my naturally calm nature. You think I cared about Rupert McLaughlin's troubles back then? No. You think I care now? I wonder also. We did not know then that each other existed. And if we had, I'm not sure it would have been a pleasant surprise. We both have a lot further to go down that road. Christ, does anyone here have a map?)

Men in uniforms arrive and they are not courteous. The tear gas gun seems to present a legal and ethical problem. So does my wallet. This inquiry takes a good deal of time and there are moments when I feel my person and my civil rights are not being totally respected. I remember being finally thrown across that famous line at the border and the look of disgust on the faces of the American officials.

Thank God for the twenty dollars hidden in my shoe.

The ride north on the bus is ashes, my stomach churning from a massive hangover. I am twenty. In San Francisco, there are places to crash, tiny apartments rented by herds of kids from places like Tucson, various dumps where people seem to sleep in shifts, the salt shakers hold ground-up marijuana, and every waking moment is punctuated with joints.

I am with my kind.

The city sells magic to kids from the provinces, everyone is going to be a rock star, poet, jazz wizard, or genius—hell, everyone is a genius, the world just does not know it yet. I fall in love with that place.

* * *

Now I have money but still I walk this city. My ankle is sprained, a thing on fire, but I must walk because somewhere in the miles I will find where I am going. This is an article of faith with me. The Tenderloin has changed, the whores and drunks and junkies are still out and about, but Vietnamese are taking the turf storefront by storefront and Oriental signs break up the old pattern of wino bars and sex shops. I hit a corner saloon, the 400 Club, a place that beckons with the stale breath of my native Chicago, and order a burgundy. The jukebox is nothing but oldies and soon Del Shannon's "Runaway" comforts my mind. It is almost noon.

The office is a block or two away, a newsroom humming with the black coffee and cigarette jangle that only a major daily can create. I am afraid to walk over there because I will be seduced instantly by one whiff of ink in the air. I drain my wine. This place was once simpler for me: She is buxom, it is eight o'clock at night, and we are eating in a small Italian place in North Beach. The year, 1967, a time when women suddenly can find work by exposing their breasts in odd situations—just across the street is a topless shoeshine parlor next door to City Lights bookstore. The woman speaks with a rich southern voice, and I wallow in the fat vowels. She is a playwright and we talk the word. The night advances, we stalk the bars, draining martinis, getting foolishly drunk. We race to catch a cable car, I jump and miss. It does not matter. I love the smell of her hair.

She has had a baby and then given it away for adoption. She will never speak of this fact. We sit in a movie theater, the actors up on the screen are in a bleak room, the doctor smokes a cigarette, the abortion proceeds. I can feel her tighten in my arms. Tears stream down her face, small droplets glistening in the half light off the glowing screen. She makes not a sound. She will not speak of this matter. Welcome to the summer of love.

I love her breasts, large, round, soft. She is on top of me, the breasts hang down, her tongue goes in my mouth. We are dead drunk.

I want to love but I am still a beginning student. Thank God the grades are easy in this course and the classes never cease. I am not fated to be a dropout. She wants to . . . be loved. She wants to be held but yet not touched, admired but not stared at. She wants the pain to stop. But she does not want risk. She never wants risk again.

She wavers. One night we go to visit some friends of hers. Her smile is generous, she has full lips, wiry hair, and when she speaks her mouth is full of those soft, southern vowels. So we go to these friends and they turn out to be two women about forty and one kind of dresses like me and one kind of dresses in a smooth and feminine manner. The living room is very clean and well ordered and the house has that odor, that astringent odor buildings seem to get when women or men live alone. I am not welcome here. No one is rude, but I am not welcome here. The two women focus on her and she drinks it up, she drinks deeply.

Like I said, she wavers. And I am noncommittal. It seems like a private matter to me, this finding love, this being loved, this seeking shelter from the storm. Especially at that time because I am very oblivious of shelter and tend to seek storm. I am strong and still drawn to hard liquor and long nights, and then the dawn slips up on me without notice and without a care.

Once in San Francisco, I pick her up early, it is maybe four in the afternoon and we go to a friend's apartment in the Embarcadero and stand on the balcony looking over the bay and have a joint. The air is cool with summer by the ocean and feels fresh against our skin. I pull her to me and feel her breasts push against my chest.

We walk into North Beach, eat, drink, and drink. We laugh a great deal and I can feel this tightening dissolving within her. Then we go back to the apartment and I sit down and she disrobes before me and we are in bed and she is eager. And then she says, "No, no," and whatever was behind her is, once again, ahead of her.

We breakfast at a cheap diner, ham and eggs. She cannot go to Monterey for the weekend rock concert. I leave. I never see her again. The walk across the city is a blur of faces, my head aches from the gin. A giant black bodybuilder in drag swishes past me in the bus station. I go south into a cauldron of sound that is called Monterey Pop. Jimi Hendrix and Janis Joplin leap from local favorites to the hard drugs of fame.

"... a man trapped ... the utterly hopeless fear ... no miracles can happen. ..."

I have another burgundy, drain it, listen to "Runaway" and leave.

The cool city air braces me.

I have always wanted to go places, drop in, take the quick scan, file, and move on. I was born to fill the cheap pages of newspapers. But now I cannot do it. I would like to think I cannot do it anymore because I am tired. That I can simply rest and then I will be ready once more to enter this fray. But this is not the reason. Nor is it because I find newspapers shallow—I was born for the saloon not the symposium. The bad hours, the lonely nights in an empty city room with just the hum off the computer, the green letters glowing on the black screen, the woman who comes in at two A.M. to file some late story and the resultant sexual energy that crackles through the tired air because she is there and I am there and the world is a very lonely place, the rain on my neck as I stand by a killing and scribble notes, the mail on the floor at my home that has tumbled through the slot and will never be answered—I love every miserable minute of this life. Especially the speed, to write in the cold hours before dawn and have the words out on the street before lunch. To make readers snap alert to things they have never imagined or wanted to know. I am an exile from newspapers because of the most grievous sin of all—I have lost my belief. I no longer believe that the front page, the business page, the sports page, the arts page can tell a story that matters. The editorial page? No one ever believed that the editorial page could forecast anything, that page was just a place for publishers to wipe their asses and call it thought. I now think that things are occurring so far beneath the daily patter of our civilization that we can both feel the tremors and at the same time ignore them. I think we are dying, and what we are dying from is from what we are. What I fear is not the decline and fall of this culture that raised me up, nor the lack of ease I now feel in filing for a newspaper. What I fear is paralysis, my own paralysis. I cannot imagine a life without an act or an act without the support of belief. I must believe . . . in order to be.

I am not cut out to brood nor is my eye on the goddamn sparrow—Christ! Look at that woman crossing the street, the way she walks, oh, ain't she fine.

* * *

I am keen about the dangers. Not out of fear but out of dread. The way I see it there are so many ways to fail and these failures are very difficult to see coming because they are all named success. I do not worry about the booze or the women or the lack of money. These things do not stop me. But there are other things.

It is past midnight and the ground is white high up here in the mountains. There is plenty to drink and plenty to snort and plenty to pop and plenty to roll. I am practicing moderation for a change but this is proving to be very lonely work.

He has been staring at a blank sheet of paper in the typewriter for three days. The huge television babbles on. Just before his face the remote dangles from the ceiling by a clothes line and every moment or so he punches out another station from 500 available on his satellite dish menu. The tumbler of whiskey sits nearby, the jar of coke, the big bag of grass, the hopper full of pills.

A sound is heard on the porch and one of the women goes and peers out. Something has not been kept at bay by the floodlights, by the beamed eyes that trigger sirens, by the menacing reputation that clings to these acres. He bestirs himself and wanders over in his bathrobe to survey the clear and imminent danger, a .45 automatic in his hand. There is a heap out on the porch, a man sprawled in the eight-degree cold and clutching his ribs with his arms. A low moaning rises off this pile of splattered clothes and busted bones. The story turns out to be simple on one level: the man is from Miami where he does some business and he was in Houston when he read the book—man! I thought this fucking book was about my life!—and then he decided to visit the man who wrote the book and, hell, he wheezes painfully, he bought a truck and then roared up into the mountains—Christ, hasn't even had the truck a single fucking full day—and then he stops at a bar and drinks for a few hours and then drops some Ecstasy and comes flying up the mountain and—who could see the fucking black ice at night?—goes off the fucking cliff. When he comes to, the windshield is busted, the steering column is driven into the dash, his ribs hurt and he crawls through the snow and up the cliff to the highway and he sees this light, all these floodlights, and he hobbles toward them in the cold.

The man goes rattling on and on as the guy in the bathrobe leans over with that loaded .45 and thinks "narc." He is debating in his mind whether to shoot the stranger in the head or stomp him to death. Each tactic has its points. But it is an ugly task to dig a hole in the ground when it is eight degrees above zero.

I point out that the man is apparently a dealer in drugs not an officer of the law.

"If that's so, how come he didn't bring me any fucking drugs?"

But the man buckled over with pain is in another place. The truck, well, he bought that with money he should have returned to a business associate in Miami, and this dereliction of sound business practices seems to terrify him more now than flying off the cliff in the night. And he has other concerns: he does not want a doctor—shit, no, his system can't pass a blood test for at least twelve more hours. And no cops, for God's sake, no cops.

We are at an impasse. The ground is too hard, the hospitals are out, the police are on a mutually agreed upon forbidden list. I throw him into my rented Blazer and drive slowly down the mountain and dump the shattered and half-frozen pilgrim at the airport.

I say, "Don't come back."

He says, "That was him, wasn't it? It was—right?"

And I drive away.

When I roll in toward three A.M. the page in the typewriter is still blank, the television still babbles, and dawn is drifting slowly toward the valley but it brings no promises to this place.

I pour myself a drink. The cold outside I can handle.

The newspaper hums with deadline. A reporter stands at the printout machine. He is finishing a story on the typical Chinese immigrant to the city. The paper has shipped him to China twice for the background. I feel my hunger rising.

For hours and days, I walk the city. I never take a cab, ride a trolley, climb up on a bus. I walk. The faces disturb me, I had forgotten the caution in human eyes when people are forced to live in cities of millions and millions. I ask a woman for a match, and watch this fear and hesitation flash across her eyes as we stand side by side at the light on Market Street. I realize I am that dangerous stranger. My pockets sag with money but I cannot seem to eat. Instead, I drink until one or two in the morning at the 400 Club. Frank the bartender is either a magician or a warlock because he seems to have an archive of old 45s in the basement and he can fetch up any song for the jukebox at a moment's notice. You have to be buzzed into the bathroom in this joint, and by God if you take too long Frank is pounding on the door wondering what the fuck you are shooting up in there. I get up at dawn and go back to walking. Constantly the pen scribbles in the notebook. I am looking for some clue and fear I will not find it.

One night I go to a café that is a self-conscious replica of a roadhouse from the fifties. It has tiny round tables jammed together, and an endless tape of old music booming. The woman at the next table is blond and talks with ease. Her escort is a good-looking man, quite young. He is a homosexual, a fact engraved on her eyes. She leans over into my face, the smile flashes. The top buttons of her blouse are undone, I feel the warmth between her breasts and she invites their inspection. I wonder how I know this one fact: you will never be capable of learning. I find all sorts of clues but reject them. She gives me everything but an engraved invitation. I cannot stay here.

"... the last land tortoise has fallen victim to the expressway. None of his kind any longer came to replace him."

I am sitting in a bar in 1967 with a friend who toils, as I do, in the string of factories surrounding the bay that everyone says are the future and that I fear are the future. We make things we cannot explain out of silicon and circuits or we make things we cannot explain out of the new natural resource, National Security. My friend is thin, has a raspy New York voice, and breaks his ass delivering an honest day's work. His wife is cheating on him, his kids are going out of control, and he spends a lot of time in his garage tuning his Chevy with its giant V-8 engine and abundant carburetors. He just loves to work with his hands and he's got a couple of St. Bernards to keep him company.

There is a war on, as it happens, and talk about this war goads my friend.

He says, "I don't want a fucking job that depends on

somebody going off to war and getting killed. If I thought my job depended on that shit, I'd say, to hell with it, you better fucking believe it."

I believe him. I believe also that his job and mine depend upon somebody going off and getting killed in some fucking war. All the jobs seem to depend on that fact by this time.

All this is a long time ago, back in that attic called the sixties (or is it a cellar?). I have a sports car, I drink rosé wine at first, the bottle between my legs as I slide around dirt curves in the coastal mountains and roar amid redwood groves. I am trying to be an eighteenth-century man, taking my women by the twos and threes, sprawled out in a belching farting heap in the forest surrounded by animals, a living thing drunkenly stumbling out of the pages of *Tom Jones* to the flailing of electric guitars. I lie down beside her on the forest floor, I fuck among the flower beds of Golden Gate Park, I grind her into the sand of the foggy Pacific beaches. I eventually recover, and replace the rosé with zinfandel and cabernet. I slide her black leather skirt off and she towers above me on a slender point of land and the gulls wheel overhead and scream.

I try reading nature books but I do not know what they are talking about. There is no booze, women seem to be shunned, the men also do not appear on the pages. There is this quality of a life without a heartbeat, loins without juice, breasts without nipples, britches without a bulge. I turn my face and walk away—ah, what is wrong with me? Also, I like guns, lots of guns, the smell of fresh powder, the crack of energy slicing the sky. Cool metal, the polish on the stock, the pure form of the brass trigger guard. The power to be left alone.

In southern California, I am pulled over, the cops approach with their hands on their guns—I am, well, unkempt—and I reach into my jacket for my wallet and license and then—presto—their guns come up fast. Or I am driving across Nebraska at two in the morning following the North Platte River and listening to Tim Buckley sing out while he busily dies of heroin when the light flashes behind me and I pull over and the movie repeats. This, I know, is the custom of the country—after all, I'm coming to Fort Laramie, coasting into that sacred ground, the Powder River country. Here Red Cloud, a Sioux chief with a track record like Sundance's—he murdered a chief in a drunken brawl back in the 1840s, counted eighty coup against enemies by the time he was a forty-year-old—finally saw the light of the new order. By the 1870s, he sneered this advice to his fellow tribesmen: "You must begin anew and put away the wisdom of your fathers. You must lay up food and forget the hungry. When your house is built and your storeroom filled, then look around for a neighbor you can take advantage of and seize all that he has." Who says Indians cannot grasp white ways? I'm standing in that humid cool of a late summer Nebraska night, the insects whirring, the cop figuring out how many felonies he can tack onto my life, the trunk stuffed with marijuana . . . and I know I should be busted, imprisoned, and reeducated. These moments keep recurring, and so does my failure to get my shit together. I naturally think it will take care itself: they all tell me I will eventually grow up. But, shades of Peter Pan, it doesn't seem to happen. So I like guns, I know I am one of the hunted and eventually they will catch me in their traps.

I sit in a stranger's apartment and he is nervous—it's

not much, about a half-kilo deal—because he does not know me. The room is rather Spartan, cheap student furniture, the stereo playing the Dead, the Family Dog posters on the wall, and a refrigerator full of nothing. His girlfriend is very good-looking, black long hair, fine face, and a body that seeks company at unpredictable times. He tells her to take a walk and we get down to business. Ah, he tenderly counts the bills. I stuff the goods carelessly in my trunk, peel out of the parking lot, and pull the cork out of an open bottle of wine with my teeth.

That fabled California sun beats down as I climb up into the redwoods. Fine homes flash by, all far nicer than I will ever live in, and everyone who lives in those homes has perfect teeth. Good genes, I guess. I roll a joint, suck down deep, take another hit off the wine. We have a loaf of sourdough bread and a hard wheel of Monterey Jack, the cheese white and crumbling. It is very good to be alive. A woman is sitting beside me, school's out, *in loco parentis* is over and she smokes a French cigarette, her fingers perfectly poised around the white wand of tobacco. I feel like I am escaping from a crypt as the cities of the Bay Area vanish from my rearview window.

The filtered light of the forest makes her naked skin glow as I lean against the rough bark of a redwood and watch her garments cascade from her body. She shakes her hair free and slides down on me and behind her is a wall of shrubs, flowers, and vines and at this moment I cannot remember one Latin name, not a single goddamn taxonomic label. The birdcalls confuse me also.

Sometimes I go to meetings—save a few fucking trees, save the mother-fucking whales, clean the air, don't piss in the creek. And I feel vile, alien, perverted, sinfully

wrong, misguided, debauched, so many things. I hide my
fangs dripping with blood from the flesh of animals. The
woman at these meetings do not wear makeup, the men
at these meetings speak precisely. No one laughs. They
say this is a club. So I go back to my dark ways.

*(He was born in this empty reach of the desert and is the
pioneer we all require if we are to fix our place in the long
march of our own history. I'm writing a magazine piece on
the town, what it was like in the old days. I go to the saloon
in the tiny desert town in the hope of finding him, but at
first the bartender is reluctant to talk. He is the oldest man,
I explain, I need him for my story. There is a hesitation,
apparently some bad blood has gone down, but then I am
told what dirt track to follow out into the desert. The trailer
is small, old, and lacks any shade. Inside the tabletops are
covered with bottles, magazines, and grime. The old man is
balding and has that lizard look that overtakes some in the
last days. He has been drinking, the fifth sits out on the
counter. When he speaks beads of drool form on his lips and
he spits at me when he gets excited. He still has his flesh and
could last a few more seasons. His feet are in broken slip-
pers and he shuffles about the small space.*

*I ask him about the old days. He tells me of a great day
in 1930.*

*"This couple stopped by the bar and we sold gas then
too, we sold pretty much everything there was to buy
around here. We were fucking IT. The guy and this woman,
she was a good-looking blonde, a Swede with nice tits, and
they said like they'd broke down out in the desert where
they'd been prospecting—there was lots of people fucking
around with that stuff back then—and could I give a ride
out for a buck or so? And I thought, I don't like the looks
of this guy, but what the hell, I could take care of myself*

then, I was a husky guy, you know. She says nothing, just stands there but gives me a nice smile and I think why not.

"So we get in my car, and he sits in back, and I think this is odd, but I watch him in my mirror and pretty soon he's a-jawin' about go left there, and take that fork there, and we're bouncing down the ruts and clawing our way across the arroyos and I think, fuck, I know where they're camped, I know every place around here but I don't say nothing. Well, after a while we get there, and by God he gets out and he comes around my side, and I think just to fake me out, he pulls a knife—why he didn't pull it in the back seat still kinda surprises me but maybe he caught me a-watchin' him in the mirror all the time. So, I'm a-starin' at him by the door with his knife held up near my face and I pull the big crescent wrench I keeps under my seat and just blindsides him with it. Teeth flew, by God, teeth flew, I tell you. And then I pops outta the car and he's a-lyin' there grabbing his face and moaning and I see a piece of firewood he'd brought into his camp just right there on the ground and I picks it up and wallops him on the head and he goes real quiet. I figures I have killed him sure.

"Well, just then I looks over at her and she's got out of the car and is looking pretty scared. She's a fine-looking woman, I mean to tell you. I got a bottle under my seat too, and I pull it out and take a swig and just look her up and down. And she begins to get the idea. I slide my hand inside her dress and feel one of those big breasts and she says, 'Okay, mister, just don't hurt me. I didn't know what he was going to do.' And this makes me kinda mad, like how dumb does she think I am.

"Well, she drops her pants and I lean her right against the fender and I fuck her awhile and she don't do nothing. And then, when she thinks she's got it whipped, why I spin her

around and pin her and slide it right up her ass and she squeals like a goddamn pig. What'd she expect?—'I didn't know what he was a-gonna do,' my ass.

"*I left'm both out there and I still don't know if I killed the guy or not. But nobody ever mentioned anything and a couple months later I went out there and there wasn't no sign, just a few bits of garbage from where they'd camped.*

"*I've often wondered what became of that Swede woman. She was something. I mean to tell you she was the best piece of ass I ever had.*"

And then he shuts up and there were beads of spittle on his old lips.)

I have this thought I do not utter—Christ, I don't want to be stoned to death or left in a cell and force-fed gran- ola for the rest of my days. But the thought persists: that the two groups I know who are most alike are environ- mentalists and pornographers. They both hate the human body, hate the soft joys of the flesh, hate their own appe- tites, hate the animal lurking within them that threatens to save their souls. Don't wear makeup—bend over bitch—leave nothing but your footprints—never let love be in your touch as you caress a breast. The obsession with orifices: one group apparently wishing to seal them off with some kind of environmentally sound cement, the other group wishing to blast through them with battering rams. Both groups are very angry, ah, such tightly wound faces. And so afraid of being overcome by emotions, of being slaves to passion. Of surrender to something irra- tional. The telephone man never surrenders, he just does his business and leaves. The nature savant never licks the bark or wants to wallow in the frenzy of the rut. The nature boys and girls know the correct names for every- thing. Both regret these . . . feelings that stir within them

and seek their penance on brutal trails or in darkened
theaters.

I am a disgrace and I know it. I like the way women
walk in high heels. I prefer Frederick's of Hollywood to
the Nature Store. My favorite fossil fuel is body oil.
Christ, the wine bottle is empty, the joint has gone out in
my hand and burned between my fingers, and I am falling
down, down, down on her. She tears at the loaf of bread,
breaks off some cheese, and I eat. I shall always treasure
the time I gave a speech to a field academy of graduating
environmentalists and a week later ran into a scientist
who had been in the audience. He said with a harsh,
clipped voice, "The last time I saw you, you'd had too
much to drink." No, no, please God say it isn't so—not
by half, amigo. There has to be more, more, more.

I drink in this place by the Lockheed plant where they
build whatever it is we need for war. The joint is huge, it
must seat a thousand, and the entertainment is topless.
The woman dancing has huge breasts—let me say it: they
can't be natural—and she's got a fucking boa constrictor
draped around her as the music blares and washes over
her perfect body. Outside the fog is rolling in and the air
has a salt tang. The woman never smiles, nor does the
snake.

Sundance needs a drink during his brief liberty in San
Francisco from his ship the *Ticonderoga*. (Ah, Ethan
Allen at the head of his Green Mountain Boys shouting to
the Brit commander, "Surrender in the name of the Great
Jehovah and the Continental Congress," or so the old
books claimed when I was a boy. My father insisted he
actually said, "Come out of there you damned old rat."
I can see the old man sipping on a quart of Drewry's as

he explained this to me and then watching my eyes to determine if I'd understood his lesson for the day.) It is 1943 or '44 and Sundance is sixteen or seventeen years old. His nerves are not so good now. He is a gunner (twenty-millimeter antiaircraft) on a carrier and he faces kamikazes barreling down the slot toward his life. One has recently crashed into the aircraft carrier's hangar and killed 220 men on Sundance's ship. First the Japanese planes come out of the sun and the thirty-eights are fired. Then as they close, the forties weigh in. And when a sailor can see the eyes of the kamikaze pilots, then, at that moment, Sundance fires his twenties. If one of the guns makes a hit, flames erupt and chunks of metal fall down on the sixteen-year-old gunner.

So Sundance needs a drink.

(The nineteenth century is tapering off, and Senator Henry Dawes explains that there remains much to be done for these Native Americans: "We may cry out against the violation of treaties, denounce flagrant disregard of inalienable rights and the inhumanity of our treatment of the defenseless ... but the fact remains.... Without doubt these Indians are somehow to be absorbed into and become a part of the 50,000,000 of our people. There does not seem to be any other way to deal with them.")

So Sundance needs a drink.

He crosses with some shipmates from Frisco to Oakland, goes into a bar, and gets drunk on whiskey. Then he takes a quart and a pint up to his cheap hotel room. He falls asleep with a cigarette in his mouth, and when his buddies return, they find the mattress on fire and hustle him out of the place before the authorities arrive. He wakes up on the dock in San Francisco, blinks and thinks, where in the hell is my quart and pint? He goes back to the room in Oakland and finds his bottles. He drains the pint instantly and passes out. Around noon he awakens and he is sober.

And that is his San Francisco.

"A chipmunk that had held out valiantly in a drainpipe had been forced to flee the usurping rats. . . ."

In 1967, I am 1-A according to my draft board (which, luck being luck, was numbered Board 13) and living amid cocktail waitresses in a cheap rental off the El Camino Real in Redwood City. The port ships napalm to the hungry rice paddies. It is supposed to be but a matter of weeks for me. I work helping to computerize the first eight years of schooling. But at night I drink cheap red wine bought by the gallon from a small shop in North Beach and punch a typewriter. I am doing the novel. The woman I am living with is taken by the experience. I have a sports car, we have a mattress on the floor, and our table is an old door, the knob still intact and standing like a monument on the plain of varnished wood.

(It is 1868, and the feds have once again made the Sioux an offer they can refuse. Crazy Horse is romping around the Powder River country and is pretty chipper—he's helped whack eighty-one troopers. When he hears of the proffered treaty he thoughtfully explains the problem to the authorities: "Now you tell us to work for a living but the Great Spirit did not make us to work but to live by hunting. You white men can work if you want to. We do not interfere with you, and again you say, why do you not become civilized? We do not want your civilization.")

Sometimes we go to the Fillmore—free apples for everyone, Richie Havens with a mouth of bad teeth and blank spaces is singing "Handsome Johnny," and when we walk out into the darkness, black faces take our measure. Late at night the radio blares, I type, she sleeps, her face like a child's, a face without a worry about the world. Her unconscious mind is planning strange menus for the next day and plotting marriage. I am deeply in love.

Dylan's *John Wesley Harding* comes over the airwaves. The man is back from the mysterious bike accident and as I pour a tumbler of zinfandel, he warns me about all along the watchtower. Immediately after this premiere playing of the album a woman calls the station and says, "He is obviously brain damaged." I finish the book in six weeks. I have not read it since. But I can still remember that night, the raw rush of the wine in my throat, and the injunction to pity the poor immigrant, the plea to the landlord.

"A parking lot now occupied most of the view from the window."

Finally, I go to the meeting that is the real reason I am in San Francisco living free and easy in this fine suite of rooms overlooking the bay. The dining room is private, the woman serving our dinner asks if I would like a drink and a bottle of chardonnay appears. I twirl the crystal in my hand and scan the fumed wooden walls. The talk is very bright and merry. I eat a salmon.

The offer is there on the table if I just reach.

Afterward, I walk into Chinatown, the magazine racks full of bare-breasted shots of Oriental women injected with silicone. The night is friendly and warm. My own child is less than a year old and half-Japanese, the eyes hooded, the face fat, warm, and brown. In a restaurant once, a Japanese man looks at my son's picture, smiles, and asks, "How does it feel to be cut out of the deal?" I realize we will never outlive racism, we all have much too much invested in the enterprise. Finally, I pause in my walk and enter Tosca's in North Beach, where the wine keeps coming, I look at the picture of my son again and wonder at the black eyes as opera pours from the jukebox. For a brief moment, I toy with taking the job because, just maybe, this is the one city in the United States where you can be half-Japanese but all American. But I know I am incapable of the sacrifice. The Polaroid is glossy and blurred but I can smell my child's clean skin.

I go with an editor to the offices of the Mitchell Brothers, successful local pornographers, where whales and fish cavort in a giant mural coating the streetside wall. Nature comes first, you know. The admission is twenty-five or thirty-five dollars a head, but the editor walks right in, and I glide up to the second floor and the private quarters. Here the pool table is sound, the bar well stocked. I crack a bottle of wine. There is a jukebox, poker tables, a moose head, and a signed poster of Hunter Thompson glowers from the wall.

I am a provincial, a man of the *despoblados,* the badlands, the backwaters, and I know this fact in the marrow of my bones. I still can't figure out the logic of the itinerary but I can sense it. I must go certain places, they will make themselves known, and then I must file strange communiqués, things that do not fit the columns, pages, and headlines of the newsroom. I must make my own medicine just as I have made my own illness. My mood begins to brighten because I feel a kind of peace with what I will do with the remaining crumbs of my life.

Also, I know I will get very drunk tonight and this thought does not alarm me. Quite the contrary. Only in drink can I find a place for the feelings within me. I need to violate myself. My hand feels the smooth shape of the cue, I shoot. I am not good tonight, there is no flow, I think the shot instead of sense it. This table is not warm.

We go out onto the balcony. Here, the sound man monitors his machine, the video camera scans the stage and throws images on huge screens. Down below, the woman is naked, she bends and her crotch opens up. Clots of men sit silently with their white T-shirts and large bellies, and they seem passive. They are the audience in this sex palace. The woman moves with fluid ease, her breasts are huge, the hair blond, her expression as blank as the grille of an automobile. After a few minutes, her stint on stage is done and she descends into the audience. I am running the camera now, sitting in a director's chair, a bottle of wine in one hand, the zoom lens in the other. Rock music booms, I zoom in on the woman, she sprays against the screens. She is wearing a G-string and it glows greenish in the half light of the audience. A man holds up a fist full of bills, she sits on his lap and begins to bump and grind. He comes in his pants and I watch the stain spread. Lap dancing.

The night continues and another dancer hits the stage, the night continues. The women pass a few feet behind my back as they come and go on their urgent errands. In the dressing room a bank of lights outlines the mirrors and they sit naked and perfect, staring blankly at their own faces. They are the women that men are said to dream of and they are here. I do not feel I am in heaven or in a nightmare or in a den of iniquity or in a state of sin. I feel I am with the dead. T. S. Eliot was wrong—no surprise—it does not end with either a bang or a whimper—it ends here with soft flesh and stained pants and with my hand directing the shots that play against the walls. You want it, we have it here. There is the Ultra Room, a glass-lined chamber where women use whips, chains, ropes, where women insert all manner of things into their bodies. And best part of all, pardner, you get to watch. I drain the bottle dry and have another fetched. I run the camera for hours, I keep drinking wine, bottles of which I keep no count. In these hours I never hear a sound from the audience or see a single expression cross the faces of the women or of the men. I am very excited. I have finally found the crucial codicil to Lord Kelvin's Laws of Thermodynamics. I am staring into the voluptuous crotch of absolute entropy. Entropy has captured the attention of every sane person for at least a century—it is the ultimate nightmare of industrial culture, running out of energy, putting the pedal to the metal and having nothing happen. And here it is, a bunch of wet pussies and a bunch of dicks probing dark holes that have no bottom.

I am celebrating the end of one future, and oh, the wine feels so good as I celebrate. I will not work for big money on a major daily and fly around the world to interview people in a Chinese village. I will not trek Nepal either. I will not wear my wool sport coat—this particular one I will eventually give to a poor man in Mexico. I drink until dawn and then catch an early flight to the desert. At the airport I will discover that I have lost my prepaid tickets. No problem, I put the fare on my credit card. I must get out of here. In this I am not alone. In the morning, the editor I drank with that night flees into the mountains and stays there two weeks. He does not drink again for months.

The paralysis has lifted. I can now look for a miracle.

"I was a man trapped in the despair once alluded to as the utterly hopeless fear confined to moderns—that no miracles can ever happen."

(Jacob Cox is Secretary of the Interior in 1870, grinding out the deals for Ulysses S. Grant as the nation holds a great barbecue. Spotted Tail is in Washington with Red Cloud to try to salvage Sioux ground and Sioux life. The buffalo are disappearing, the great dying has begun, and Cox leans over the negotiating table and offers some free advice to the chief.

"A man must expect some trouble in his life and should face it in a manly way, not by complaining."

"Tell him," Spotted Tail informs the interpreter, "that if he had had as many hardships in his life as I have had in mine, he would have cut his throat long ago.")

My definition of a miracle may differ from that of the priests on some fine theological points. I do not seek evidence of magic flights, sudden bounties, unexpected cures, auras of light signifying grace. The corpse can rot with corruption and still I will see evidence of saintliness. I seek persistence, struggle, and a refusal to surrender.

It is March 1540, and Hernando de Soto lands at Tampa, Florida, and then swings up through Georgia with six hundred men, two hundred horses, war dogs, swine, and a passel of black and Mexican slaves. He is rich from the conquest of Peru and he wants more. As a young man with the bandits of Pizarro, he rode his horse up so close to the seated Inca that breath from the steed's nostrils fluttered the red threads hanging from the emperor's crown. He is not a man to respect much of anything beyond booty.

In North America, he leaves a generous swath of ruin in his wake. His slobbering mob enters a state called

Cofitachiqui, the land of the people we later call the Cherokees. The capital is a spot dubbed Talomeco and it is ruled by a young and beautiful woman. She travels in a litter sheltered by shades made of fine linen, crosses a river by canoe, and confronts the conquistador. She plucks a strand of pearls from her neck and puts them in his eager hands. Her eyes catch his lust.

She says, "Do you hold that of much account? Go to Talomeco, my village, and you will find so many that your horses cannot carry them."

Talomeco turns out to be a charnel house, the long buildings stacked high with corpses. The diseases of the new people have preceded them. De Soto makes her a prisoner and stomps onward. He sees mountains in the distance and surely there will be gold in them. Eventually, they pause on the trail, the woman must relieve herself. She scurries into the bushes and disappears. We know no more of her. She disappears from our books and scribblings. Hernando de Soto marches on, slaughtering at will, poxing the people with organisms none can see or understand. He dies from the plagues he has brought. His men sink his body into the waters of the Mississippi lest natives have their way with the corpse.

Now we cannot find the woman. We cannot ask her questions. We cannot know her fate. I think she is still out there. I have caught glimpses of her for years. Not in the sex palace in San Francisco where I splattered images on the wall. I did not see her there. But still I have seen her at times out of the corner of my eye, peering through the leaves, breathing faintly. I have more faith in her existence than I do in the American dollar. That is my miracle. She will have different names but this is not a problem for me since no one seems to know her actual name. Her tribe will vary. She exists, she will not give up. There is no surrender in her eyes. And more remarkably, no hatred. Anger, yes, she's got some of that. She is a spunky woman. But no hatred, a basic drug of my era.

So I will not cut my throat. I can smell the freshness of the linens draped over her litter as she glides through the green world I seek.

She does not fear that she will fall. She fastens her jaws on the male's neck, and there she rides secure. They mate while in flight, a seemingly needless risk that long puzzled scientists. Why is this ride necessary? True, there are a lot of bees and butterflies and whatnot that fornicate in the air. But this species of wasp could have accomplished the venture without leaving the good and solid earth. So why are they behaving this way? And what—the impossible question we are trained never to ask—do the hammer orchids make of it all? For we know, and we insist, the orchids cannot think. Or see. Or in any way we will ever admit, know. And they are up there in the trees, clinging while the male flies and fucks with the female down below.

The guayacán was blooming with blue fire against the hot ground about the time the young man died near the old church. I did not hear the shot. I did not even know of his death as I roared north—rolling down from the tropical forest into the short-tree forest, past the stand peddling ceviche by the truck stop, and on into the Sonoran desert. Last night I drank too much because I knew I had to leave to make some money up north and so now I drive through the caprice of Mexican traffic with a hangover.

(In the 1840s, artist George Catlin saw a bunch of Sioux come to a fort on the Missouri and trade 1,400 buffalo tongues for a few gallons of whiskey.)

Last night she said, "I don't want you to go." And I said nothing because there was nothing to say. It was not just the money, though God knows I was running out of it. It was the desire for the road. To move, for me, is to act, and I have a desperate need to act. Once I was talking to Sundance on the phone, dangling off a receiver in the desert, while he rolled along in that monotone of his from his skid row lair in Los Angeles, and he touched on this need to move. He said he was once up in Steamboat

Springs, Colorado, just drinking and hanging out, and this guy decided to head out to Tucson, Arizona, way down there in the desert. "This fellow," Sundance continued, "he left town with a saddle horse and a pack horse. I have always wondered about him, about riding with those horses down the highways. The traffic would be dangerous. And the pavement is very hard on the horses' hooves." Did he make it? I asked, knowing that in these stories neither Robert Sundance nor anyone else ever knows the answer to such a question. This morning as I drove out of the small town nestled against the mountains I noticed the dead horse by the side of the highway, one killed the day before as it bolted out of the maze of trees into someone's headlights. Yesterday, the animal looked brown, and sleek and dead. This morning, one leg had been neatly sliced off—I could hear some smiling Mexican saying, *"Buena comida, amigo."*

I have engineered this trip with a phone call to a magazine in New York, sold them a bill of goods, and now for a week or two I will be in various states, plus Los Angeles, maybe the Caribbean. All for the bucks so that I can continue living in a forest swatting mosquitoes and scratching the festering bites on my legs that never seem to heal. The death happened while I drank. The message simply has yet to arrive.

Things exist at three points in time, I think. When they occur, when we learn that they have occurred, and when we forget them. The last point in time is in many ways the most important one for me because I believe that in the instant we forget we commit a sin. I do not know if God forgives this sin but I know that I do not—not in others, not for myself.

The man dies this way—he is taken out to an old mission in the American part of this desert and shot through the head. Or he is shot in the head, falls dead, and then is scooped up and taken out to the old mission. When this happened, as I mentioned, I did not hear the shot, the thud in his skull, the sudden drop of the body to the bare earth. He lay there for a long time, months and months, until he became simply bones. The dead man is the cousin of a live man I know in Mexico and both are products of the drug business. It is obligatory to deplore the drug business. I will not do this. Once, it was simply a way for people with no future to find a future by smuggling and selling drugs. I know a little about one country, my own, and I know that many people in my country cannot face the day or the night without drugs. Then, when the business of blood orchid raising began to go slack, this drug business became the premise for a war. People pissed into cups as part of their employment application, were taught to wipe their asses with the Bill of Rights, had their homes and haunts searched, and forfeited what property they had when the suspicion of drugs crossed their lives. It is all in the cases snoring down in the basements of the courthouses. Hardly anyone objects.

But I do. I object to gun control, liquor laws, urine tests, fingerprints, computer-filed credit records, dog licenses, driver's licenses (let the highway be the judge), mandatory use of seat belts, mandatory installation of air bags, the DEA, FBI, CIA, NIA, INS, BIA, IRS, FAA, the National Park Service, Bureau of Land Management, Department of Defense, curfews, blue laws, the omnibus crime bill, cooling-off periods (some like it hot), the draft, riot statutes, transactional immunity, nonprofit organizations (if the government approves of their actions, it is a moral certainty I will not), RICO statutes, Department of

Justice strike forces, obscenity laws, fagophobia codes, burial codes, tax exemption for churches, narcs, taxes, and borders as defined by the authorities.

(In 1867, General William Tecumseh Sherman is out on the North Platte as part of a peace delegation to the Sioux. He figures it is all a waste of time. After all, he is a warrior, and the Sioux look to be the same stripe of people. Sherman is kind of a hero of mine—just how many other Civil War generals were taken from the nuthouse to the battlefield? As he listens to the drivel of the treaty conditions he gets impatient and finally blurts out, "The railroads are coming and you cannot stop [them] any more than you can stop the sun or the moon. You must decide, you must submit. This is not a peace commission only; it is also a war commission. Without peace, the Great White Father who, out of love for you, withheld his soldiers, will let loose his young men and you will be swept away. . . . Do the best you can for yourselves. . . ."

Red Cloud is up again in the Powder River country when he hears this bold talk by the half-crazed general. He sends back a reply: "If the Great Father kept white men out of my country, then peace would last forever. The Great Spirit has raised me in this land and has raised you in another land. What I have said I mean. I mean to keep this land.")

When I go south into Mexico, I anticipate another country, but the fucking orchids have reached here. Whomp whomp whomping over my head are seven choppers financed by the American treasury. They are supposed to do search-and-destroy missions on local botanical favorites. This plague is everywhere.

(I want to say several things right now, get them out of the way. I feel flickers of lucidity coming on and experience has taught me these moments are unlikely to be sustained. I wish to address the community, the common good, the

commonweal—all that nurturing and sacred stuff. UNION PACIFIC. *Okay, here goes: We are takers, to a man and to a woman and to a child, and we have conquered this ground. And we are willing to fork over the cash—in the 1870s we spent $150,000 for every dead Lakota.*

LITTLE HOUSE ON THE PRAIRIE.

"You are fools," said Sitting Bull, an early expert in the field of home economics, "to make yourselves slaves to a piece of bacon fat, some hardtack, and a little sugar and coffee."

We cannot face this fact so we hide behind the feel and the image of the taking, the days of the pioneers, the vestments of the cattle industry, the pageants of the Neolithic cultures we gutted, the image of the gun, the memory of the roar of our firepower when the trigger was pulled.

"I was willing," John Wayne explained to the boy in his last movie, The Shootist.

We will be forced to leave if we do not change because this conquered ground, it is merely sleeping, and when it awakens, it will breathe fire and kill us softly with its night sounds.

SHE.

We need to look at ourselves, with love, with doubt, with clear eyes. The last buffalo, that black stare, blood pouring from the nostrils.

I once watched a prairie falcon kill a dove—the silence weighed more than a meeting house. I once saw a flower bloom on a grave by a desert trail and the bright colors screamed.

The new AK-47 is on the polished coffee table. I shoulder it, smell the oil. This lucidity business is not coming easily.

We need to look at ourselves, with love, with doubt, with clear eyes.

We are lovers or we must become so.

Please, just one more drink!
Nat Turner, pass the shiv.)

That is why I pay attention. That is why the deaths matter. That is why it is a sin not to notice them or pretend they never happened.

As for the dead man found with that hole through his skull by the old church, I have visited with his cousin, relaxed in the cousin's orchard, tasted his hospitality. He is a man in his late twenties with intense eyes and a stomach that will no longer obey him. He is overweight, very nervous, and many men have tried to kill him. He has killed men, four I know of in the States—the numbers in Mexico are beyond my knowing. Imagine you are sitting at your kitchen table at night with your family when a gun cracks, a bullet comes through the glass window, and then you spill forward onto the table and are quite dead. That is the procedure for one of his four kills in the States. He carries six driver's licenses all bearing his photograph and different names. He dotes on his ulcers. His youngest wife is very lovely and has a soft smile and perfect skin. He murdered his own cousin because he burned him on a deal to the tune of $100,000. When his bones are found, his family comes up some six hundred miles and pays for a casket and the transport home with twelve crisp one-hundred-dollar bills. The bones merely fill a small bag but the coffin is necessary to comply with the laws and besides there are standards of decency and respect.

Things exist at three points in time: when they occur, when we learn that they have occurred, and when we forget them. This last, of course, is a sin.

There is an elaborate calculus in my life and this swirl of numbers batters my brain. Carmen, down the street from my Mexican home in the barrio, has been deserted by her man and she and the three children need food for tortillas. The girl from the village who stops by to use the shower has just had a miscarriage. Old Teodoro is losing the use of his legs and, damn his lazy bones, can no longer work at age seventy-six. The dog has worms and medicine must be bought. The forest is slinking away each day as bulldozers tear it down for grasslands to feed America's need for cheap beef. The fight against these facts drains thousands from my paltry reserves. And now the goddamn president of the republic has raised the price of beer. So I am roaring north, burning up the road at eighty miles an hour, dodging crazy truck drivers who take up a lane and a half, passing new fresh wrecks with the bodies stacked neatly by the shoulder. Because of all these—factors?—I am going to fabricate a tale about the plight of modern environmentalism, that is the angle for the magazine, how the movement is really all just a media event because that is the only form of utterance now readily understood. The media are no longer the message, but the media simply are—there is no longer a message or a need of one.

I come to this story, to this particular deal, because of a voyage I once made. In some ways I never exist in the present moment but am always trapped in some cloud of experiences that I call the past. This vast country of things that have happened to me, this region remains very vivid to me, and often I am listening to someone or watching something and yet I am not really there, I am back in this past. I can recall the scent on the nape of woman's neck that crossed my life ten years ago. I can feel the anger in a wind that died long ago. . . .

The ship rocks on ten-foot waves and everything is gray.

My clothes are damp and stink.

The shower is cold and the rice and vegetables and the rum may be running out. In the lounge Mick is arguing and the veins on his neck are growing larger. He is very muscular, in his twenties, and pretty much recovered from falling off his motorcycle. He is also a Jehovah's Witness but none of us knows this fact at the moment. For three days he has been fucking one of the cooks but this disturbs no one—though there are few women on the ship, there seems little competition in this particular area of our lives. Besides it does not affect her cooking, which remains terrible. One night we had a fish that washed up on deck, and I swear to God the cook wore a gas mask so as not violate her vegetarian sensibilities. So fuck her, Mick, no hard feelings. We are having an argument over another matter. Mick is one of those impaired people who cannot seem to grasp the notion of argument and swiftly moves to a state of war. Not that he can really grasp the notion of war—during the engagement when we were ramming and tearing holes in other ships he emerged from his cabin drunk, was tongue-lashed by a small woman who kept the engine room running, and then crept like a whipped dog back to his lair and did not come forth again for two days. Perhaps the cook, who I must note has beautiful long hair and skin like cream, brought him some carrots. But this time, as the argument moves Mick's Jehovah's Witness brain toward war, something is different. He is standing in the gangway amidships and moving menacingly toward this other man. His nominal opponent appears calm and relaxed. He plans to put a choke hold on Mick, strangle him to death, and toss him over the side. Failing this, the captain stands behind Mick with a flare gun. He plans to send a rocket into Mick's back, kill him, and toss him over the side. I stick to rum and my notebook. And then, Mick, perhaps receiving a message from his strange God Jehovah, backs down, lowers his whining voice, and slips swiftly down the ladder into the hold and his normal oblivion. The incident passes and never receives mention in the story I write. Nor if I had written of this episode would it have been published because the ship I am on is an environmental vessel going about the business of our new Green God, and while a little downside is allowable, a dark side is not, no, is not allowable. And we all know this without being told.

Fear also must be husbanded in such an environmental tale. A touch of fear is good, it shows that the characters are human and recognize risk and by this recognition make themselves capable of being heroes to the reader. One night during a tropical storm, the waves average twenty feet, the winds roar at over forty knots. Water pours into the bridge and anyone stepping out on the deck would be overboard and dead in an instant. None of the life gear on board seems functional. The captain loudly denies this, but he knows and he knows that I know. There are these survival suits, odd contraptions with a flotation device, a skin that protects one from the cold of the bobbing waves, a radio transmitter to beckon rescuers as one rocks upon the waters in those long hours and days after a ship has gone down. We have three such suits for twenty-four people. Hardly anyone knows what such suits are (standard gear on commercial ships in these waters) and hardly anyone knows that there are only three on board. They are tucked away in the captain's cabin and he knows this and I know this and she knows this. Who is she? Another character who seems doomed to fall on the cutting room floor of this movie.

The hair is blond, the body hard, she stands like a man with the feet firmly planted, and yet she moves with the grace of a woman. Her scent is fresh and yet she works all the time scraping rust off the hull, painting walls, cleaning the deck. Her the smile is slight, like that of a little girl, and the eyes often small as if she is peering through a gun slit at a disappointing world. The hands are callused from work and rough when they touch and she is very strong. Once she grabs me from behind, puts on a choke hold and I begin to go black into unconsciousness. Then she giggles and releases her hold and light floods back into my brain and I marvel at her strength and caprice. Her cabin is tidy, the small bookshelf a haven of herbal teas and dietary supplements. She has two gallons of rum. And a .357 magnum. She does not trust the captain and knows of the three survival suits he has secretly stashed. She tells me that she read once that "real captains go down with their ships, and if this motherfucker goes over the side in a survival suit when things go bad, I'm going to make him a real captain." When we ram other ships and the air is shredded by the scream of metal tearing and rupturing, when the sea crashes into these new wounds as we bob a thousand miles from any coast, at the moment that we take the idea of green things into a new place, into a war zone, she is always on the bridge, always near that captain—I have looked over videotape footage and she seems always in the frame—and under her heavy-weather gear she is packing that .357 magnum.

Fear, always fear, fear of drowning, fear of being caught out when I am afraid, fear of vomiting for hours when the bad storms hit, fear of what the other vessels will do when they find out we are not peaceful, not peaceful at all, but filled with anger and violence and a readiness to push things past a point of no return. Fear of the icy water that will kill me within two or three minutes if I go over the side, fear of missing the key moment that could occur suddenly out of the gray soggy sky, the moment that sums up days, weeks, years, centuries, millennia in one snapshot of action or gesture or word or emotion. Fear of buckling when the collision comes and we all discover whether we are really willing to put our lives on the line for other species, other bloods, other strands of DNA spiraling toward madness in this endless and boring expanse of ocean. Fear when I look up into her eyes and she asks, what do you want me to do, ah, the fear that I will tell her, tell anyone the answer to that question. She lights a cigarette, smoke curls from her full lips, and she says, "You are a child, a naive child." And I hope and hope. Fear.

The others on board call her the Biker Broad and are careful how they speak and act around her. For her part, she says little and that very little is said softly and with very little inflection. There is a thing about her that I never quite figure out or pin down: she takes up space like a man, she imposes herself upon the world and seems to be a statue that you must walk around, something that will not budge. And yet she moves with this catlike grace, her footfalls are silent, her muscular frame cutting through space without stirring the faintest breeze. When she weeps, and this occurs only once, she is ashamed and turns away lest anyone catch her in such a moment.

A .357 magnum.

Fear.

What do you want?

Fable, a thing more powerful than fact, defines the content of stories. First, we must be innocent. Second, they must be guilty. Third, there was a paradise and our job, by God, is to restore it. Fourth, always, always, it is not our fault. These are the rules of the fable and its hold is stronger and more binding than that of the finest steel. Paradise is essential in all stories, such is the power of the fable. There was a time when there was no boss, no rich man, no tyrant. There was a time when there was no war, no violence, no rape, no killing. There was a time when the men and women were not at each other's throats, or, if you wish, a time when the women were at the men's throats and under a matriarchy all was better in the various lands. There was a time when all living things maintained a harmony and none were present in too great a number and the forest resounded with song, all the springs bubbled with sweet water, and love was in every eye. Then this went away. Some say an apple did it. Some figure it was a capitalist. Others believe industrialism did the deed. Or racism. Or sexism. Or speciesism. It could have been the uplift bra. Or the fully automatic weapon. Not to forget The Bomb.

(Red Cloud is still at that fucking peace conference in Washington, D.C. It is 1870 and they've shown him their cannon, their big ships, their domed capitol, taken him to the White House to meet the big chief. But Red Cloud is unfazed and this is driving them nuts. He say to them, "Look at me. I was raised on this land where the sun rises, now I come from where the sun sets. Whose voice was first sounded on this land? The red people who had but bows and arrows. . . . I came here to tell my Great Father what I do not like in my country. . . . What he has done in my country I did not want; I did not ask for it; white people going through my country. Father, have you or any of your

120

friends here got children? Do you want to raise them? Look at me, I come here with all these young men. All of them have children and want to raise them. The white children have surrounded me and left me nothing but an island. When we first had this land we were strong, now we are all melting like snow on a hillside while you are growing like spring grass. . . ."

Fable. The innocent garden. When she was good. God, we all seem to need that.)

I push the pedal down hard, I am going eighty-five on a bad road. I do not believe the fable. I do not believe much of anything at the moment—I simply calculate the elements I need to fill out the flesh of the story—the sound bites, odd moments, little clumps of statistics, that will provide the grist. I am at work as I pull up to the American line and enter into the indignity of customs. Always, I fail here. I have the wrong attitude. They ask, What do you do for a living, and I say, That is none of your business. And I truly believe it is none of their business. In my dim memory of the American Revolution, it was nothing about having appropriate employment. But there is a great distance between Valley Forge and this fat creature in a uniform at the border who is demanding to know what I do for a living. There is the problem of where I live in Mexico, a town notorious for drugs and murders. Once I state where I live the officials always pull my truck out of the line and direct it to a stall where the real search begins.

There is a sameness to this experience. The agent eventually will say, "If you keep that attitude, I can make this as hard as you want."

Then I will say, "Go ahead. I've got the rest of my fucking life."

They'll first check underneath with mirrors to see if the bolts are clean on the oil pan, they are very keen on wily tricks like that. Then they'll make a big show of tire thumping, go under the hood, flip the seat forward and stare at the all the junk and dirt that lives back there. They'll glare at the bumper sticker—NATURE BATS LAST—and then I'll open the shell over the truckbed. Before them will be a maze of compartments and boxes and they'll ask, what's in those? I'll say stuff. Then they'll crawl inside—and this is the part I like—and eventually I'll hear a yell. The whole truckbed is littered with cactus needles. They'll say, pulling a thorn from their hand, "Where do these come from?" And I'll say, "Cactus." Technically, I should say cacti, but I would rather be understood than be correct. Much like the thorn itself.

Usually in ten or twenty or thirty minutes, I am allowed to roll out there and enter the country of my birth. Actually, I love my country but I'm not fond of its gatekeepers. Los Angeles is still a long haul and it will be first light before I get there. The best hours seem to come between Blythe and Palm Springs, that long pull against the dry honesty of the Mojave. There is less evidence of a human presence on this stretch and what evidence there is seems to be apologetic and in retreat. Then I drop down into the L.A. basin, slip through the maze of freeways, and pull up to the curb in Santa Monica.

There is a switch somewhere in my head that automatically clicks when I begin to do a story, and as I get out of the truck and look at the office of the environmental organization, I can hear it. I become that camera noting things without a clear scheme for them: A big glass dolphin dominates the office and the bookcase archives the writings of nonviolence and the plight of a planet. Out

the window women walk by very expensively dressed. . . .
The man in charge of the organization, the captain I once
sailed with, explains he cannot read easily, he scrambles
up messages, he cannot tie his shoelaces—something mis-
fires in his brain he says. Imagine, he asks me, being a
sailor and not being able to tie a knot?

The story takes over, days and days of interviews, dinners, drives, phone calls, bad coffee. There is the cruise in
the Caribbean where, if I go, we will sink a goddamn
ship. There is the cruise out into the Atlantic, where if I
go, we will board the *Pinta* and *Santa Maria* reenacting
Columbus's voyage to a New World, we will board them
with dozens of Indians and send THEM scurrying home-
ward to their fetid European ports. All this, as I said,
takes days and days with dinners, glasses of wine, traffic
jams on the freeway. The captain tells me his mother died
when he was young, his father beat him, he kept running
away, the sea, the sea, the sea. And there are all those
headlines and sound bites on television and still photographs of life at the edge. It is quite a package, it will sell.
They will want to know this because it will entertain
them and best of all it will not threaten them. Saving the
earth—that big ball of dirt I have never seen in person
although the snaps from space look impressive. I have the
opening scene: we are driving down the freeway, he has
one hand on the wheel, and he tells me the car is a dona-
tion from a Deadhead up in the Pacific Northwest and
then he segues into reading Joseph Conrad during a
typhoon in the China Sea, and suddenly his mother is
dying, he runs away—but wait, suddenly he remembers
those whores in Thailand, the grace of women in Japan,
the years at sea, he is reciting now, somehow he has a
photographic memory and poetry and pages of prose spill

out of him, his hand, just one hand, rides on the wheel and he seems not to look ahead and we cut through traffic and he is enjoying talking and he admits he cannot explain his crusade to save the seas, why he is so obsessed with saving wild creatures, and I ask about his mother and we drive on and on in growing silence. And so I have the beginning. The rest is cookbook, a vignette here, one there, the critical voices—I make sure I get ahold of colleagues that have left him and now denounce him, for I am objective—and all I really think of is that he ran away to sea at fifteen and has the kind of brain that cannot remember how to tie a knot and somehow he faked everything on a Norwegian tramp steamer. And I have been sent here to put him in his place and I am willing to do this for money and of course, my need for money is completely defensible and my aim is true. The ending, why that is simple: his obsession with the code of the samurai, his deep need for the ways of the warrior. A wrap. Now he is in his place and I have built this place for him.

The part that sticks in my mind is this: three musicians outside the office of the save the seas organization are playing "La Bamba" at a Santa Monica street fair while I munch on free carrot cake. The three singers are all recent Russian immigrants.

I write the story and this is an easy thing to do. My God it pours out of me. I just write and drink black coffee and forget to count the days. Then I let it sit for a day or two and rewrite and rewrite until it is tight and there is no escape: the environmental movement as a media event, as a series of media events, and the man who cannot tie his shoes is a P. T. Barnum of this world. I put the story in a large manila envelope, address it to the magazine in New York, carefully include a list of my expenses which by this time are eight or nine hundred dollars. And I never mail that envelope or do anything else with the material. For months I do not think about the story or why I do not mail it. Nor do I answer any messages from the magazine. I have never had this happen before—no, no, that is not quite true. I have always had it happen but each time I claim it is something different and each time I quit my job or leave my marriage or change my state so that I do not have to recognize that something is going on that has gone on with me before. I slowly and surely—this time I think it is not just an act or a rehearsal—commit a kind of suicide. This time I want it to be deliberate and final. I have only one apparent way to make a living—filing these stories—and I proceed to explode this way. Months later in the soft hours of the night I am drunk in Mexico and a dark-skinned woman says she wants me and I do not mail that envelope either. A man high on a mountain offers to go to sea with me with his guns and cunning—he has killed 150 times before—and I do not mail that envelope.

I cry wolf, howl like a goddamn beast. The wolf no longer exists where it once existed and there is a great deal of debate about bringing the animal back. Tracks are missing on the land, scat lacking on the trail. Or perhaps it is spawn gone from the stream, a howl absent from the high clouds over the canyon? Much is said and written. I decide to put that animal back. There is not even a moment's gratitude. (They are never grateful. We should be glad. Gratitude would be an expression of slavery.) There is no story here. Such an act is considered a crime and when you write about your crimes they call it a confession. It is a clean thing. We have, as you know, been drunk one hundred years. Thank God for this fact, it helped to pass the time. The women, they are right down there below in the pit of the theater jacking off the customers. And come, take my hand, we can go to the Ultra Room and watch them shove things—do you like zucchini or would you prefer the humble cucumber?—up their vaginas or (tell me, what do you like?) up their asses. Whips or chains are an option. Do not worry, it is all permitted. We can't go back after all. Please pay at the door, the one that leads in. You can guess the rest. Didn't you always tell me you wanted to find the border, the edge?

And that is how I spend my time, month after month, year after year. I cannot tell if I am waiting for someone to kill me or waiting for someone to turn on the lights. There are just these trips that melt into one another, these assignments, articles. Stories. Fables. It is hot, summer is ending and once again I am racing back toward Tucson so that I can recross the border. I have been up for days, been on the road, trying to make that money to stay in Mexico. I stop to pick up a check and this guy who owes me money—Jesus, more people owe me than any other deadbeat in America—this guy says, "Did you know that Josie died?" Ah, Josie, sixty-one years old, Mexican-American, the woman who knit clothes for my son when he was born, the woman who brought over soup when I was sick, the woman who lit candles for me in the church. I wrote about a sliver of her world in a book called *Red Line,* a look at drugs on the border and the lack of values in my life and everyone else's. Part of the book was about a Mexican-American named Arturo who was an ex-narc. Josie was his wife. She felt fine, went to the beauty parlor, started feeling dizzy in the chair, passed

out, and died six hours later in the hospital. A blood clot
to the brain. She dyed her hair blond, and she always was
laughing and talking, pressing food on me, asking me if I
wanted this or that. The soups were very good and she
made tortillas every day. She worried about her weight
and went to the mall every morning before it opened and
walked round and round in circles. When she died, the
family gathered to sign the death certificate and that is
when her children learned that she had left school in the
fifth grade to bring money into her family.

She had been dead four weeks when I got the news and
I did not feel good about the delay. A thousand-year war!
that smile and she is talking to me, asking, asking, asking
me if I wanted more—no? oh, yes you do—and her warm
face masking a sternness that could overcome anything
and for six decades did just that. So, I abandoned my
plan of returning to Mexico that day and I tracked down
Arturo, who drives a limo part-time to funerals. I found
him outside a church. He looked like a broken toy. He is
leaning against a stucco wall wearing a short-sleeved
shirt, a tie, and staring down at his shoes. They had been
married forty years. We drank all that night and into the
day. He complained about the widows who suddenly had
begun calling him. He felt he was not ready yet. I said,
"Let's go to Mexico. You will feel better." And so, after
a while, we went.

We arrive for the fiesta of Mexican independence, the
sixteenth of September.

My house in the barrio is intact, it always is—my
neighbors are very kind. I walk in and there is a musty
smell and spiders fleeing up the cold walls and out in
back the indecent plants of the tropics are blooming—
they are like flashers on a city street corner, flies open,

very erect. We break open the Seagram's and then the peasants start stopping by.

The campesinos are very poor this year, the federales have been well financed by the Americans' DEA and much of the crop has been taken. Those seven helicopters with sprayers have been in town for two months, there is a fixed-wing spotter plane, there are of course the federales, professional killers to a man, and as a side dish, hundreds of soldiers. Three soldiers were machine-gunned two weeks ago. The air is heavy with intentions. In El Mesa, a tiny *ejido* (collective village), the federales, my friends tell me, came a week or so ago, and took five thousand plants. They caught two men in the field, took their guns and money but let them go. The campesinos had failed to pay protection so they lost their crop. It can go that way. This has happened in many villages and so, for the third straight year, there is no money.

We go down to the cantina and drink beer. The air reeks of piss, over toward the wall a drunk sleeps sprawled against a small wooden table, and a man sits down beside me and says, "Carlito, do you still wish to buy a boa?" And I look down expecting to see a swirling hoop of energy in a burlap bag at his feet. Then, the official tempo changes—I say official tempo, because the tempo in the cantina and the tempo inside my head are not in sync—and another man sits down at the table and says do you want marijuana? His face is crooked with desire and I go through a pantomime of being wise—is he setting me up? Is he part of some gang that will club me to the floor once the money is on the varnished wood of the tabletop? Oh, I am so shrewd, and so I smile. The barman stalks me, hovers about the table like a fighter plane in a holding action, and I cave in and think, I am tired of living. I look up and catch the man's ready eye. He slaps down a lid and says it was cut five days before. Other Mexicans I know come over, they pull me aside, they say do not buy it, he sells bad shit and it has too many stems and seeds. Finally, the man who shines shoes on the plaza convinces me to not buy.

So we go back to my house, crank the stereo up (an expensive indulgence of mine at 110 watts a channel), and I give Arturo a joint. He says he feels nothing and then for five hours does not get out of his chair by the banana tree in the patio.

That night we go to the plaza and it is crowded with people eating and laughing and walking around in circles. Men drink openly, something that cannot normally be done on the town's streets. It is about thirty hours until El Grito, the cry of Independence that Father Hidalgo gave to his Indian charges in 1810 when the revolution began and the blood started flowing. The priest came out of the mountains with forty thousand Indians wielding pikes and machetes. Everyone is building up toward El Grito when the crowd will roar, "Viva México." Art and I buy taquitos from a stand and sit on a curb. Next to us is a guy in his twenties and with him is a beautiful black stallion with a silver bridle. The man says his name is Leopoldo, and he has been working up in Daly City in the Bay Area.

> *I am going to sing a corrido,*
> *Give me all of your attention.*
> *A corrido about the cruel and cowardly way*
> *They killed Valencia.*

He had a car in California, he says, and made good money, but he came back for the horse. I am a poor judge of size but this horse is very big and black and very calm.

129

Leopoldo and I move up under the portals of an old colonial mansion on the plaza and the animal follows, reins trailing. We sit on the steps, the horse towering over us like a thunderhead, and from time to time, Leopoldo gently strokes its nose and speaks softly to it. It is a wonderful horse and it knows how to dance. This is an esteemed thing in the sierra—for a horse to dance to the music of a hired band while the man sits astride, usually drunk, and rocks along to the melody. The training takes a long time and the horses have great value. In the villages, one can usually first spot the signs of the life not by gold chains or new pickups but by the presence of fine horses. The place will have no electricity, the houses will be mud and twigs, everyone will be shoeless, and then one will notice the fine horses, coats glowing.

Leopoldo is very cheerful and speaks easily. Tomorrow there will be many dancing horses and they will form a semicircle around a band and every reputation will be on the line. Ten thousand peasants will pour in from the sierra and they will watch these horses and everyone, every man, woman, and child, will know which horse is truly the finest, which horse has the best ear, the most graceful moves, which horse is most attuned to the music. There will be no award, there will be no ribbons, but everyone will know and for a year they will talk of this knowledge. Leopoldo is ready. As we speak he continues to groom his horse, which follows him everywhere in the plaza like a dog, the bridle hanging.

The women are all ripe and smiling and as we sit chewing the tacos they stream past in bright colors and masked faces. This is a different dance, the one of desire. Leopoldo seems to absorb the energy, and swell with it. He wears a fine black leather vest, tight pants, and a winning smile. He speaks clearly but without force, his words

130

a gentle brook flowing out into the plaza. This is the
place of dreams and this is the night for the dreaming.
The year is all jobs, fists, bills, hot afternoons and here,
right now, the temperature is perfect, like stepping into a
kind world. I watch the women and listen to his words
even though I know the women are wonderfully deliberate fantasies and his words are an honestly constructed
fraud. California, the job, ah, yes, and then came the call,
the letter, the postcard, and he must return, return
instantly. For the black stallion. His job up there in the
Bay Area, it is never quite openly stated. The reason for
the return is also left unclear. There is only one sharp-
edged image: I left an automobile for this horse. He seems
to know what he is about and I envy this fact.

The next afternoon Arturo and I are sitting in the alameda, the key ground for every Mexican within fifty
miles. Dozens of horses are circling this tiny park and on
the curbs girls and young women sit in their very best
dresses, acting indifferent, and praying for a rider to stop,
boost them up, and ride off with them for many turns
around the alameda. This is an important part of the
fiesta, a major step in the carnal dance. We sip beer and
behind is the town's statue to motherhood. A campesino
I know joins us. He and Arturo talk and the man slowly
realizes that Arturo is a significant find—an American
(and of course all Americans have money) and one
recently widowed. Ah, a possible gold mine. He sends a
girl off to find his niece—a beautiful girl of seventeen
who sometimes uses my shower, a girl who has just had
a miscarriage. I remember the last fiesta, how she laughed
and squealed in the shower in my house, how she and her
girlfriend seemed to stay in there for hours preparing
themselves for their big night.

Her history is a tattered thing: she lives in the campo in

a house with dirt floors, flies, and three times as many people as rooms. Her mother is dead, her father has abandoned her, and this peasant family with too many mouths to feed has accepted her as one more mouth it will feed. For a while she worked at a small stand on the alameda that sold *elotes,* ears of steaming corn. She quit after a week. She explained it simply by saying, "I am lazy." Half the time she lives in town a few doors down from me with her godmother—here the web weaves finer and finer strands. Her godmother is the woman with a fistful of children whose husband has run off with a man and abandoned her, the woman who comes to the door because she needs a few pesos for tortillas. They all live in one room with the privy out back and the television, black and white, is always on and everyone sits there in a coma watching the snowy screen. None of this seems to bother the girl, in fact very little touches her. At the last fiesta she met a man who rode a fine horse and he boosted her up and they circled and circled the alameda while we all watched and the air was full of hope and possibility. That evening they rode off and he took her to his mother's house and he told her he loved her and then he fucked her. The next day she discovered he was married. And then she discovered she was pregnant. This, she said, was no problem, she would have the baby *sola,* alone. And then came the miscarriage. Now it is early fall, and a strange thing has happened to her since the miscarriage. Her body has been transformed from one of a girlish chubbiness to the full figure of a woman. When she is in my home, she is very quiet, but I catch her eyeing me from some corner of her world. Her silence does not come from shyness. Now her uncle is alive with hope as he glances at Arturo. There is a flurry of Spanish and he sends another girl off to fetch his niece, pronto! He tells Arturo he can have her and she is very fine. I can understand—one less mouth to feed. Arturo is horrified, grabs my arm and says, "Let's get out of here."

Nobody knew for sure,
The reason why Valencia was massacred
With no compassion.
It was the Saturday of Glory, the Saturday of Holy Week.

We move down into the arroyo where thousands of drunken Mexicans live in the sure knowledge that there is no tomorrow that matters. The cantinas have been closed by the police for the duration, as has the liquor store, but beer is sold in the wash. The average wage is four or five dollars a day if one finds work and the beer costs a dollar a can. Mexicans are buying us beers. There are no white people here today. We begin talking to a little old man from a village in the hills, a wizened creature of seventy-seven with a couple of teeth and a weight of maybe one hundred pounds. He is joking with another campesino, asking if they have gotten their crop in yet. I do not have to ask which crop.

The old man turns out to be Leopoldo's father, and we move down the wash to watch his son dance drunkenly on his fine black horse. I gnaw on an elote, throw down yet another beer. Near me stands the cop who guards the bank. He is very drunk, but so am I. Suddenly, overcome by the beauty of the horses, he jerks his 9mm from his holster and empties a clip into the serene air. He is dragged away to sleep it off. I ask the gnomelike old man if he knew a man named Chalo, a professional killer who worked this area for Caro Quintero, the one-time drug king of Mexico. Chalo died not so long ago when someone pumped seventy rounds from an Uzi into his body. Ah, the man says, he knew Chalo. He pats his shirt pocket and says he has a list there with seven names on it, including Chalo's. Now Chalo is dead, another name is in prison and five more remain. It seems a year or more ago, one of his sons was killed. That son owned the fine black stallion that his other son, Leopoldo, is riding today.

Who would imagine that at El Rancho Zapote
He will encounter death.
Some friends, they told him,
"José, they are looking for you."
And José, laughing, he answers,
"I am waiting for them."

In 1912, during an early round of the ten-year killing spree that rocked Mexico, Emiliano Zapata and Pancho Villa met with their armies in a suburb of the Mexico City they had just conquered. Both men were of peasant stock, suspicious of anything larger than family or town or known faces. And now they had to create a government, in their eyes an act akin to implanting a cancer. Their conversation that fourth day of December was recorded and is often cited to show how little they knew or could imagine. I think they understood it all, they simply couldn't figure a way out of the trap of the powerful state.

Villa opens simply by saying, "I do not need public positions because I do not know how to deal with them. We will have to see where those people are [the politicos and intellectuals then flocking to forge a new state], we will only let them be in charge as long as they don't create problems for us."

Zapata listens and replies, "That is why I warn all the friends that they should be careful, or otherwise the machete will fall on them. I trust that we shall not be betrayed. We have limited ourselves to prodding them, taking care of them, taking care, taking care, on one side, on the other, to keep them in the pasture."

"Ah," Villa responds. "I understand very well that we ignorant men make war, and the cabinets have to take advantage of them; but they should not cause any more problems."

Zapata rejoins, "The men who have done most of the work are those who enjoy those sidewalks less. Only sidewalks. And I say for myself: the moment I get on one of those sidewalks, I start to fall down."

I start to fall down. Right in front of me is a woman of about twenty-five on a dancing horse. Her skin is brown, the cheeks rouged, her teeth white and even, the teeth of an herbivore though I am sure she eats meat. As the animal sways to the music, so does she. She wears a charro outfit with painfully tight pants. The old campesino looks up at where I am staring, licks his ancient lips, and says of the mount and the rider, "That horse has the best ass." And then comes a cackling, a breath springing from the dry dust of remembered lust. I open another can of beer. The black stallion, Leopoldo, Chalo, the details. The young girl whose breasts have swollen since her miscarriage. The old man, he is not disturbed. He is long past that. He explains his world as Leopoldo on the black stallion dances next to the woman in the tight pants. He says some men came to his son José and challenged him to a race, and he accepted. He rode off one day into the forest to the appointed place and when he got there six men opened up with a volley of gunfire and his son died.

> *Everybody was laughing at these things.*
> *They couldn't see his situation.*
> *Three narcotraficantes got close to him.*
> *And they got ahold of him.*

Chalo organized this killing. Now the old man and Leopoldo and the rest of his family, well, they have the list. They are armed, of course, since the surviving five know of the list and are trying to kill them. Leopoldo is adequate to this work. A few years back he was sent to Islas Tres Marías, the Mexican prison off Nayarit that is on a barren patch of ground bobbing in an endless sea of sharks. His crime: importing Uzis. I drink and drink and remember how Chalo died. He was riding on his rancho when a hail of bullets tore into him. The local people say Chalo took seventy rounds and that the man and the horse and the dog trotting beside them, that all three fell as one, fell dead to the warm forest ground.

My friend who was trying to pawn off his niece on Arturo awhile earlier rejoins us now. He and the old man talk softly. My friend says, "We are *limpio,* clean, how is your village?" The old man says, "We are still packaging." Then their eyes brighten—they have decided to entertain the two strange Americans. Another six-pack is bought by the old man and he calls over a band. The musicians circle us and he requests a corrido, a ballad. They sing out loudly and the old man smiles with deep satisfaction. The song details the murder of his son.

> *He wanted to draw his gun*
> *But it was now too late.*

Death was waiting for him,
Waiting in the middle of the day.

Leopoldo rides over, takes a beer, leans back in his saddle, and pours it on the sweating stallion's rump. He gently rubs the cerveza into the fine black coat, his face aglow with pleasure, his body at ease as his eyes hunt the crowd for the five men who, someday, will come for him, will come silently to kill him. He is very happy, his horse has performed beautifully. He tells me again, "I left my car to come back here but that is nothing for such a horse." Perhaps, in a year or so, there will be a song about him.

The light begins to fade and the night seeps into town. On the tops of the old buildings on the plaza candles burn in paper bags. The women are beautiful and walk past like goddesses. Their eyes are rich with scorn. The men and boys are in their tight pants and best hats. The night is truly gentle, the way is clearly plain. I come from a place, a culture, where there is much trouble, but we do not carry lists in our pockets, we carry causes in our minds. Gun control, the glass dolphin riding in the window of the organization's office in Santa Monica, recycling. The inner child. The girl is at my elbow, I can sense her, her dark eyes alert and yet know ing, her body assured, the grave waiting but the night ahead. She is ready and I am not and I can prove that she knows very little of the world. She is lazy, don't you see?

I'm going to sing a corrido.
Give me all your attention.
A corrido about the cruel and cowardly way
They kill Valencia.

The band is roaring now as the dancers prance in the evening air, a woman is singing, her skirt short and tight. The men never remove their hats as they dance, the women never soften their eyes. At midnight El Grito swells up from the streets, various bands stumble drunkenly around and serenade anyone who is not swift enough to escape their joy. A group—guitar, drum, horn, bass—wanders into the patio of a small inn and there is no one up and the caged parrot sleeps under its sheet and does not make a sound as the men slowly snake around the *pila* and the plants and play their song against the very old and lonely walls. There has to be a ground on which I can stand, a far ground beyond the brambles of the clever, and this ground is not across the river and in the shade of the trees. I will make a list. I cannot ride a horse, though the black stallion is such a fine horse. The animal is always calm, the animal survived the murder, the animal can dance to the music. The girl is very sure of herself. She has no fear of the future. Or of the past. The old man of seventy-seven, his life is simply five things to be checked off. I can see his bony fingers patting his frayed pocket.

Imagine the problem is not physical. Imagine the problem has never been physical, that it is not biodiversity, it is not the ozone layer, it is not the greenhouse effect, the whales, the old-growth forest, the loss of jobs, the crack in the ghetto, the abortions, the tongue in the mouth, the diseases stalking everywhere as love goes on unconcerned. Imagine the problem is not some syndrome of our society that can be solved by commissions or laws or a redistribution of what we call wealth. Imagine that it goes deeper, right to the core of what we call our civilization and that no one outside of ourselves can effect real change, that our civilization, our governments are sick and that we are mentally ill and spiritually dead and that all our issues and crises are symptoms of this deeper sickness. Imagine the problem is not physical and no amount of driving, no amount of road will deal with the problem. Imagine that the problem is not that we are powerless or that we are victims but that we have lost the fire and belief and courage to act. We hear whispers of the future but we slap our hands against our ears, we catch glimpses but turn our faces swiftly aside.

I am no better. My guts roil with fear. This is how the future comes to me, how I stumble down unmapped lanes and suddenly am in front of that cathouse where she waits unloved, her face of indeterminate colors, the lips smiling and the eyes knowing far too much. I am always walking, sometimes in a forest with pink amapas bending over me, their petals carpeting the ground, sometimes in the desert with every shrub and tree and plant raking my skin with thorns. It is very quiet, soft purr of a breeze, brief bursts of birdsong, whir of insects, and I hear this roar, she comes as a locomotive is flying across the ground, smoke belching, steel wheels screaming, no engineer in the cabin, and behind this engine is an endless strand of boxcars—no tramps looking out because the doors are closed—and there are no tracks, never a single length of track, this express goes its own way. It will all happen too fast for me to react, too fast for me to close my eyes, shut my ears, turn my body, and I will briefly face the future. I cannot remember it and be honest because this future is unlike the pasts I like to pretend will be the future. This time the future is alive. And then it will be gone. Sometimes this happens in the night and I see the glow of the lights as it vanishes into the land.

This future is palpable, and no charts of economic growth or of population growth can possibly suggest its routes or cargo. There will be no first hundred days for this future, there will be no five-year plans. There will be no program. *Imagine the problem is that we cannot imagine a future where we possess less but are more. Imagine the problem is a future that terrifies us because we lose our machines but gain our feet and pounding hearts.*

Then what is to be done? I watch as two women struggle to make their feet fit a fine pair of stiletto heels. For one woman, the shoes are much too small. For the other, the shoes are much too big. They both insist the shoes fit perfectly. Imagine the problem is not physical. There is nothing to fear. But the bridle, it is silver, the stallion black, the woman on the dancing horse, ah, the best ass of all.

> *Fly, fly little dove.*
> *Fly to all the ranchos.*
> *Go and sing the corrido*
> *Of Don José Valencia.*

Months before, I published a story in an American magazine about the drug world in this town and there was talk here about me and my words. The local Mexicans had a copy before I did. One came to me and said, "We had a meeting and decided to hang you." I thought he was joking. And then others looked at me with different eyes and I was not sure what they thought. There were other messages. I decided there was nothing to do but stay. A fiesta was going on that night. I went down to the arroyo where the drunks sleep under a fig tree that is deconstructing a stone wall, where I knew the men would be and the dancing horses. I sat down and drank for hours while in the darkness men and conversations fluttered around me like the barely visible yet almost electric movement of bats hunting in the night. Nothing happened, and after that no one threatened me. And it all died down. On the other hand at a fiesta about ten miles away, a visitor asked too many questions about the local business. The village schoolteacher taking his morning walk found him in the morning with his arms and legs cut off and ice picks in his eyes.

The genitals were severed also.

Fly, fly little dove.

(Almost five centuries have spun through this ground since the conquest. In that time, no group in Mexico has ever achieved power through a ballot box. Not once. A half a thousand years have weighed down on this nation like stones. In that time, wealth has never been divided except by force or the threat of force. What you want you take. What you get you share. What you think, you will tell no one. What you are . . . is alive. And I will haunt your towns, your cantinas, your fiestas, burials, baptisms, birthdays, and saints' days yearning for your blood, envious of your smile, greedy for your laughter. I am the specter on the edge of your lives, a soulless creature hungry for your sense of God and place. I am a gringo and my skin is light, my eyes are blue, and I have everything you want, except a life. I live on a giant reservation. They have taken my campo from me and the buffalo, the buffalo can barely be found. We are casting new ones at a foundry and soon I am told the moaning will be back.)

I keep returning. I am starving in a place where no one has money, yet they all seem fed. I must get a grip on myself. I must maintain my poise, my mask. I tell myself:

Pull that chair over here, open that can of Tecate, now look at the bloom on the banana tree where the hummingbirds are feeding. Ignore the noise out front, the one hundred fifty cases of beer cooling on a ton of ice, the pile of wood waiting for the eighty pounds of *carne asada*. Focus on the greedy fig trees in the patio—those biological bombs whose roots will in God's good time pull this ancient building apart.

Yesterday, it seemed so simple. I had come down to check up on Leopoldo and his dancing horse. See how he was progressing with his list of names. Take in the fiesta, Cinco de Mayo, commemorating the time the Mexicans walloped the French. Everything was to go according to plan.

Then a man called Chuy phones from Mexico City, and says he's coming in for his wedding. This will not help. That's why the fifteen-piece band arrived by bus a few hours ago complete with a lead singer, a woman with thin hips, a perfect face, and one polio-ravaged leg, which she drags slightly. Still, I've got the chair pulled over, the beer is cold in my hand and beads of moisture collect on its red metal hide. The federales are out front, that's true, and packing as always. And Chuy's private plane landed at the town's little strip and he's helling around the area getting ready for the hop. I must relax. The book is in the can and for the first time in over a year I'm not looking over my shoulder and I'm not being followed and I'm not carrying a nine-millimeter with fifteen in the clip and an extra clip in my pocket.

There will be murders in the next few days, hard drinking, snippets of the official war on drugs, cocaine snorted off the hoods of pickups. Women with hungry eyes. A dead woman with empty eyes. There will be love. People will laugh often. It will be pretty much the way it always is in these parts.

But what about her? She's been dead what? Thirty hours? And already buried. They don't waste time down here. Remember the first time you met her? It is in this patio, maybe twenty-four months ago, and she turns to another woman and says, "I want him." Her skin is dark, she is from down south where the Indian blood still pounds through the veins, and very short, maybe five foot at a stretch, the eyes quick and the teeth very white and small like a cat's. She shows you a color photo she treasures. It is of her television set. She smells like fresh laundry just taken off the line.

I think now of my arrival a short while ago when I learned of her death. The woman who told me said, "Ah, poor Carlito, now you will never make love to her."

Drink. Don't think of that tiny body, aged thirty-three forever, sleeping in the Campo Santo, her eyes staring up at dirt until the end of time when everything will be righted. She left four children and always smiled.

I can hear the noise rising out front. There the mix is beer, scotch, cocaine, the Mexican government's narcotics strike force, and drug dealers. But I wish to stay with my Tecate and my barely cold dead.

The owner is at my side now, he shakes my shoulder and says, "You've got to help me. Chuy's pissing in my washing machine."

And by God, he is. So I meet the enemy and he says he is in love.

In some ways Chuy's wedding has a familiar ring. Back in January he partied for five days, rented a couple of hotels, and hired a band. He also held a fete at his ranch where he had bulldozed a parking lot in the forest to hold more than a hundred gleaming pickup trucks with chrome roll bars and darkly tinted windows—the standard transportation of those in the life. On that occasion the boys fired nine-millimeters and Uzis at the stars around midnight and celebrated the fact that they were alive and some of their enemies were not. In fact, Chuy had done everything a groom could do at that wedding. Except he forgot to get married. He is going to try again.

I have come here to see a man about a horse, a man whose mount is renowned for its grace and beauty and its skill at dancing. A man who the last time I drank with him was working on that list of seven names, of all the hombres who had murdered his brother. Two of the names were scratched off, and he had a light smile as he explained there were only five to go.

But that man is nowhere to be found—ah, I am told, he has gone off on some errands. I am also told that "there's a lot of lead in air right now." The marijuana is harvested this month but no one is able to move any. The government bribes have become impossibly high, they say, and various organizations in the industry are killing time by killing each other over market share. There are many details to work out but one fundamental reality: the last time Chuy stayed here he would arise each morning and come out of his room with a pistol and then he would say, "Buenos días" to the district attorney who was wearing two pistols and the comandante who was wearing one pistol.

But not today, for this is the time for the wedding. One reveler from last night's anticipatory celebration is still sleeping. He is lying in a wash with the pigs and, during brief flickers of consciousness, vomiting generously.

I left my inn earlier. The sun hammered me as I wandered in the wash below the town among the horses, musicians, and roving squads of señoritas, all gathered in critical mass to celebrate Cinco de Mayo. Chuy was running a bit late—he had yet to make it from a local cantina to the ceremony and his bride. So I walked down the calles to join the fiesta for the national holiday. The cerveza was still going for a buck a throw, and the wages hadn't gone up. As I stood at the beer stand, a nicely dressed gentleman rattled his car keys on the counter and explained to the bartender: Yes, you have paid thousands of pesos for a beer permit, but now you have to pay me. A solution was reached and the beer began to flow. A hummingbird hovered by a sign next to the beer stand that declared that drinking in the wash was prohibited. I bought another beer while two customers drained their cans and pissed against the stand itself.

A Mexican told me the government was asking impossible bribes in the marijuana industry because it wanted to take over the industry and be the industry. These negotiations had made things *"muy caliente."* For example, awhile back there was that dinner party. A group of wealthy Americans were at table in their fine home when some men with Uzis walked in. The story circulating in the American community is that the bandits said, "Give us your money," and that one American grabbed for an Uzi and was killed. The women also were sprayed with a few rounds but lived. The Mexican version varies: The American hosting the party had failed to pay for a 150-kilo load and what the gunman said was, "Give us *our* money." The American grabbed for the gun and was blown to pieces. As the gunmen left one of the women flipped them the finger, which led to another burst. The man's corpse was removed by his family. They came to fetch it in a Learjet.

When I got back to the hotel there were new delays. Chuy had finally swept in, commandeered his band, grabbed six cases of beer, and gone off to celebrate Cinco de Mayo. I cracked open a beer and a book.

Chuy is a tall man in his late thirties with a winning smile. He is wearing cowboy boots, tan jeans, a guayabera shirt, and a straw Stetson, and has stuffed a .45 automatic into his back pocket. When a friend and I are introduced, Chuy becomes very alert. By happenstance my friend, Arturo, shares the same last name as a renowned drug family that operates in precisely the same city as Chuy. A few years back a member of this family irked someone, was tied to two separate motor vehicles and torn in half. Chuy's eyes briefly darken as he ponders my friend's name, then that wonderful smile returns, and he shakes my friend's hand and says, "*¡Muy pesado!* A heavyweight!"

After a brief chat, I turn my attention to attacking the mountain of beer. The grill is fired up and eighty pounds of steaks begin to sizzle. The gateway to the hotel is blocked by a bus, armed guards check the guests as they enter, and wherever Chuy wanders among his fellow celebrants, two or three men with cold eyes and willing pistols follow. Dogs slink around the edge of the crowd as we await the bride.

La Banda emerges from its quarters and it is a proud sight to behold. The musicians are dressed in black and armed with two French horns, two trombones, three clarinets, two cornets, snare drums and cymbals, conga drums. And a menacing tuba. The group has no amplifier or microphones. The first note knocks me off my chair, and as I sprawl on the cobbles and wonder about possible broken limbs or cracked ribs, the sound waves pound me against the stone patio like surf crashing against a cliff. All this before the tuba weighs in like a tidal wave. La Banda is clearly in a class by itself—Chuy is paying them $10,000 a day, plus free hotel rooms and food. I encountered some of them at breakfast and they were dining on T-bone steaks. They seem to know but one song. Chuy is sitting off by himself with three other gentlemen, apparently guests of honor. He is beaming at the beauty of the music. People come up to pay their respects. One young guy is angry. He is one of Chuy's folk and that very afternoon another guest at the party had insulted this loyal pistolero during the public fiesta. His honor demands something be done about this outrage.

The manager of the hotel notices something that distresses him: the guests at the wedding party tend to sport pistols that peek out from their back pockets. So he calls up the mayor and demands that the police disarm his guests. This idea has several flaws. For one thing, Chuy has hired some of the police force to guard the gate. And second, as the mayor explains, "I can't send in the police, Chuy has more firepower than we do."

Her name is Ofelia—no, was Ofelia. Besides the photo of the television set, she showed me snapshots of her sofa, her kitchen table, the refrigerator, an end table, a stuffed chair, and an electric clock. When she kissed me, she plunged her tongue into my mouth. Her husband is the best waiter in town and usually drunk. A little while back he was driving her and a daughter down a dirt track, lost control, and they rolled. He and the daughter are still in the hospital and they will live. That first night and in the days and nights that followed, these facts did not seem to command her attention. She asked if I would call her from the States. She asked if I would buy her things. She seemed always happy and seemed to dance above the brick patio on her little feet.

I was not sociable back then. I stayed in my room in the hotel and worked through a thousand pages of bank documents. As my tired eyes scanned the columns of numbers, I watched billions of dollars disappear into the dark void of what prosecutors called gigantic fraud. A fan slowly twirled over my head and I drank black coffee hour after hour. I was beginning a book that would devour more than a year of my life. I was surly with everyone. I would make sense of the numbers, I would win. So I did not leave the room. I am the gringo, the work-obsessed fool.

Suddenly, she is at my side. She has entered silently. The room is dark except for a sliver of light from the barely opened shutters and this slice of the sun falls precisely on the documents. There is a twelve- or fourteen-foot ceiling, a fireplace, cold walls, and the soft whomp whomp of the fan above. She presses her hip against me as I sit crouched over the endless numbers. There is a smile on her face. She wears a dress and high heels and it is nine in the morning. I place my hand on her leg and she begins to grind against me.

You have another woman in the States, she says, that is no problem in Mexico. Then she shows the photo of her sofa—it is protected with a clear plastic slipcover. I smile, finger my bank documents, and want a drink very badly. I am tired of trouble. I am going to be good, the first draft of the book will have almost five hundred footnotes,

I will be a real person. Maybe mow the lawn, paint the white picket fence, subscribe to sturdy, sensible magazines, and fret about crime. She grins; her teeth are perfect and white. She calls out, and her daughter enters. I stand and we are introduced. Then with a flick of Ofelia's tiny wrist the daughter disappears through the door. And her tongue is in my mouth again.

Will you call me from the States? she repeats. She is as hungry as a lioness. I point to the imposing pile of bank documents—my work, my . . . She will have none of my nonsense. A burro brays, a rooster crows, the life of the town pounds against my cell. Her friend enters beaming with some joy. I cling manfully to my columns of numbers. The faint breeze from the fan plays with her curly black hair as Ofelia speaks.

After a little while, a man in a military uniform storms into the party; his bearing is very erect and he does not smile. Soon Chuy and his colleagues are in a deep conference with the man, who is the local comandante of the Army garrison. He demands their weapons: if Chuy does not turn over his gun, the comandante is coming back with a couple of hundred soldiers. Some pistols are stashed in a car trunk outside the hotel walls. Money changes hands.

Calm returns, La Banda roars on. There never really was any possibility of the party getting out of control because the authorities are at the party. That man over there in the white T-shirt sitting by Chuy's side and bending his ear is part of the federales' special antinarcotics strike force. As are some of the other guests. They have traveled hundreds of miles to attend this ceremony. No one asks them to surrender their *armas*. After a while, the mayor shows up for a bit. Chuy is a respected citizen in this town. For years, his father was a functionary in the mayor's office. Chuy lives in a different city now and he has made many friends. His brother is the federal attorney there.

Chuy has done time on Islas Tres Marías, Mexico's version of Devil's Island. He has also done time in American prisons. He makes a point of telling my American friend, "They treated me very nice." He has reportedly murdered seven people. Leopoldo, the fellow I came down to visit, the man with the hit list on his mind and the wonderful horse, the man who cannot be here because he has errands to do, he is Chuy's good friend.

The bride arrives around nine P.M. and she is lovely. Gold bracelets grace her arms and a maid of honor attends her. Chuy rises briefly from his chair, grabs his dream woman, and for about five seconds dances. Liters of twelve-year-old scotch circulate among the crowd (they go for $37 at the local liquor store). The local judge refuses to come and officiate because she was duped once before at the aborted January wedding. Chuy appears to take this setback in stride and beams as people come up to congratulate him on his non-wedding wedding. When I ask a Mexican why Chuy persists in these failed ceremonies, he looks at me with pity and says, "Because he loves to get married." He already has a wife in the States. His brother is there also—in the joint.

Toward midnight the angry fellow who was insulted in the wash seeks to redeem his honor. He attacks the fellow who showed disrespect. The other man is not too stunned and has the presence of mind to whip out his pistol. The car trunk has been reopened. Chuy disarms the man and then kicks him in the ass. This is a very forgiving culture.

In front of me I see the wife of one of Mexico's former district attorneys dancing up a storm with the pistoleros. A few years back, her husband was cut down while sitting right next to her, quite possibly by some of the guests at this wedding.

As we celebrate someone leaves and goes out into the campo. I do not realize this fact at that moment, I am drunk after all, but I learn of it later. A peasant in a village I know has come down off the sierra with a load on pack horses. He is going to do an independent deal, he is going to be rich. It is all within the reach of his dark, callused hands. He is sitting at dinner, venison stew from a deer he has just killed, and he and a friend do not hear them in time. They are quickly cut down, the 75-kilo load is taken. It is all very efficient—the killers are federales. They deliver the load to the prearranged pickup point, help toss it on the truck and pocket the money. I can see Ofelia's friends laughing and drinking and flirting and seeking romance. One sidles up to me, she has hair the color of dark honey, a tight skirt and is very trim. Her voice is soft and feels like the glow of a candle as she speaks to me in the shadows. It is getting toward the fortieth or fiftieth hour since Ofelia died. I am not angry any longer. Life is for the living so long as the living live.

(Spotted Tail is the great chief, the wise man, the one who sees what is ahead clearly and never flinches. He stares out at the rubble of Lakota life and offers this thought: "There is a time for all things. Think for a moment how many multitudes of animal tribes we ourselves have destroyed; look upon the snow that appears today—tomorrow it is water. Listen to the dirge of the dry leaves that were green and vigorous but a few moons before! We are part of that life and it seems our time has come."

It is now August 1881. Little Crow Dog waits. Spotted Tail is slaughtered on a dirt road. The snow is now water.)

When I awaken the next day I find the hotel a semi-ruin with a few mountains of beer bottles and many scotch bottles scattered about. The man who spent yesterday vomiting in the wash with the pigs is better now and says, "It was a glorious drunk and a delicious *la cruda.*" The party is to resume in a few hours. The wedding rolls on for five days and five nights. The ceremony gets lost in the swirl of joy.

I catch brief moments through the drink. I walk down an old narrow street, the roar of La Banda pours from the doorway of an inn. The bride-not-to-be is on horseback and the animal dances in the street to the music. She is blond and slight, her hips screaming from tight Levi's, and her face is serene as her body sways to the rhythms of the half-ton animal beneath her. I enter and find Chuy, his federale bodyguards, and a horde of hangers-on sitting at tables amid the rubble of empty bottles. Orchids grow on the trees of the patio, bougainvillea clings to the old walls. There is said to be a tunnel from the old inn to the old church, a secret passage that once linked the priests to their women. All these towns are rife with tales and ghosts. Everyone knows these facts and phantoms.

I order a glass of red wine. Chuy will have none of this—"Order a bottle on me, I do not do little things." His face is relaxed from scotch, his eyes alert from cocaine.

Now he must do a big thing. This marriage matter is not so casual. The woman is the daughter of a major cocaine mogul and he is part of a family that runs a large chunk of the white powder business in Mexico. When I am told this by a friend, he adds, "Never say his name out loud." The father has his standards and one is that Chuy make an honest woman of his daughter. Or he will have him killed.

But Chuy's thoughts are elsewhere. He looks over at the damage his matrimonial instincts have created and smiles. He explains, "I am in the meat business. I think it is time I got back to selling a little meat." I can understand why, he has spent somewhere between $50,000 and $75,000 in the last five days. Each day I hear him on the phone ordering money to be flown in. When I ask how this is done—wire transfer?—a friend looks at me in disbelief and explains, "Chuy does not have money delivered by wire but by briefcase."

Ofelia's husband used to be a waiter in this very inn. I drain my glass of wine and have another and another. The federale sitting next to me is fat and dark and watches me write in my notebook. He is a very talented man, he explains. Once he commanded the elite unit of the antinarcotics strike force in the region, before he was temporarily broken down in rank for firing "a premature burst." Still, he is a man of power. Are guns desired? He says he can bring them south by the truck. The same for whiskey and scotch. His colleague, another officer in the unit, nods. Then the man gets up, approaches a woman who is nicely dressed, and they disappear into a room. Two days later he is found dead. I am told "his heart stopped." When they discover the body, the sheets are a mess, the woman is gone, and the dead officer has a white powdery mustache riding on his cold face.

But that is not on my mind now. Ofelia is leaning toward me, her skin so dark and rich looking, her face is beaming as she shows me a photograph of her stove. She licks my ear. Her body is like a child's and she is so eager.

The stove is yellow and perfectly polished like heirloom silverware. I say I must work. In the United States, this tactic is always successful. She looks down at me huddled behind the bunker of my bank documents. Her hand runs through my hair, the other slides up my pant leg.

Do you love me? she asks.

There is a machine now, the man says, a machine in the sierra that compresses things. A kilo can be reduced to the size of a cigarette package, or to a thin wafer. And when these little packets arrive in the United States, they can be returned to normal size by the simple application of some kind of fluid.

I am back in my room, the same chamber where I was felled by Ofelia's hungers. She is dead of course and I am drunk and La Banda has left, everyone has left. The party is over. Chuy has stiffed everyone—the band, the hotels, the liquor stores, the restaurants. No one has been paid. He cannot be found. An entire world has sunk beneath the waves like Atlantis as the drug killings escalate. A friend has to visit the capital. Before he leaves he instructs his wife: Here is a blank check I have signed and if I do not return in one day empty out all our accounts and leave. She does not ask questions. The campo is not safe, they are strafing passing vehicles with machine pistols. The town mechanic is found on the highway. His finger-nails are missing, the wrists slit and packed with salt, the . . .

I do everything within my power. I go to the capital, dine with a powerful publishing figure. We eat and drink for three hours, the steak is an inch and a half thick. Two good-looking women—the dresses tight and slit, the bodices oozing cleavage—eye us across the room. Do you want them? the man asks. Let's throw them in the car and go off, he continues. In the evening, he explains, the muchachas come out along this avenue like frogs after a summer rain. But I am all business. I give him everything—Chuy's name, his brother the federal prosecutor's name, the rank and names of the federales, the bride-to-be's father's name, everything. He nods this is very good and taps out a number on his cellular phone. Instantly, he is talking to the attorney general, rattles off the names and hangs up. No problem, he says, he will run a check. It seems so simple: I will have the files, fill in the details, know the dimensions of this portion of the business. It will all come belching out of the deep brain cells of a Mexican government computer.

Two days later I return and stay in the very best hotel—I must maintain my image, the gringo writer, the seeker of truth, the carnivore who can tear asunder any piece of *carne asada*. I go down to the bar and the man sitting next to me is very well dressed and fine gold chains hang from his neck.

He says he is in the pharmaceutical business.

Oh, yes, and where does this commerce take you?

Why I have just been in the Sierra Madre. He smiles.

Do you go to the States?

Why yes, he beams, we import our wares there.

The barmaid has an almond face, young eyes, and the firm body of her eighteen years. He speaks to her, tells his room number, and yes, yes, she says, she will be up there at eight P.M. The bartender eyes them, comes over, she whispers to him, and he is assured of his share of the price.

I make a call to the publisher. Surely by now the attorney general has run those simple names through his big computer and come up with the sheets. But the publisher cannot come to the phone, his secretary explains, his stomach is very upset. She thinks it is the flu.

This is a very serious stomachache. Calls are made for months. He can never come to the phone. Or call back. When I run the same names through contacts among the American authorities, they draw a blank. I have been dealing with phantoms.

You want me to denounce drugs? I will not. You want me to endorse drugs? I will not do that either. Three days ago, I delivered a message. A mother wished to find her daughter. A friend checked for me, made the calls. The voices told him to back off, to let it alone. Yes, we know her, they said. Back off, stay out of this. Their words rumbled with the bust that was making their mouths water. The daughter is a whore, she is living in a crack house. She has no right to our hearts. We all know that. I have no position on drugs. The blood orchids, I think, make them necessary for many. The lack of real work, the lack of real power, make the drugs delicious. I have been to the drug war but that is not the real killing ground. The people who can piss into a cup and pass, they are also casualties, standing everywhere around me with their hearts pumping blood out onto the tile floors, the sticky wet fluid spreading, the therapists gathering to feed, the eyes of so many now looking like deer in the headlights. They seldom complain, these brokenhearted people, they seem not to feel a thing.

It is night now, Chuy is God knows where, the uniforms are creeping around some house, eager as wolves to take down that crack house, sweep up the girl, turn on the bright lights in the interrogation room, and make a good bust. After I told the mother about her daughter, I sat on a hillside that was soon covered by flocks of blue-birds. A peace descended on me, my heartbeat slowed, the sun caressed my skin, and out the corner of my eye I could see the flicker of a white-tailed deer moving through a bosque of mesquite. And at that instant a jet armed for tank destruction roared by 150 feet off the deck. And I wanted a drug.

The wall in my room is covered with spiders and they are motionless as they wait for the kill. It is the end of summer now, Cinco de Mayo is a memory, and for all I know Chuy is lying by some roadside, his fingernails missing, his wrists slit, perhaps the small puncture wounds on the arm where the ice pick went in and out and in and out for the bone tickling. The genitals neatly sliced off and packed in his generous mouth. I do not know. There is no one to ask at the moment, talk has ceased, a silence has descended broken only by small arms fire.

I remember the last time I saw Ofelia. I had worked until midnight on my bank documents, and then fallen into bed preoccupied by a fifty-million-dollar black hole in a Panamanian shell corporation. I left the door open to catch the night air, and the sounds were burros braying, roosters crowing, and now and then a singing drunk stumbling home along the calle. Dogs also snarled and howled and made love in the velvet blackness of the tropical night.

I did not hear her enter but around four A.M. felt her ass against my naked body. She offered no photographs.

She said, "Do you think this is a dream?"

They say she died of too much dieting, that this ruined her stomach. Or they say she died of cancer. Or they say she died at age thirty-three and left four children, a drunken husband, a stack of photographs of her sofa, television, chair, stove, and things. They will not say what has become of Chuy. There is very little talking now, my phone is dead, the spiders wait motionless on the wall. I am not drinking, I am cold stone sober.

She said, "Do you think this is a dream?"

She left before dawn and I can see her looking over her shoulder and smiling back at me. I am standing under the front portal, she is disappearing down a dirt path into blackness. As she melted away she crossed the exact ground where Chuy's second stab at a wedding would take place.

That night is when I sinned. I never slept with Ofelia, not at all. I felt it was not right, she was married, she had a family. I refused. I ruined her dream. I know now she felt this thing inside her, this finger of death probing her young body and she recoiled from that icy finger and a hunger surged within her that she needed to feed if she were to live, to ever live at all. And I said no. And I will live with what I did not do until the day I die and I will know every minute for the rest of my life that the priests have never, not once, understood what flows through us and what makes us live and makes us create life around us. I can smell her hair at this very moment.

I can't get rid of what I see and feel. Ecology, pornography, murder, and breakfast all seem to flow together. This is my river and I am afloat upon it, come what may. The Sioux are gathering for a Sun Dance. The thing in my bones, I will beat it. Nine, four, buffalo. Order a whole bottle. Call me from the States. It is time to sell a little meat. What would you like me to do?

I cannot be made acceptable. All this . . . stuff gets in the way. This is not what I had planned. By now—ah, let

me check my career schedule—I was to be nicely garbed
and seated at a solid table in my tweed jacket. A cup of
fresh-ground coffee cools at my elbow, the fine bone
china saucer giving a welcoming click as I delicately
set the cup down. The manuscript is before me—I have
told the help to hold all phone calls while I work—and
I etch in yet more fine lines with my $180 gold-tipped
fountain pen. I make visitations at conferences and share
my artistic angst with audiences sedated by large suppos-
itories of Literature. At least that is what is on my schedule. Somebody's fucked up here. What are these goddamn
spiders doing on the wall, and where is my proper
wardrobe?

Clouds of bluebirds.

I am not drinking, as I have said. But perhaps this is
one of my many mistakes.

The other matter is not simply a mistake. I know in my
bones that forgetting what has happened is a sin. And I
struggle not to commit this sin. But now I have sinned in
a way I never knew before was possible.

Do you think this is a dream?

She smells like laundry just taken off the line.

The male and female wasp do not hurry, no,
not at all. They remain locked together in
fornication for hours. And they do other things.
The female for the first time in her life is off the
ground, in flight. The tunnel-digging predator
now kisses the sky. She does not waste this rare
opportunity. The male hauls her from flower to
flower and here they both feed, continuing to
fuck all the while. For first and last time during
her time on this earth, the female tastes nectar.

While the male and female wasp are
slurping up nectar and fornicating, the male, we
think, is also scoping out the forest floor. Sex, we
believe, does not distract him from this great
task. He is looking for a good place to drop the
female later, after the bash, a piece of ground
rich in beetles where his kind can thrive, where
his descendants will prosper. Just how he does

this we do not understand. But we feel confident that however strange it may seem, he is actually the explorer of his world, the Columbus finding the new country and the new future. And the hammer orchid that cannot watch, watches; that cannot see, sees; that cannot know, ...

Blue teeth glowing in the dark. Blue uniforms with ripe sunbursts of red on the blouses of the dead boys at Gettysburg. Blue bodies swelling in the June heat of Little Bighorn. Blue shirts slogging through the snow that cold day at Wounded Knee. Blues slithering out of the black dirt of the delta. Blue eyes of the Wehrmacht trudging across the icy steppes. Blue, the official color of the Krupp cannon works. Blue over my head as I look into the eye of God and Götterdämmerung. Blues for Mr. Charlie. Bluedicks crying up from the ground in spring. General Custer, sir: you blue it. We will not eat blue food, it is a fact. Blue-sky deal. Blue heaven. Blue teeth glowing in the dark.

It was then for the first time that I saw the state of my testicles. . . . I remembered that as a medical student I saw, in the famous Houssay textbook, a photograph of a man who, because of the enormous size of his testicles, wheeled them along in a wheelbarrow! Mine were of similar dimensions, and were colored a deep black and blue.*

---

*Nunca Más, 24.

Our country has always been known as a land of dei-
ties; shall we now permit a horde of dogs to stain it? . . .
From the moment they arrived with their ill luck, happiness and peace seem to have departed from everywhere.
—*Vietnamese appeal for resistance against French, 1864*

In a high pass at 13,000 feet, we come upon a natural
grotto. The wind howls through the rock crotch and
snaps our heads back. The grotto holds a small statue of
the Virgin, dozens of candles, a pile of money, and countless scarves tied to a string, the multicolored bundle
whipping in the wind like an international flag.

The soldiers passing by on foot with their rifles slung
across their backs fling songs into the raging wind.

"When we sing," the captain offers, "we forget we are
tired."

She is sitting by my side, and she is very thirsty. Her hair
is blond and when she walked across the room to my
table it trailed down her back to her ass. I touch it and
the strands feel like straw from savage sessions with the
bleach bottles. She is twenty-three—they are always
twenty-three. It is, according to custom, the right age.
The roots are black, black as obsidian. I love her roots.
But she will not admit to their existence as they line up
like row after row of tree stumps on her head. I am in the
place where no one ever says, *"Yo soy indio."* I understand. There are things all of us wish not to admit. On
the plane to this place, I sat next to a man and his wife
and their two young children. I was reading a book on
artists and other control junkies who flourished in the
fifteen years after Waterloo. The book is about the birth
of the modern, that wave breaking just past the horizon.

I am a sucker for the beginnings. I am, at the moment, also draining a half carafe of red wine. I sense where I am going. And the man sees the cover of the book—its English and obscure title—and seizes upon me as a harbor in the storm. He has married a woman of the nation to which we are headed, knows not a word of the language, and from the hard glances from his wife, few of the customs and habits. I keep drinking and we talk about long-dead people who created things or wanted to create things in those brief years after Waterloo.

That was many days ago. Now I am in-country, I have succumbed. I am in a whorehouse near the center of the city on a warm summer night. I am on my knees to her, I feel that much reverence. But she cannot sense this gesture of devotion because it is all taking place in my mind as she smiles, her lips full and red, her teeth white, polished, and nicely even. Yes, I am on my knees, the hard Spanish tile floors grinding against my cartilage and joints, the darkness shaking with North American music, the other patrons small mushroomlike clumps in the inky air, the men never smiling, the women softly and insistently stroking their companions' crotches as if checking on a delivery that is coming express. The man at the door charged twenty dollars to enter and there was a stairway and then things got dark, the walls barely glowed. The bartender bends over washing glasses and takes me in with hooded eyes. Women in short shorts, Capri pants, and miniskirts sit on stools nursing small glasses filled with a dark fluid. It is the midnight hour and the trees are in leaf, the streets purring with lovers and motor scooters, taxis and strollers and soldiers and police, and out there the scent of flowers floats over everything and everyone. In here, it is not the same. But it is very safe. The nation prides itself on certain standards of honesty. Your suitcase is not pilfered by the maid. You are not mugged on the busy streets regardless of the hour. I am sliding into drunkenness and have fifteen hundred dollars in my shirt pocket as a large-breasted woman leans against my shoulder and plies her trade in a whorehouse in a provincial capital of the nation. How can one be safer than that?

> Women were interrogated in the same manner. They were stripped naked, laid down on a bed. . . . With women, they would insert the wire in the vagina and then apply it to the breasts. . . . Many of them would menstruate. . . . With them they only used the telephone. . . .*

The air is thick with cigarette and cigar smoke and I chew it slowly as my eyes adjust to the near-blackness. Earlier, I ate a dinner of beets, carrots, and chicken along the avenida. I have been craving green things, roughage, in this nation of carnivores. I watched two sixteen-year-old girls in tight pants and blouses lean against a wall and stare at me while they smoked cigarettes. Their lips were deeply reddened, their cheeks seemed rouged, and around the eyes swirled coronas of black and blue. When they pursed their lips, smoke would pour forth like a river seeking a sea. Their blouses were low cut and they displayed cleavage while birds crackled in the trees over my head. Now I have come to a different place. Of course, a cabdriver helped and the fare was only four dollars. Other matters intervened, this often happens. I drank a 750-milliliter bottle of wine, and it was very good. They are proud of their wine here, particularly the reds.

---

*Nunca Más, 37.

She is licking my ear, now she turns my head, I feel her tongue reach into my mouth like an ice breaker. Spooning. They have somehow dimmed the light and I pull back and look at her, that long mane of blond hair, and someone—the bartender with the hooded eyes?—flicks some switch and a black light takes over this cellar and she smiles.

She tells me she is from the capital and has been in this provincial city merely three weeks. Ah, that smile.

Her teeth are blue.

I am lying in a tongue of black volcanic boulders just above the barracks. The mules feed in the stone corral—mules are the form of transportation for the authorities in the high mountains and move at about six kilometers an hour. They are less tender of foot and more sure of foot than horses, and they are strong. They are also stubborn. This morning when the muleteer was shoeing one, he lost his patience and staggered the animal with a hard blow to the head.

I ask, "Do the mules have names?"

"Sí, they all have one name—ass."

"From the Bible?"

"Sí."

At this altitude, the mules last two or three years and then are sold to the farms in the valleys. The men last thirty-five years.

They call the experience *la margarita,* the daisy. Other new terms are required. When you vanish you are *chupado,* sucked up. If you are tossed out of an airplane, you are *traslado,* transferred. Or *mandado para arriba,* sent up.

[America's] Pacific era . . . destined to be the greatest of all, is just at its dawn.
—*President Theodore Roosevelt, San Francisco, 1903*

The Vietnamese are slaves by nature. They have been ruled by us and now they are ruled by the French. They can't have a very brilliant future.
—*Sun Yat-sen, leader of the Chinese revolution, speaking to a Japanese statesmen, 1911*

The room is plain, windowless, and brightly lit. You cannot see, there is that hood over your head. Your arms are tied, at times so are your legs. You do not know where you are, you will never know where you are or have been. It begins mildly, almost chastely. First, perhaps, cigarette burns on the arms, and other body parts. Your hair is pulled, your face slapped. There may be pinching. There are various instruments for stretching, tearing, and puncturing your flesh. You feel a kick, then another. A fist plows into your face. You cannot see the blows coming, you cannot see anything. There are voices of course, angry voices, contemptuous voices, strange voices. Sometimes there is a pause and a question will suddenly thud against your torn and bleeding ears. You may know the answer to this question or you may not know the answer. No matter, you will give an answer. Everyone does, every time.

You may wonder why this is happening, just as you wonder where this is happening. Do not bother with such thoughts. It is happening because it is necessary. And it is happening here, which, in time, is everywhere. You are product, you are part of a new process of living. You do not realize it yet, but you have become a key part of the economy.

You may try to seal a part of yourself off from what is happening by focusing your mind, by that act sometimes called disassociating. The mind localizes the pain, builds a wall around its presence, drowns it in a witch's brew of chemicals. The football player finishing the game with a broken leg, the soldier taking a bullet and continuing to move forward. Your ribs ache, some are broken, your eyes and ears are swollen, your back feels crushed, there are burns scattered about your hide, your mouth bleeds from the stumps where there were quite recently teeth. It is a tall order to seal this off, but it is possible. We know this from the experiences of the heroes and the saints. You visualize, perhaps, a bunch of grapes, and for each locus of pain, you pluck one grape in your mind and the pain diminishes or disappears. There are many images, you can find the one that suits your nature. You think the word blue, you say silently to yourself: the moon is blue. You are floating, and with each lap of the waves against your body, the pain ebbs and goes away like a stain slowly leaving a fine white shirt.

Then you are suddenly picked up by the hair and the legs and thrown on something metal and cold. It feels like a bed frame. Your hands and feet are tied to the corners, you are spread-eagled. With the first surge, you almost break your limbs when your body snaps and contracts. And it does not stop—surge, after surge, after surge.

Finally, they drag you down a hall—it dimly sounds like a hall and not a room—and toss you into what feels like a small chamber. A cell. You lie on the floor and it is covered with cold water. Your battered body swells up.

You are not a hero or a saint. You can no longer disassociate. The surges batter through all defenses.

And there is one other thing you will soon realize that you cannot do. You cannot die. That is no longer within your control. You will live as long as others decide you should live. You lie in the cold water, hooded, shackled, and grow like a monstrous flower as your body swells.

Out of four prisoners, we had to kill three; out of ten, we had to kill nine and keep only one for interrogation. These were our orders.

—*Soldier LeCalic, testimony, 1931*

La capital bloats with more than ten million people, the thirty-mile-wide tongue of a brown river rolls past like a sea. The air feels temperate even in the heart of the summer and the tree-lined avenues hint at the calm of a midwestern town. There are things named after the Liberator, but hardly a reminder of the time of the Leader, Juan. The cabdriver charges the normal rate for a ride from the airport—forty dollars. No one pretends to understand the economy here. I look out the window and see a world that is cleaner and gentler to the eye than any possible ride from the airport in Chicago or New York or Detroit or Phoenix or Los Angeles. Women walk the broad boulevards in skin-tight pants. There is a hypersexuality here like that of a ghetto. I drink a cup of coffee at the Buffalo Hotel and then stroll two blocks to meet my contact. Her hair is black, her bones are fine, and her eyes sparkle in her face. She is fluent in Spanish and German, and puts forth her cheek to be kissed. The sultry summer air pours through an open sliding glass door and I bathe in it as she talks to headquarters in Germany. I have not really slept for twenty-four hours and it is easy for me to excuse myself from her attention.

The country I see from this seventh-floor office is the eighth largest in the world, slightly smaller than India, has around thirty million people, and keeps getting forgotten.

At the beginning of the twentieth century, the nation was a contender and rode at that magical takeoff point with Australia and Canada. Then something happened and everyone in this place wonders at what that something was and is. And will be. For it never seems to end.

Que el mundo fue y será porquería
Ya lo sé, en el 510 y en el 2000 también . . .

That the world was and will be a pigsty
I know; in 510 and in 2000, too;
That there have always been crooks, schemers and
    suckers,
The happy and the embittered, ideals and frauds.
But that the twentieth century is a display of insolent evil,
No one can deny.*

Vietnam represents the cornerstone of the Free World in Southeast Asia, the keystone to the arch, the finger in the dike. . . . Vietnam is crucial to the Free World in fields other than the military. . . . We must assist the inspiring growth of Vietnamese democracy and economy.
    —*Senator John F. Kennedy, June 1, 1956*

The sound of horns drifts up from the street below. I hear the woman's voice arguing over a phone with other voices in Germany. My itinerary is very exact, with three thousand dollars in airfares plus Teutonic fantasies of buses that leave on schedule, army trucks, airlines that

---

*Enrique Santos Discépolo, "Cambalache," 1934. In Nicholas Fraser and Marysa Navarro, *Eva Perón* (New York: W. W. Norton, 1980), pp. 18–19.

never lose luggage, phones that work, and mail that always goes through. I am to rendezvous with mules. That is the image: huge mountains white with snow and ice, men on muleback braving the stone teeth of the cordillera, and me, the Sancho Panza scribbling *un mundo fantástico*. I have no desire to enter into the negotiations crackling through the phone line so I thumb through the major newspaper. A headline tells of an investigative piece: the secret military squads are being reformed. They will counter terrorism, they will be ready, they will protect the poor and seek out the corrupted fruit of *la patria*.

At night, you will be walking down a street, the lamps few, the houses darkened, the air sweet with flowers. Your head will be filled with ideas, your body with fine red wine, and the clicking of your heels on the sidewalk will tap out a rhythm for the visions swirling up from your soul.

> *Vivimos revocados en un merengue*
> *y en un mismo lodo todos manoseados....*
>
> We live wallowing in the mess
> And we're all covered by the same mud.

You will be thinking of your woman, you will be thinking of your man, you will be thinking of love and gardens and fine meals on clean plates, you will be thinking of an embrace, the smell of a baby, the mouth at the breast, the hand on the breast, the glory of God, the smell of clean sheets. A man will get out of a small parked car. The car will be dark, probably black as it happens. The man will ask you to go with him. There will be no identification, no badges, no sacred seals and holy oils. It will happen very swiftly and you will, believe me, get in the car. And no one will ever see you again.

¡Hoy resulta que es lo mismo
ser derecho que traidor! . . .

Today it makes no difference
Whether you are honest or a traitor,
Ignorant, wise or a thief,
Generous or crooked;
All's the same, nothing is better.
A donkey is the same
As a great professor.
There are no failures, no hierarchies;
People without morals have brought us to their level.

TOP SECRET

AMBASSADOR HAS OVER-ALL AUTHORITY FOR HANDLING OF NEWS-MEN. . . . CORRESPONDENTS SHOULD NOT BE TAKEN ON MISSION WHOSE NATURE SUCH THAT UNDESIRABLE DISPATCHES WOULD BE HIGHLY PROBABLE. . . . SENSATIONAL STORIES ABOUT CHILDREN OR CIVILIANS WHO BECOME UNFORTUNATE VICTIMS OF MILITARY OPERATIONS ARE CLEARLY INIMICAL TO NATIONAL INTEREST.

—*Top secret State Department cablegram to*
U.S. commanders in Vietnam, 1962

It is forbidden to dance anywhere at all.
—*Article 4, Morality Law, Laws of the Republic of*
South Vietnam, May 24, 1962

Dancing with death is sufficient.
—*Madame Ngo Dinh Nhu, June 22, 1962*

I put down the newspaper. The president himself has denied the reports. It is all being blown out of proportion, he advises. The authorities say this is not a matter for alarm, merely a prudent and normal action and there are no plans or thoughts of . . .

The woman puts down the phone, she has kept the Germans at bay. They sit in their offices at this moment and look out windows at a gray sky and an endless drizzle. They will eat turnips today and never smell a flower. Her eyes say that we will be different, we will walk past lush tropical blooms, dine at sidewalk cafés, drink rich dark coffees, sip robust wines. Her eyes say I will smell a woman because here it is the thing to do. We will disappear, yes, but disappear into love, with candles flickering against a dark wall. The window will be open, the curtains will faintly rustle in the night breeze, the sounds of the city will softly enter like the purring of a huge beast. And in the morning, no one will regret anything.

She hands me a publication, a small book of color photographs of the native people of this continent. A group of campesinos and their families huddle under trees. No one is smiling, a pregnant woman stares out with her arms folded above her swollen belly, small children look out blankly, the men display mouths as hard as a knife's edge. They are in rebellion—big estates have taken their land and this has made them angry. Turn the page and the camera softly embraces the face of a young man as he smokes cocaine. Next a black monkey wears a yellow cap and a white cassock as a young woman smiles at him and her body sings with brightly woven native textiles. And of course, the essential and eternal photo, one entitled *Hombres de la Limpieza*, the Men of Purity. They stand at attention, rifles on their shoulders, hard metal helmets on their heads, the uniforms dark, the boots stout and ready for the kick. All this is pictured in the plaza where before them a man with a long handmade broom sweeps the refuse of a gutter into a dustpan fashioned from a slashed five-gallon lard can.

I go out on the small balcony. The city looks rich, European, safe, and sensual. The boulevards are lined with buildings that seem transplanted from France. I continue flipping through the photo book—almost every image is of an Indian in native costume. Or an Indian naked. We are suddenly in the green jungle by the great river, the women wear a small cloth riding a string that rests on their big hips, their bodies are decorated with large red rings, their black hair is cut like a Dutch boy's, their heavy breasts hang down without a care. Or it is *carnaval* in the metropolis by the sea. The women are tanned, oiled, and glitter with gold. Their nipples are dark, and their smiles recall the pleasure of a cat lapping a bowl of warm milk. A pigeon lands on the balcony railing and begins to coo. It has only one leg, yet it rests in balance and carries on as if it were a perfectly normal pigeon. After that it is a quick taxi to military headquarters.

We are along the waterfront. There are stands for refreshments and slabs of offices like sides of bacon curing black in the sun. Flags fly from huge staffs, people in uniforms form little clots on the street, and the sky above beckons with summer and love. The biggest single center was down here. That fact no one disputes, not the guests, not the hosts. The nation is a military machine, and this is machine row. The cabdriver cannot find where we are going, we circle, we dodge, we pull over and ask. Over there, I say, that building. It's my bad Spanish, clearly.

Finally, after half an hour scurrying along five hundred yards of avenida, we arrive. Over there.

The building squats with massive antennae and big white dishes on its roof. I pass the armed guards and surrender my passport at the lobby checkpoint and fasten an orange identification tag to my shirt. The interior is very dark and hardly a light bulb is burning. The elevator stops on the fifth floor, an aide appears and moves me toward a large room with a big dark wooden conference table. I sit, a man dressed in white enters silently and places a demitasse of coffee on a fine china saucer before me. I automatically note the age of everyone I see in this building. If they are over thirty, then they were in it. This is almost a certainty. There were at least 350 centers—no one can be sure of the exact number because of the bulldozing and the fact that you had to wear a long black hood every minute of every day—and the men and women of this service functioned as guards in each and every one of these centers. Sometimes, of course, they asked you questions also.

> Si uno vive en la impostura
> Y otro roba en su ambición. . . .

> If one man lives in imposture
> And another steals through ambition,
> It's the same if you are priest,
> Mattress-maker, King of Clubs,
> Huckster or stowaway.

At first they felt sick and had some diarrhea, then they began to feel it hard to breathe and they had low blood pressure; some serious cases had trouble with their optic nerves and went blind. Pregnant women gave birth to still-born or premature children. Most of the affected cattle died. . . . River fish floated on the surface of the water belly up, soon after the chemicals were spread.

—*Cao Van Nguyen, M.D., reporting on U.S. chemical attack, October 3, 1964*

Weapons used by American and Vietnamese forces also have become controversial. One of these weapons is the .223-caliber Armalite rifle, introduced in combat. . . . The rifle has a muzzle velocity so high that its metal-jacketed bullet virtually explodes when it hits a human being, causing a huge jagged wound. The effect is similar to the Dum-Dum expanding bullet outlawed by the Geneva Convention.

—*AP dispatch from Saigon, March 25, 1965*

Government expenditure for the development of chemical and biological agents has grown by $175 million—to $275 million—in the last five years. Hottest areas of research are psychochemical agents—e.g. compounds that induce temporary, partial disabilities (blindness, deafness, paralysis, amnesia).

—Chemical Week, *April 10, 1965*

After ten minutes I am taken down a dark hallway and come to rest in a medium-size office. The comandante rises from behind his large desk, expresses his pleasure. And asks for the proper papers. He examines them minutely and then with a small movement of his hand suggests I sit on the leather couch by the coffee table. He produces a leather folder, flips it open to orders, communiqués, documents of many types and all splattered with seals.

Ah, yes, yes, he says, you will be met at the next airport by soldiers, all is arranged. There are many stamps, there must be a radio communiqué made to the forward base. The comandante looks to be fifty, is fine-boned, his hair trimmed, his body still relatively hard. He speaks with authority but there is a softness in his voice. Out his window I can see a bank of other windows framing offices just like his own.

¡Qué falta de respeto, qué atropello a la razón!
¡Cualquiera es un señor! ¡Cualquiera es un ladrón!

What lack of respect, what an assault on reason!
Anyone is a gentleman! Anyone is a thief!

Then a race by cab to catch a plane. Watching from the small window at 20,000 feet, I see the green coast give way to the dull farms of the plain, then this grid of rectangles surrenders to the brown paste of desert. Finally, the wall of cordillera heaves into view, we descend and land in the green path of a river valley rich with vineyards.

In theory, the nation is very rich. The land is bountiful and the war of liberation in the early nineteenth century left it with a generous portion. For decades the nation's army was semiorganized brigands, wild men on horseback from the vast grasslands. They systematically destroyed the people they discovered living in the immense interior. They called them natives. This is a commonplace repeated in many portions of the planet during the stage called settlement. By the end of the century, the nation's ruler decided he wanted a professional army. He bought cannon from Krupp. He founded a military academy and brought over ten German officers to run it. This force kept itself busy for decades tidying up frontiers and making menacing gestures toward neighboring nations. But there was a weakness deep in its vitals: it had no actual enemies. Mountains, oceans, and giant rivers secure the nation's boundaries. The land rolls on and on. *Lebensraum,* that obsession of the various Reichs, should mean little or nothing here. Of course, the military wanted to be like everyone else and for decades proposed the doctrine that if the nation did not physically expand, it would sicken and die. Claims were made to barren islands, icy polar stretches, desolate portions of neighboring nations. In the soft hours of evening while their wives busied themselves with needlework and their mistresses awaited their visits, officers would sit in their quiet studies and pen essays and small books on the need for the nation to expand and the need of a big military machine to foster this expansion. Nothing much came of these efforts. To expand meant testing the military machine, and tests, while promising victory, might bring defeat.

Around 1930, the military came up with a solution to this impasse. It attacked the nation itself. This was not so difficult. The governments that came and went were messy, boisterous, and unseemly to an orderly mind. The elected officials haggled and argued and said things that offended logic and efficiency. The training of the military prepared them to have a contempt for politicians and voters. For decades they periodically seized power from the civilians. They formed deep bonds with the militaries of Adolf Hitler and Benito Mussolini. And then with the second great war of the century and the defeat of all that they admired, they were left at sea again, a passion lacking an object, much like a prisoner dreaming of a woman.

The military fed off what was then the fifth-richest nation in the world—they had more cars per capita than Britain, more doctors per capita than anyone in Europe except maybe the Swiss and Hungarians. The leaders ardently believed the nation should be a player on the world stage, should use its treasure to add luster to its name. Eva, the beloved Eva, donated food and aid to Italy and Spain after the second great war. She gave money to the poor of Washington, D.C. The military sought a mission worthy of this affluence, a mission commensurate with its vision of honor. The French came to their rescue. They became the new teachers of the military and they taught a doctrine called counterinsurgency. There is this belief system called communism. It can be anywhere, moving silently like dry rot in a ship. It can be invisible, buried in the consciousness of ordinary-looking men and women. It can be under the bed. Counterinsurgency is a body of expertise that trains one how to root out this plague. Or other plagues. By 1966, the military training manual explained,

> Communism wants to destroy the human being, family, fatherland, property, the state and God. . . . Nothing exists in Communism to link women with home and family because, proclaiming her emancipation, Communism separates her from domestic life and child raising to throw her into public life and collective production, just like men. . . . [T]he father is the natural head of the family. The mother finds herself an associate of this authority. . . . According to the will of God, the rich should use their excess to alleviate misery. The poor should know that poverty does not dishonor, nor making a living with work, as the example of the son of God proved. The poor are more loved by God.

And so armed with a way of thinking, honed in a technique of doing, the military naturally progressed to the inevitable solution, the destination taken by so many others. The garden of the blood orchids. There was this time years ago, when the children of the rich and the children of the middle classes became guerrillas—estimates of their numbers vary from a few hundred to a couple of thousand or possibly up to forty thousand. Anyone can make an estimate, just as no one can ever really know. Whatever their numbers, they were sufficient for the second-largest standing army on the continent to consider serious adversaries. No quarter was given. Soon, the military ran out of children of the middle and upper classes who had flirted with radicalism or gone whole hog into kidnappings, killings, and bomb tossings. But this detail did not affect productivity or slow down the process of justice and purification. Few successful armies ever seek to shed their soldiers and shut down operations. It is simply not done.

Two soldiers await me in the terminal—a noncom and a private. They wear khaki, black boots, berets. I get in the rear of the Travelall. There are no interior door handles in the back seat.

> One of the most infamous methods of torture used by the government is partial electrocution—or "frying" as one U.S. advisor called it. . . . Sometimes the wires are attached to the male genital organs, or to the breasts of a Vietcong woman prisoner. . . . Other techniques . . . involve cutting off the fingers, ears, fingernails or sexual organs of another prisoner. Sometimes a string of ears decorates the wall of a government military installation. . . .
>
> The Viet Cong prisoners were interrogated on an airplane flying toward Saigon. The first refused to answer

181

questions and was thrown out of the airplane at 3,000 feet. The second immediately answered all the questions. But he, too, was thrown out.

—*Beverly Deepe, dispatch from Vietnam,*
New York Herald-Tribune, *April 25, 1965*

Spoons, spooning. You lie down, you must be tired. Your legs are spread. The air is stale from cigarette smoke. You can barely smell this through your blood-encrusted nostrils. Your nails are broken and thank God you cannot see them. You are almost grateful for the hood. Spoons. . . .

Now everything blooms in the roar of January and I crawl on my hands and knees among the low plants. The flowers are red, rose, pink, purple, lavender, orange, yellow, and white. Moss lathers over boulders until they look like strange green rocks. I listen carefully to the language of the mountains. A soldier has explained it to me: "Some days the wind does not come until noon and then it will blow through the night. And sometimes it blows at dawn and never stops." The cordillera speaks through the wind and it whistles, wheezes, purrs, roars, pants, screams, shouts, stutters, murmurs—all without end. Below me I can see clouds boiling up and dissipating. The wind eats all. White bones of guanacos gleam in the black rocks around me.

It is months later and I am standing at a red tile kitchen counter looking out at the wash where the trees are quickening with spring. The heads of the male house finches in the shrubs redden before my eyes, the blood is up, and every living thing knows that it is time to drive it home. The females extend their stubby wings from their fat bodies and flutter them at their sides while the blazing males come over and pop seeds into their yawning mouths. The ducks down below on the pond are swimming closer and closer to each other. I am listening to the blues. The sparrows are on the north side of the house huddling from the wind, the small bath I built is shimmering, the fountain is shooting water up two feet, the cardinal feeders hang in place, the hummingbird stations are ready, the mounted screen is smeared with peanut butter and ground-up bugs, the block of seed is sited for the quail, and the coveys are fairly large despite the stinginess of the winter rains. I have planted thirty-five perennials for wildlife and tomorrow, I promise, I will get the delphiniums and larkspur into God's good earth. I will plant them because they are blue.

Since I returned, I have kept a seven-day votive candle to the Virgin of Guadalupe burning. The altar is rich with items: a photo of a woman at a baseball game in Comiskey Park, Zuñi fetishes of a duck, a badger, coyote and buffalo, Seri images of the moon and the woman who is the moon, a Huichol yarn drawing of a shaman dreaming (and he looks pretty damned fucked up lying on his back in what appears to be a wheelbarrow with a bird flapping overhead, a bow floating near his feet, and peyote dreams spewing from his mouth like vomit), and a Huichol yarn-and-feather wand with which I regularly cleanse my doorways to protect me from evil. There is also a photograph of General Francisco Villa bolting ahead on horseback (one taken at the time of the reported revolution), a label from a case of fruit in the 1930s with a large-breasted woman smiling at the words BUXOM MELONS, a bundle of sweet grass barely singed by my devotions, a passel of images of Betty Page smiling and buck naked as she stokes the fires of boys in the 1950s, a medicine pouch in which I do not look because I have been taught manners and morals. Of course Christ is there hanging from his Tarahumara cross, a bull, various santos, Shiva, Buddha, the Virgin of Guadalupe surrounded by a wreath of pink roses, the basic gang. The goat can be trouble depending on your theology. I bought it from a Tarascan Indian woman who lived in a one-room shack a long drive down a bumpy dirt road in Michoacán. The men cut the wood for the kiln, the woman make the *figuras*. When you lift the goat's body off its base, a man and a woman heave into view. They are innocent of clothing, her feet are up in the air, her legs are spread, he is erect, on top, and driving as hard as any clay man can. There is also a squirrel god, images of the moon, sun, birds, musicians, mermaids, frogs, Atlas who is not shrugging, roosters, and drunkards. A flying Eskimo hovers about the altar and there is that candle. My mojo is working.

There is another candle in the shape of a woman almost eight inches high, the wax red, the breasts inviting. I bought it at a *curandero* stall in a small town against the Sierra Madre and a white wick pokes out of her kindly head. The man running the stall said it would bring me a woman. Here are his instructions: Merely see the woman in your mind, then light the candle, and she will come. Cost me five dollars American. I have never lit it.

I am standing at that red tile counter over the stainless steel sink with a long and slender bottle brush in my hand. The altar is very near at hand. I am scrubbing a tall glass that once contained a seven-day votive candle to the

Virgin. But I failed in this particular devotion. I was gone to a far place, sitting in a cellar with a woman whose blond hair trailed down her back to her ass and when I touched that hair it did not feel like part of a living thing but more like straw.

While I was gone, the wick leaned in the night or the day—I will never know—and burned against the glass and the glass blackened and went dark with carbon. I have soaked it, I have put it in ammonia, I have put it in vinegar, many soaps, water heated on the stove. Still patches of this blackness persist. And I am determined to scrub it off, no matter how long it takes, no matter how boring the grind of work. I find the bristles are not adequate, but when I bend the brush and the metal stem scrapes hard against the glass the blackness seems to diminish. As I pursue my task to cleanse the Virgin, I am thinking of the Germans. They paid me to go to the place with the cellar and the woman who is exactly twenty-three—she is always twenty-three—and when I came back and I wrote the story for their magazine, they became very unhappy. It turns out my story was not what they sent me to the place to report.

I have a fax in my pocket—they love to rocket faxes from their dark bunkers where they recline in lederhosen while slowly turning *Untermenschen* on a spit—and it is to the point. The *Volk* are nothing if not exact.

Where are the mule rides? Where are the men and their camaraderie? Where is the heroic toil against the great mountains? I know, you will say these are very German questions? Well, our readers are German and you should remember that.

Ah, I am remembering now. I scrub and scrub and I cannot get out that splotch of carbon where, in my absence, the wick tilted against the glass and left its dark mark. I have exhausted my chemical lore, I have devoted time—for a week the container sat in a rich broth of chemicals lapping against the glass—and still nothing seems to remove the stain.

There are other serious signs. The cardinals have not come to the house, despite my feeders. I see them, sometimes a hundred feet, sometimes a hundred yards from my house, and yet they do not come. I have water, I have special foods, I have a feeder that cost me almost forty dollars that no creature but a cardinal and his near kinsmen can feed from with success. They do not come. I see their brilliant red plumage flickering in the brush just below me as I scrub the vessel that held my offering to the Virgin. And they will not come.

I think of lighting the red wax candle in the shape of a woman. But this I do not do. I think of the Germans, wallowing in their *Gemütlichkeit,* and I can hear cuckoo clocks pecking against my head and they will not cease no matter how much I beg. Once an hour, the birds leap out-of-doors in these clocks, and a sound peals, and the whole machinery insists the world is orderly, safe, and known. When this happens, scraping the carbon off the glass that held the votive candles is not enough. When the cuckoos call, I want to kill every one of them.

Stonewall Jackson was wonderfully simple in his approach. Once an officer came to him and said there were Union forces on all sides of him and what should he do? Jackson said, "Kill them." I thought that was pretty wonderful. "Kill them all." . . . Religion and military life

are wholly compatible in my mind. You can't go into this
disciplined life . . . without spiritual support. . . .
—*Lieutenant General Victor H. (Brute) Krulak,*
commander, Fleet Marine Force, Pacific,
Life, *April 30, 1965*

The skin is stripped from the soles. Your hood is lifted
just a bit, and you see a bloody rag and they tell you
these are your wife's panties. Then, the electrodes are
placed on the teeth. And of course, there are the beads.
They are a narrow strand, each nodule a jewel-like elec-
trode. You find them difficult to swallow because you are
vomiting all the time, but with encouragement you swallow them. When the surge comes, each bead radiates and
cuts deep within your torso, and tears and slashes. You
are strangely silent, you have sailed off into a country
that is not beyond pain but is beyond sound. For several
hours afterward, you shake but you do not eat or drink
for days. You fear convulsions.

We have been riding in the back of a truck for hours and
I am sprawled out over sacks and cases of supplies. The
dirt road is rutted and bumpy. The men smoke and drink
hot tea and talk. They could pour tea during an earthquake and never spill a drop. They are a friendly lot, the
military bearing vanishes in the absence of an officer.
They explain to me why the military is a good choice for
them. One says, "I was raised in a farming area and as a
farm worker I made two hundred dollars a month. Now,
as corporal in the military, I make six hundred seventy
per month. I can have a family now."
When we slide down into the valley, the ground goes
green with vineyards, and small houses appear among the

lushness. The truck lurches to a stop, one of the soldiers hops out. A woman in a blue blouse and tan skirt stands framed in the doorway. She is thirty-something, her hips heavy, her hair stringy from a day of household tasks. She smiles at her approaching man, a small boy races across the yard, and by the entrance to their home a rose blooms. This is the ground beneath all the terrors.

Eva fought death with the same valor she had faced the other demons of this life. And the nation felt this and was moved. A city hoped to change its name to Eva. The Congress declared her *Jefa Espiritual de la Nación*. She was awarded the necklace of the Order of the Liberator, and this crowded her neck with 753 precious stones splayed out in six different emblems, among them the condor. The national flag hung from her scrawny dying neck in gold, platinum, diamonds, and enamel. It was during her time and her rule and the years of her early adoration that the nation began to catch on the breeze a first whiff of terror and torture and vanishing acts.

A waiter directs me to a club a block off the main avenida. It is pitch black and at eleven P.M. still largely empty. The show, the bartender explains, will begin at one-thirty in the morning. I drink a beer, one named after the great range that protects the nation's flank. Rock music plays loudly, secluded red lights cast a slight glow around the cavernous room. Women come in one by one. They carry large handbags and disappear behind the stage. Soon they emerge wearing short pants and halters. Every one of them is fat. It is the *estilo,* apparently, of the establishment. A woman slides silently out of the darkness into the seat beside me. She is thirsty, I order her a drink. She wears a white and black polka dot halter and shorts. I can barely hear her over the roar of music. She takes my hand and puts it under her clothing and on one enormous breast. The skin is warm, the tissue feels like rock. An implant.

She says that her name is Charlene.

"What would you like?" she asks. "You can have what you like for fifty dollars."

I go up to the bar, buy another beer. A man sitting on a stool asks the woman next to him a simple question: Is there another club where the women are not so fat? Yes, she answers kindly, and gives him a name and address. And that is how I came to the place in the basement and the woman with the blue teeth.

For days I have been peering into the low green mysteries of the plants, life forces that persist in a high mountain desert where the growing season is a twinkling in the flow of a year's time. The soldiers look on my crawling with justifiable amusement. The plants are spare, low. There are no trees, wood for the fire must be hauled up from the valleys. Finally, I explain my interest: the plants can stay here, we cannot.

And no one has anything to say about this queer notion of mine.

So we stand in a circle and drink the native tea and lyrical local Spanish with its Italian inflections fills the air and is punctuated with frequent laughter and yet more cups of tea.

I am in a provincial capital, a city of maybe 800,000. Trees line the streets, people swab the sidewalks with kerosene in the soft light of morning. Then the breath of summer comes on, the quick business of the early hours, conversations over coffee at the tables lining the rumble of the avenida. The small cups are delicate, the espresso black and strong. The women are fair-skinned, their blouses undone at the top, the breasts uplifted. Cleavage runs like a white line down the highway of this life. The women strut. The men swagger. The soldiers tell me that in the evening this is "the avenue of tits." No one can complain of a day that begins in this manner.

My days are consumed by the military. I am a suitcase other people carry around, I am checked and tagged, and shipped. The first evening, the local comandante carefully briefs me. He holds a pointer and vigorously stabs at a large military map stuck with pins and flags. The map is entitled INTELLIGENCE. Main bases are identified and sub-bases and forward bases—nineteen bases in all in this particular zone. And *La Frontera,* the border, a red patch on the map, ah the *zona rosa,* the fantasy line contrived by humans and sketched against a wall of rock and snow, the place where constant winds bend everyone over. While the comandante speaks, his aide-de-camp beams with a wide smile. The comandante's hatrack holds helmets, a garrison belt, his holster and .45. Christ hangs from his cross over the desk. The wall is lined with photographs of earlier comandantes, a row of faces going back almost fifty years, each looking stern, the hard eyes peering out from upswept caps that mimic the German army that has taught them all. A ceiling fan slowly stirs overhead.

The comandante tells me, "People can come here to see wild land the hand of man has not ruined."

The provincial capital is a miniature of the national capital's dream: we are Europeans, we are an outpost of civilization in a hopeless sea of brown ignorance and sloth. Shops hold European fashions. Here the Indians hardly exist. There are but a hundred thousand left in the nation and they are short brown beggars on the edge of the life. The wars of the last century finished them off and no one misses them or hears the croaks of any ghosts. The population is from Europe and most came in the late nineteenth and early twentieth centuries. The face of the nation is not mestizo, the skin is not dark. In fact there is no simple face. In the capital, the psychiatrists flourish and the typical patient is having an identity crisis. Blue eyes crying in the sun.

In the morning at first light, the soldiers come to the hotel. They are very friendly and laughter fills the truck. The trip is to take but an hour. Of course there is a flat tire. But all in all it goes smoothly. More soldiers await in the small rural town. Then it is off to another comandante and a major and a captain and a lieutenant. We sit at another large table, drink coffee from small cups, plan my journey into the cordillera. Later there are steaks in the officers' mess and good red wine. On the wall are drawings of national heroes and paintings of historic moments. The television never goes off; a waiter waits like a statue two feet behind my chair.

I could not be treated better, and the flash of teeth with all those smiles is a constant relaxant. What do you think of our women? I am asked. And of course I tell them the truth.

Spoons. Your vagina flaps open and you can do nothing. You are embarrassed. You are naked except for that hood, and you cannot see. They are watching you, you sense this. You try not to imagine what you look like, beaten, bloody. Burns dancing about your soft flesh. Your belly huge and swollen. Over the doorway, someone has written THE PATH TO HAPPINESS. Yes, spoons.

> In 1969 the U.S. set a goal for the Phoenix program to "neutralize" 20,000 NLF agents during the year, and at the end of the year GVN authorities reported 19,534 agents "neutralized." The figure was unsettling in that there had been no corresponding decline in Ameican estimates of NLF agents at large. Who, then, were the 19,534 people . . . ?
> . . . A large percentage of the "neutralized agents" were simply people whom the Phoenix herded in and out of the police stations in order to fill their quotas. . . . A conscientious village chief discovered the local Phoenix agent was extorting gold and jewelry from the people. . . .
> —*Frances Fitzgerald,* Fire in the Lake

Eva said that she was driven by "a sense of outrage against injustice."

She was very passionate on this issue. She made that clear: "As far as I can remember the existence of injustice has hurt my soul as if nails were being driven into it. From every period of my life I retain the memory of some injustice tormenting me and tearing me apart."

When she lived they called her a whore, a fascist, and a saint. When she died they drained her blood and filled her with chemicals and varnished her with a clear, plasticlike material. She was going to be the nation's mummy. But plans changed, new rulers decided the nation did not need a mummy, and she was secretly buried in Italy under the name of an Italian woman and everyone pretty much forgot about her. She was thirty-three years old, just like Christ. She claimed to be thirty-one.

I remember drinking on the avenidas, the beautiful green trees arcing over my head and the promenade of men and women and boys and girls flowing by my evening table, and asking myself, "Who now passing was involved in the *guerra sucia?*"

All I hear is silence. All I truly smell is the musk of sexual desire floating like a sweet ribbon through the throng.

They have all been raised on the doctrine of a saint named Eva. No one can get rid of her memory. Second grade textbooks taught the prayer: "Our little mother, who is in heaven . . . Good Fairy who laughs amongst the angels. . . . Evita, I promise you that I will be good."

Goodness, simple goodness. A general explained. Once woman in a wheelchair disappeared. How could such a creature be a menace? "One becomes a terrorist," he answered patiently, "not only by killing with a weapon or setting a bomb but also by encouraging others through ideas that go against our Western and Christian civilization."

You try to regulate your breathing, to pace and calm yourself but it is no good. You feel them probing you. They have been trained very well, trained in a base in Panama by the giant sister republic of the North. And they have improvised, gone beyond even this fine training. You are tied to a cold metal bed frame. You are blind. And you feel something metallic entering your vagina.

The wind blows cold across the desert ground at twelve thousand feet. The land is the color of earth—brown, tan, rust, red, gray—and the plants are low, clinging, and few.

The light burns white on the stone where time and rock have almost fashioned a tiled floor. I see small streams gathering into rivers as the sun licks the snows above and water oozes and then crashes toward the deserts below. My head is woozy from the altitude and I feel at home. Deserts are my language.

I spin around, a young guanaco scampers. The animal is said to be the relative of a camel, isolated here long ago when the tectonic plates lost their love for each other and drifted apart and we all became separated on our rafts of stone and soil. Until recently there have been few bridges—that span in the Bering Sea, the caravels, aircraft, now missiles waiting to pierce our hearts like Cupid. The animal lopes, its head small, the coat light tan. I am transfixed. I have no thoughts. It simply is and this seduces me.

Below, where the water runs off the range, a green tongue forms of moss and grasses. I look hard and can see herds of guanacos there, ten, twenty, thirty, forty . . . and then I stop counting.

When I look down at my feet I see the tire tracks of motorcycles everywhere incising the soft, sandy soil. Sometimes I will follow the tire tracks across a tundralike plain. Where the treads ate into the soil, the plants now seem to flourish more than in the ground that remained undisturbed. The garden seems to like the machine.

I have wandered for days and not seen a single tree or encountered a plant that rises higher than my ankle. At night the stars are very near, the air scented with smoke from the fire. No one lives here. I am in an enormous emptiness above the clouds, which I watch each day boiling below me in a futile effort to create rain.

* * *

I nuzzle her stiff blond hair. Her smile is a joy, even with the blue teeth. Her breasts bother her, too large, she repeats, too fat. But overall she handles life well. She has a son, she tells me, who is four years old. The father has left her. And then with a little flutter of her delicate hand, she indicates that this desertion is of no importance. A calm settles over me and she is inducing this calm. But not with her requests that we go off together for a while. The other people in this cave are not calming. The men sit stiffly, never smiling, their faces masks. The women all smile.

They are normal. Everyone I see and speak with and listen to is normal. The nation is a giant mirror and everywhere I look I see myself. I do not ask the woman about the dirty war. She is not a woman interested in affairs.

It is a spoon, a metal spoon, gliding up your vagina. At first the spoon does not seem to stop its exploration. And then it pauses. It has probed up and up and now rests against the fetus harbored in your swollen belly.

The captain in the course of many conversations mentions two things that stick in my mind as I drink vino tinto in the thin air. He says, "What no one ever admits is that it was a real war." And he says, "In the mountains you don't know when." I swallow the red wine and think the number is at least thirty thousand. The government admits nine thousand but in these matters, the authorities have a tendency to undercount.

They later explained that they were civilized men and women. They would inject them with sedatives and then load them in large transport aircraft. Out over the ocean, they would open the door and pitch them out into the soft night sky above the green waters. Once they took four nuns on this trip. After that the sisters were referred to as the flying nuns.

The captain is a very nice man with a wonderful smile. He loves to listen to Bob Dylan—back at the base I could hear his stereo roaring for hours with a voice explaining that the answer is blowing in the wind. Five years ago, the captain's wife died of cancer. He is now engaged and will marry in four months. But what I notice is his age: he is old enough to have been there when the war was fought with black cars arriving in the night hours.

There is very little difference between the captain and me. Except of course for this matter of rank. I do not have the makings of an officer.

There was a couple that lived in a small house, and out of one room the man ran a facility that put bubbles in beverages. One night they came for them and they disappeared. No one has seen them since then. They were both blind.

> The program to neutralize the Vietcong infrastructure . . . is called Phoenix. . . . Phoenix is the offspring of the CIA. . . . Phoenix does involve killing. . . . The central government . . . assigns quotas to the provinces. . . .
> —*Robert G. Kaiser, Jr., dispatch from Saigon,*
> Washington Post, *February 17, 1970*

The captain is not happy. The men and I have been drinking since perhaps noon, drinking flagons of red wine. Our hut at thirteen or fourteen thousand feet leans against the black rock of the volcano, and in midsummer snow still covers its slopes. At night it freezes, during the day the light is brilliant, the sky blue, and you can fish for trout in the nearby laguna. The other country is but a few miles away. Sometimes their guards come over with jugs of wine, and the guards I drink with feed them beef. There is little to do up here in the mountains, there is no danger from men, just weather. The men play cards and cook and joke. I give them a magazine full of photographs of naked women. They are astounded at the pubic hair—blond! blond!—and the willingly revealed vaginas. Then the captain seizes the copy—something about morale, he tells me—and clutching it disappears to his bunk.

By nightfall, I am drunk and so are my companions. I have sampled the wine of several nations and declared that of my hosts the best. I have had history explained to me—the Liberator, it seems, was simply a mercenary who wanted to be the king of England. We have become quite friendly. I do not ask them about the dirty war, about the disappeared. I know they will tell me it was necessary, that it was a real war, that subversion threatened the nation. I have no desire to argue. We have been together for days. They are like me and I know it. No special selection was necessary to find them. For the rest of my life, I will meet them everywhere, every day.

Around midnight, I seem to lose my normally sweet temper. I tell the captain his nation will never amount to anything until it is a democracy and it will never be a democracy until the rich and the armed and the privileged share power with the population. I am pounding my fist on the long table, spilling my wine as I gesture. Freedom, power, equality, an armed citizenry, forty acres and a mule, honest elections, freedom of speech, the right to bad talk. It all pours out of me. One of the key Liberators

hated freedom except for himself. He wrote against pop-
ular elections, he described a free politics as "criminal
clemency." He set in motion a war to the death—bring in
twenty heads and you can be an ensign, thirty will make
you lieutenant, fifty a captain. "Democracy on my lips,"
he said, and then tapping his chest, "aristocracy here."
So, I thunder on, it began on the wrong foot. I sound like
a weird version of a Rotarian luncheon speaker. More
wine too—thank you, Señor. The men listen attentively,
the captain storms off to his bunk and my magazine.

Suddenly, a five-gallon pail of fruit mash appears—
home brew. We drink it by the mason jar for hours. Perhaps it is the altitude or the hours of drinking or both,
but I feel a great peace, a peace like that of a condor riding the high winds. I am in the garden and have in this
failed nation found a successful nation. It is the ultimate
product: the way of war as life itself, a thing so pure and
inviolate that real war itself can be dispensed with. From
time to time, Jews, union members, writers, professors, a
visiting Scandinavian girl, radicals, stray Italians, students, doctors, some French nuns, lawyers, just about
anyone, can be rounded up, questioned, tortured, murdered, and buried. Or the bodies can be burned, or
thrown into the sea. The orchids will flourish, their blossoms open and feed, the roots run at will across the face
or the back and drink deeply. *La margarita, por favor.*
The ideal economy of the garden can be pursued, endlessly. It is self-contained, it is perfect.

Around three in the morning two soldiers are still
standing. We go outside where the national flag flaps in
the wind during the day, piss in a circle, and drink some
more. We sing songs—the Beatles, "Louie, Louie," what
have you. After each big drink of wine, one soldier says

his only phrase in English: "Verrrry, gooood, verrrry gooood."

Wires are connected to the spoon, the spoon rests against the fetus, the fetus rests under your big belly. The surge is 220 volts and it comes again and again. This does not always happen. Sometimes pregnant women are segregated, and when the child is born, it is taken from the mother. There are couples in the military, in the service of the nation, who are childless. They are given these babies. Tonight, this very night, they are raising them, loving them. For others, the spoons.

> The solatium payment [compensation to Vietnamese civilians killed by military action] for those over 15 years of age that are killed is 4,000 piasters [about $7]. Those under 15 years of age is 2,000 piasters [about $3.50]. They do not keep figures on the number of payments that have been made. However, the total payments made last year amounted to 114,713,440 piasters or $972,000.
> —*Information supplied to Senate Foreign Relations Committee by John Paul Vann, chief, U.S. pacification program, February 18, 1970*

There is a small alcove just across the clutter of tiny tables in the cave where I sit and drink with the blond woman with large breasts. In this alcove is a couch. I can peer into it at this moment—a shower curtain has been pulled to one side. If you pay fifty dollars, you can go in this closetlike space with a woman in a tight sequined dress, her breasts almost spilling from her top, eyes radiant with interest and affection. Her skin will be soft and nicely scented.

A man and a woman at a nearby table stand up. They enter the alcove, the shower curtain swings across the opening. But it is a curtain not tailored to this particular doorway and rides at the bottom about a foot off the floor. I can see her ankles and stiletto heels. He is sitting on the couch, his trousers down around his shoes.

The blond woman at my side is almost purring now. Let us do that, she is saying, let me make you happy, anything, anything you want. Her tongue is in my ear.

I say no.

Her mood does not change. She continues to smile. Then she says she wants some coins, some coins from the United States. I reach in my pocket and produce a quarter, a nickel, a penny, a dime. Washington, Jefferson, Lincoln, Roosevelt. I explain the faces to her. All are presidents of my particular nation, the great republic of the North.

I ask her, why do you want these coins?

For good luck, she says softly.

We sit there sipping our drinks. She puts her head on my shoulder, and we quietly watch the two sets of ankles under the shower curtain. Her breast feels soft and loving against me, and fills me with a feeling of tenderness.

They came as a professional couple. He was a doctor. Usually, he would be asked questions first, but on this occasion the order was reversed. As La Margarita shot 220 volts through her, he heard her cries. He said, "My love, I love you. I never dreamt they would bring you into this." This last phrase was somewhat clipped as they applied an electric cattle prod to him. His questioning went on a long time as she listened through her hood. Then came a loud shriek. Then silence. She never heard his voice again. It was the twenty-eighth day of June.*

Down near the notch where subterranean rock forces skim water to drift across the sand, and the oaks hide on the slopes by the scars of old mines, the barn owl is nesting on a clutch of eggs. I stand in the tall grass and look. The round gold head pivots. Just below the house in a tall velvet ash tree, a great horned owl is doing likewise. They have been hooting for a month, fucking through the dark hours. I have been ailing, the energy not there, the fist unlimbered. *(It was then for the first time that I saw the state of my testicles. . . .)* Days slide past, I make a fire, watch the coals, turn over soil for flowers that do not yet exist. I refuse invitations, cancel talks, ignore the mail, no longer listen to the telephone. *(With them they only used the telephone. . . .)* I do not know if the owls believe in the future. I do not know what owls believe. But I can see their actions and feel the glare from their stony dark eyes as they sit on the big nests of twigs high in the trees. And they shame me. I am suspicious of messages from some place called nature—especially when they are delivered to others and then translated for my benefit. But I feel the owls. I go out on the porch and look down at the grove where they wait for their eggs to hatch. Everything here hates them. I have seen them spooked out of hiding during the day, and birds come from everywhere to mob them. They are the killers of the night when most things are blind and helpless. They persist. I once sat in on a talk by one of the world's leading ecologists. It was a kind of panel and most of the players talked of the deep mean-

Nunca Más, 172.

ings they had found in the wild. Finally, a man spoke up. He said, "The only purpose of the game is to stay in the game."

Blue teeth smiling in the dark. Ah, my breasts are fat, I know.

The spoon, gliding.

At night, they can drive me wild with their hooting. It is unseemly, it is naked and raw and I am here alone with nothing but a fistful of Beethoven and a glass of wine. Ah, I hear a throbbing, yes, there out the window over the hill where the white-tailed deer browse in the first hour of light, a helicopter hovers, seeking its prey. Forbidden people. Forbidden plants. Me. They come here often. I am only four or five miles as the owl flies from one of their borders. They are protecting me from enemies. I know this. I have spoken with them. They ask, what are you doing out there all alone. I tell them I watch birds. I do not get into any details about the owls.

There is a bit of testimony that should be entered. It was collected after everything was over. It is about a world of no exit. It comes from the report of one of those commissions that clot the flow of modern life. "As for example, on the occasion when, showing me more blood-stained rags, they said these were my daughters' knickers, and asked me whether I wanted them to be tortured with me or separately. . . . The most vivid and terrifying memory I have of all that time was of always living with death. I felt it was impossible to think. I desperately tried to summon a thought in order to convince myself I wasn't dead. . . . At the same time, I wished with all my heart that they would kill me as soon as possible."*

---

*Nunca Más, 23.

*   *   *

Yesterday, a gentle rain walked across the valley leaving soft footprints of mud, and when it briefly cleared, a double rainbow framed the earth to the west, pure bands of color beginning purple, then blue, green, yellow, and ending in an outer ring of red. Later coyotes sang at the edge of the pond. A male and female cardinal have finally showed up and come to my feeder. So have the hummingbirds. The flowers are in finally and drink the sun. Rats scurry in the gray hour before dawn and consume the seeds spilled by the profligate birds. Military jets have been cruising the valley a few hundred feet above the treetops, as have more large helicopters. Police and other agents hide in the bushes and eye me as I drive down the dirt road.

Clouds are rolling in. The land is dry and needs to drink. Out the window an immature golden eagle soars. They are very powerful and can dive at 120 to 150 miles an hour. They can live for decades, build nests that take a truck to move. They tend to dine on squirrels, small birds, and the like. But we refuse to believe this fact. We insist they devour our lambs, threaten our livestock, wage war against us, so that we can justify our war against them. We kill them often, though this is technically against our laws. But what do the laws know of our needs? We give them many common names—bird of Jupiter, calumet bird, king of birds. American war bird. War bird.

In February/March, the Task Force ... organized a "Course in Fighting Subversion" to which representatives from different ... countries were invited. The course was held in the School of Naval Warfare. ... Each country gave a lecture, which was recorded. This consisted of an introduction to the country and a review of the nature and methods of repression there. Another report covered the most effective methods of torture and its different phases, physical torture (with diagrams of the most vulnerable points), psychological torture, isolation, etc. They also prepared a dossier with photographs, description and background information on the people they were looking for. . . .*

He says, "I was born in the mountains. For example, as a child I was in the mountains. For me the mountains have secrets. When you know the secrets, they are more beautiful."

He is upset. A few days earlier, three blind Spaniards with a sighted guide had walked up a monstrous local peak. Like many who love mountains, he does not want their embrace to be purchased cheaply.

He is speaking softly in the twilight. "It is necessary to love the mountains," he advises, "to learn the secrets. When you have a storm and wind and a white-out—no book can teach you that feeling."

I ask him to explain.

He will have none of it.

"No, no, no," he snaps. "Now we talk about the mountains, but tomorrow you will feel them."

Four days later I am bending in the wind on a high knoll of desert pavement. A palisade of boulders stabs up toward that other nation a short way to the east. Suddenly, a young guanaco races into view. The beige animal moves effortlessly through the thin air, steep slopes, and

*Nunca Más, 134.

rock outcrops. A large black form floats up, a condor riding the winds of the high mountains looking for the moments of death.

The republic is fashioning a new hymn and I hear the tentative bars of this music being hummed everywhere on the avenues. War is no longer something we prepare for, nor is peace something we seek. Nor is the military some group separate from us. We are all committed to campaign whether we wear uniforms or not. We believe peace can kill us. So we live in a permanent state of war. We no longer can contrive a way to run an economy without war. But we almost never use that blunt word; it is too crude for our tastes. We now have actions, operations, sorties, feints, and so forth. Just as we do not live in a police state but rather a drug-free nation, a place of soon-to-be-registered guns, a place of identification numbers and cards, and the constant testing to ensure the purity of our cells from the Satanic forces that surround us. Should we falter, the authorities are listening, riding their Clipper Chips through the Sargasso Seas of our lives. We must be free of certain plant products, of certain images of fornication, of inappropriate song lyrics, of gender preferences, of sexually based words. We must not buy war toys. And we must be absolutely one hundred percent free of violence. The state will not share a single second of this emotion.

We are on the threshold of our Golden Age. We have fought world wars, we have fought cold wars. Now we are entering an age that promises never to end. History, we are advised, will end, but not this new age of wonders. Come, it beckons, the time of the eco-wars where we go tooth and fang against everyone to protect our

access to materials—fuels, fibers, minerals, nutrients. Forget the old and humdrum standards of gold, gems,
buxom women, opium, slaves, booty. Now we live in an
elevated state beyond such tawdry and vulgar goals.
Given our planet's human numbers there is no likely way
for us to be cheated of endless adventures in this war.
And after our depressing but hopefully brief season of
stagnation, this green war may prove to be the finest
ground of all for the blood orchids.

For a century we have proven that, almost without
exception, there were too many members of other species
and so we have lowered their numbers, or retired them
entirely. We have taken no guff from the bison and spotted owls of this world. And now this game is almost over
and we have tasted the joy of close to total victory. Our
ark is spacious and has many empty rooms with more
chambers opening up daily. The next Noah will work a
short shift.

Soon our generals will march under banners of breach-
ing blue whales or of ivory-billed woodpeckers. Our
cause will be sacred, we will tread the bloody ground
reluctantly, and we will grieve over our killing and we
will murder solely because of our concern for the rights
of others, the little living things that need a space to
thrive. The blood will flow for the good of the creatures
of the planet. We will seek not booty but ecological management, resource management, human management. We
will, of course, slaughter, we will sweep islands, plains,
mountains, deserts, jungles, seas, and nations.

Our old nightmares will prove false. We have fooled
ourselves with imaginary horrors: the yellow peril, the
niggers, the Third World, the illegal immigrants we do
not pity, the Jews, the shanty Irish, the dagos, the

bohunks, the beer-swilling, blockheaded krauts, the spics, the sand niggers, queers, dykes, and all the other motherfuckers. It turns out they are not worthy adversaries coming dangerously near our precious throats. They are moths flying to our flame. They think that if there are more of them, we will be outnumbered. They do not realize they are a commodity, and a bumper crop is wonderful for our prospects. They still believe in progress, development, bootstraps, open discussion, process, probate, civility, and all the malarkey we have force-fed them. We know what it is really about. Taking. And no one on God's good earth has ever been our equal. In a better world, they would retire our jersey and number, play the national anthem, and then we would take a bow and officially quit the game. But they do not ask us to retire. Because they do not understand the game and we do.

Ah, you ask, who is this we? And that is the point. To be a player in this game you never have to admit what you are really doing. Not once. You merely have to play along. And we have.

We are coming for you. We look like doctors or we look like scholars or we look like ecologists or we look like gardeners or we look like nurses or we look like you or we all look alike. We always look like professionals and we have our papers in perfect order. We sweep down the lanes, the streets, the boulevards, the avenues, the tollways, the freeways, the hideaways. We will put out your cigarettes, pour your liquor down the drain, grab that syringe from your trembling fingers, deny you fatty foods, chase the demons from your mind, or remove your mind from your body. We will recommend fiber. We will take you for a run. We will lock you up. We will offer universal care, we will clean your air, purify your water, guarantee your food, clarify your speech, remove the bullets from your gun and the gun from your hand. We will destroy the high heels, we will rule your womb, we will count the trees, take the ax from your hand. We will listen to your conversations, read what you write, check your accounts, monitor your files. But do not worry, you can trust us. And you can trust no one else. We ride huge steeds, steam roars from their nostrils, their black bodies tremble with excitement, they whinny in delight, but you do not hear us. You hear almost nothing. You are in your room, the set is on, you notice very little, and when it is necessary for you to be informed, we flash the message before the your eyes on that flickering screen. We will supervise your children. We will let you fuck and, from time to time, we will insist you bear children. We will teach you safe sex and promise the vaccine is on the way. At other moments, the light will go red, and we will tally the offspring and tell you that is enough.

We will kill your sense of smell, deaden your wet tongue, make numb the tips of your fingers, end that quiver and hardness in your nipples, still your loins. And should you resent this—which will never happen—we will serve up cyberspace and virtual reality.

We will let you have anything you desire, except power. And we know you will not complain because we will be very good to you. We love you, we pray for you. We watch you with ever vigilant eyes. We know the answers, we have been to the schools, we have sat in on policy discussions. We are the future, and you will not change the channel because we are too compelling. And if you do, we are everywhere. We are your dish.

(A vermilion flycatcher comes to the catclaw tree. The

bird is brilliant red and black and worries its way down from limb to limb. Now it sits poised and then dives into the water, lifts up like an osprey with a kill, and alights on another limb. This is how a vermilion flycatcher gets clean. I watch it sit, dive, rise up, and ruffle its feathers again and again for maybe twenty minutes in the early morning light. Getting clean is no simple task.)

I can feel the roots moving across the land, gouging new channels through our eager flesh, seeking blood. The flower will bloom, the fragrance will remind us of good times. We will go willingly with a smile on our lips and love in our hearts. We will go because we do not want to learn another way to live. We would rather die.

Or, perhaps, a voice will come down from the mountain, a bush will burn, new tablets of stone will heave into view like spacecraft. We could turn it all around and kill the garden. We could share food with the hungry, shelter with the people freezing in the storm. Love with the people who are crying in the rain. Take power. The answers are as simple as the questions. Kill the commissions, strangle the study groups with their own entrails, send the therapists to the showers, tell the president he can drop his pants again—it's okay, Bill, we don't need you anymore. We are an exceptional model of the human race. We no longer know how to produce food. We no longer can heal ourselves. We no longer really raise our young. We have forgotten the names of the stars, fail to notice the phases of the moon. We do not know the plants and they no longer protect us. We tell ourselves we are the most powerful specimens of our kind who have ever lived. But when the lights are off we are helpless. We cannot move without traffic signals. We must attend classes in order to learn by rote numbered steps toward love or how to breast-feed our baby. We justify anything, anything at all, by the need to maintain our way of life. And then we go to the doctor and tell the professionals we have no life. We have a simple test for making decisions: our way of life, which we cleverly call our standard of living, must not change except to grow yet more grand. We have a simple reality we live with each and every day: our way of life is killing us. Call the doctor, honey, Code Blue is blooming in the garden.

Still we could be free. We could walk out the door. We still can walk a little or least crawl.

We can, actually, do anything. Anything at all.

Except, as we constantly tell ourselves, we know better. We tell ourselves that we live in a global village. But then why do we have no neighbors?

> Agents fingered villages and villagers for extinction, the former by B-52 strikes and artillery fire, the latter by death, often after torture. A major at the Central Intelligence Agency operation headquarters in Da Nang . . . was the coordinator for the Phoenix program. . . . According to Ambassador William J. Colby, until recently in charge of the parent program, the Civil Operations and Rural Development and Support, run jointly by the U.S. and South Vietnam, the purpose of the exercise is "to provide permanent protection" for the villagers.
>
> —*Mary McGrory, Washington* Evening Star,
> *August 3, 1971*

At first, people asked me what it was like. And I told them it was just like here, only more expensive. I always mentioned that a cup of coffee at the airport ran $4.20. They would express surprise, then nod knowingly.

Or they would ask, what were these people like who laid out pregnant women on metal bed frames and gave them electric shocks? And I would say, well, they're just like you and me. And without exception the person questioning me would snap, "No, they're not." And I would look into their eyes and know. Yes, yes, yes.

Now no one asks, and I do not have to tell them anything at all.

When people ask what I am doing, I tell them I am studying orchids. A silence follows and then they usually smile as if they were on to my strange, small joke.

Mademoiselle, I am not so mysterious as many believe. On the contrary, I'm a very open man. I hide nothing. . . .

But the Americans do not persist. They kill for five minutes; then they give four minutes breathing space; then they kill again. They are Vietnamese like me. Deep in my heart, I don't like it. But I also know that to stop the war we have to bomb them. . . .

Mademoiselle, *j'aime la vie.* I love life. . . . I said my prayer to the Holy Virgin. . . . Every Sunday morning I attend Holy Mass in my chapel and every day I pray. I pray for my troops. . . . I went to the church of Saint Mary for the Advent. . . . I'm a real Catholic. . . . Mademoiselle, I like to do well whatever I do, whether being converted, playing tennis, riding a horse, waterskiing, staying in office as president. I like to assume my responsibilities, and this why I don't share the power and I'm the chief. *Oui, je suis le chef. Mademoiselle, demandez moi: qui est le chef ici? Moi! C'est moi! C'est moi le chef.* I am the chief.

C'est tout? Is that all? I hope you are satisfied, Mademoiselle. I hope you are because I did not hide anything from you. . . . I'm made like that. Would you have ever expected to find a guy like that? . . . Sometimes I feel like there isn't anything else to do, anymore, but pray to God.

> —*President Nguyen Van Thieu,*
> *interview with Oriana Fallaci,*
> *Saigon, December 30, 1972*

The end came unexpectedly. For the first time in over a century, the military attacked something besides its own people. It was over a matter of some barren islands where a few shepherds lived. The war lasted seventy-three days and when it was over the military was defeated and disgraced. The junta fell from power and the civilians reclaimed the government for a spell.

The Commission was created to investigate the disappeared ones. Its work was difficult. All the files had been destroyed. Few of the graves could be found. Many of the torture centers had been erased from the earth. A handful of officers faced a limited trial. No one was really punished. The military demanded amnesty. The thing was too dangerous to pursue. And so the entire matter drifted away and went to the place where memories are buried.

But the Commission did issue a report and hundreds of thousands of copies were snapped up by the people. A curious fact emerged in the report. When the Commission would take a handful of people who had survived to the places it suspected they had been tortured, the survivors would look around and yet could not identify anything. And then when they were blindfolded, they could find the rooms where the electricity was applied, find the cells where they sat for months and years with hoods on their heads, knew exactly how many paces this way and that way everything was. Once they were blind again and could see, they acted as if they owned the place.

In June of 1978, the admiral explained, "Let no one think of the country as fragmented into private feudal manors, let no one put the interests of individual groups before that of the community. This is a statement about responsibility and therefore it is a moral statement.

"There are judicial norms and standards which do not apply in this instance: the right of habeas corpus, for example," the general of the nation explained in 1980. "In this type of struggle, the secrecy with which our special operations must be conducted means that we cannot divulge whom we have captured and whom we want to capture: everything has to be enveloped in a cloud of secrecy."*

What's a nice girl like you doing in a place like this?
Choppers, bodies black, blades whomping the air, we are swinging in low, the grass bends and whirls below us like green hair in a spring breeze. We open fire without warning, the tail gunner hesitates at first, he sights on a man racing toward the shelter of the trees, he can see the man's face, he can see right into his eyes, so he chokes with his finger on the trigger, the endless belt of cartridges ready to reel through his weapon. They always do the first time or two. The gunner looks deep into the soul of the man below—we cannot cure them of this hocus-pocus thinking, but then his finger moves and he stitches the son-of-a-bitch, flowers of red spring from the soil of the man's back, and he goes down and he will stay down and

Nunca Más, pp. 273, 397.

we will go on. We are saving the lungs of the earth, we are saving biodiversity, we are saving the great river, the endangered species, the vast ecosystem that belches and farts day and night and gives us the good gases that keep the sun from killing us all. We are green, the dead man's back is now red. It is a necessary thing.

The doctor will see you now.

We are in the basement but they do not know this fact. We never let them see, we never reveal the face surrounding our voice, we never surrender the slightest clue as to our location, or what day it is, or whether the sun has risen or the sun has set. We deny them the phases of the moon. We have signed an oath never to say or write on a piece of paper what our work is. We do not tell our wives, we give the most general kind of answer to our children. The neighbors simply think we work for the government, analysts of some kind. We prefer the women, especially when they first arrive. They crack almost as soon as we strip their clothes off, the way they stand there blindfolded with their delicate hands covering their breasts and vaginas. It is almost touching. Then we make them suck us off. None refuses. We can tell they think this will buy them something. Then, the enlisted men serially fuck them on the floor. They usually go limp and the troops say it is like fucking a corpse. We throw them in a room with water on the floor, they lie there wet and cold, we can hear a soft weeping. Then we kick them, break some ribs, crush the nipples. One guy always takes them in the ass, every time. Then they are ready for the wire. We have questions, they give answers. They never get the answers right. It is impossible. We know that. This is not a test. It is a necessary message. Eventually, we let them die. The bodies are the only problem. Oddly enough, the women last longer than the men as a rule. They are simply tougher. The children we destroy in the first hour.

I'll never lie to you.

We fly in tight formations, the targets are easy, not really targets but zones that must be constantly cleansed with napalm, bombs, cannon fire, rockets. We have no schedule, but still the work is constant. Of course, the new pilots have to educated. We still are born deficient in this matter of mission. The border with Mexico is difficult because the fires never end there; the raids are so numerous, there is always a curtain of black smoke rising up from this border. The same is true of the zone between China and Siberia, constant fires, they just never go out. Latin America has been left to its own time-tested devices, so for the most part satellite monitoring is sufficient. Most of the Middle East is calm since we leveled the cities. Africa is not an issue—simply enough low-level strikes to remind them but really famine and disease do the basic maintenance. India is where we train, endless targets for practice. First-time pilots always remark on the throngs of cattle that wander the ruins of the cities. They just can't get over these starving herds. At night in the mess halls, there is talk of ranching possibilities once more open space has been created. There is so much work to do but it is successful and satisfying work. We can see that off the wing. The forests are growing, the grasslands returning. The air is sweeter and even the smoke from the burning is minor compared to gases that the cities used to release. It is the only solution and we know that.

All I can tell you is that the people there seem perfectly normal. They treat their children kindly, the dogs look fed, the parks are very pretty. There is a great deal of laughter and they make excellent coffee. Hire them as babysitters any day. A lot like you or me. Of course, she says her breasts are fat, *gorditas*. And her hair is very parched from all that bleach as it trails down like straw to her insistent ass. I am sure if I had been more willing she would have told me of the bad men she had known, of the one great love of her life, of her dream as a child, of the color television she wishes to own. Of the places she would like to visit—shake hands with that smiling mouse and ride those rides. And the men, I loved their laughter and they make damn fine wine. I can see that they are excellent with orchids. In my native land I have been around experts at their cultivation.

> I was asked to bring in a body count, not to bring in prisoners. I did what I felt my superior officers wanted me to do.
> —an American first lieutenant court-martialed
> for allegedly killing civilians

They have kept the faith. True, they wonder where their daughter and her husband are. They go to the church and they ask and "Father . . . sent us to Monsignor . . . who told us that the young people were in a rehabilitation program in houses that had been set up for that purpose and where they were being well treated. . . .

"He told us that [the general] was the charitable soul who thought up this plan to avoid the loss of intelligent people. . . . He said that the work was carried out with psychologists and sociologists, that there were medical teams to deal with their health, and that for those who could not be recuperated, it was possible that 'some pious

soul' might give them an injection to make them sleep forever."*

Spooning.
Spoons.
Ah, daisies.
Lucky coins.
Blue teeth glowing in the dark.

---

*_Nunca Más_, pp. 250–51.

We are in Australia, the wasps are mating just below and orchids, particularly hammer orchids (Drakaea) and elbow orchids (Spiculaea), seem to notice. The hammer orchids, for example, have a strange labellum—that tonguelike projection in the middle of the flower. It looks ... just like a small, fat, wingless female version of the Thynnid wasp. The imitation is damn near perfect—shiny head, round, faintly hairy body, ass tilted up a bit into the air. The scent also—that delicious pheromone the female releases—is copied and wafts off into the air from the hammer orchid. It is floating across the forest, it is sexually inviting, perhaps maddening, and the orchid, which cannot possibly know, now it hears the rush of wings approaching it, though of course it cannot possibly hear either.

The fake female wasp rides on the end of

a little hinged arm that sticks up from the flower of the hammer orchid. She bobs up and down in the wind, she looks so alive and of course, there is that scent. The male descends—ah, the moment is at hand that evolution has been waiting for, the moment that so stimulated that crabby old churchman Charlie Darwin as he battled his illnesses and fears in his dark English study—grabs the female impersonator, wrenches to take off into his mating flight. And then the hammer comes down, a thing delicately called the column, and on its end are stigma and pollinia. The male wasp is already trying to probe that uplifted ass with his genitals when—wham! the hammer hits, and suddenly the male senses this is not a real female and he departs. It has taken less than a second. And glued to his back are the reproductive cells of the orchid. There are four species of hammer orchids. Each attracts a specific species of Thynnid wasp. And they do this by mimicking a female that spends all of her life tunneling in the forest floor far below. Except, of course, for her few hours of flying, fucking, nectar slurping, and fun.

No one sees it coming. The war has blinded so many of us.

We move without plan up the long steps—I assume there are long steps, such temples always seem to have these grand approaches in order to diminish us.

We speak softly to each other, we can not quite believe what is happening or what we are doing.

At first we had gathered around a huge statue. Does this statue exist? What or who is the statue of? I do not know. These places always seem to have monstrous statues made of cold stone or cold metal. I notice that the lips on the women are thin flat lines across their faces. The necks of the men grow red with anticipation.

We pulled this statue down by tugging at mighty ropes. The fragments now lie dead on the pavement.

That was before we raced up those endless steps.

At the door the guard looks surprised.

We kill him instantly.

And sweep on, like a straw broom, into the Pentagon.

There was a time I dreamed of killing deer. I would lie in my bed as endless panels of ballistics charts streaked past my eyes, wonderful arcs of statistical power inscribing the bullets flung by .264s or .270s or 30/06s. I was in love with guns then and I admired their power and their functional design and the fact that their work could be converted to numbers—to feet per second, foot-pounds of energy, and the like. Bullets also fascinated me, full jacketed, soft, hollow pointed, banana peel, such variety of metal forms to gouge corridors through targets. And, of course, the smell of powder pleased my nostrils.

In my dream, the deer was always a large buck emerging from a mesquite bosque at dawn. First would come a tentative doe, then another and another and another, and finally, in the gray light strode the buck. He had been careful, he had been cunning, and his antlers were very large and fearsome. The animal dropped like a stone from my fine shooting and when I gutted the deer the intestines were warm and sticky against my fingers. I was twelve years old and I had my dreams.

The B-52s and B-47s roared overhead all the time then and they made the desert cower. They drowned out the rattling sound of the cooler motor on the roof. The pilots said they were targeted for China but no one really knew if this fact was true. We did not expect to be told the truth then. We believed in our national security. I can remember very little questioning of these matters. The teacher in my school built a bomb shelter in her backyard. She was a spinster, overweight, and fond of Shakespeare. The planes would just go over some nights hour after hour and I would know a red alert had been called, that somewhere back along the Potomac, or in that mysterious mountain in Colorado with its underground headquarters, wiser heads had caught the whiff of danger over the horizon and sent their angry birds out on station. Of course, the planes carried nuclear bombs, but who would have it any other way? It was the late fifties and the Reds had to be watched and if the opportunity occurred, cold-cocked. I remember the scent of the citrus blossoms pouring through the room, the roar of the bombers, and the deer in my dream falling dead at the command of my trigger finger. I never for a moment worried about nuclear war and the instant death of everyone. Never for a single instant. Hell, I'd knelt by my school desk during bombing drills when I was seven or eight years old. Besides, atomic war was so easy and clean and quick. Everything ended in a flash of fire and no one had to ever deal with anything again. It did not sound that bad to me, a lot better than facing the ugly world that increasingly was hurtling down the pike at my life.

I also thought of breasts and lips and hips and parts of girls I did not really know as I lay there a twelve-year-old boy dreaming of imaginary firepower as real firepower streamed across the roof of my bungalow home. My mother had already found a copy of *Playboy* hidden in my bookcase and asked me about it. I had smiled dumbly, as was the custom.

There was a Cold War on and our side had to win it or the world would end. It would be years before I caught a glimmer of the truth and when I did no one would listen to me.

We were losing the Cold War. Just losing it more slowly than the other side. Ah, this is the place, I suspect, for that universal opiate, the thesis statement: We have been at war for over a century now and it has bankrupted our treasury, destroyed our land, corrupted our people, and fouled our bed. We are creatures of fear, suppliants, and we expect to be taken care of by something and we do not expect to be loved or give love. For me, at least, the last item is the most telling. We now have sex but have lost our sexuality.

No one ever dropped the big one on Moscow as it turned out. But they nuked New Mexico. And Nevada. And everywhere else where I go to seek love in all the dry places. I think of this now that I've finally gotten older and gotten my hands on the girls and they've gotten their hands on me.

The corridors are very clean and smell of powders and soaps. The linoleum feels like the skin of a corpse, the dull lights on the ceilings echo the blank eyes in a lifeless face. Water fountains are carefully spaced everywhere. It has all been planned, that is certain.

We break into groups:

Farmers from around Hanford, Washington, all marked with curious stigmata from their original and fascinating cancers.

Downwind people from Utah, the women striking though off-balanced, what with their single breasts.

Navajo uranium miners walking slowly but deliberately with their wheezing lungs.

I must not forget the beasts—squads of wolves, grizzlies, and lions, storming off to discover just why they were displaced, why those National Forests were cut flat.

Old ranchers with Winchester .94s, the rifles cocked, crazed to find the map rooms where their ground was marked off forever and buried by a grease pen with the words gunnery range *or* bombing range.

Mothers from Oregon with bizarre-looking children, the entire group wearing orange clothing like a uniform.

Bands of buffalo, those curved horns so black and beautiful, hooves clattering across the polished floors, steam pouring from their flared nostrils, old bulls in the lead—as they pass I see the flattened form of a general on the floor, the face mashed, could be any man's.

Strange glowing rodents, tortoises, and birds from the sacred ground called Trinity in New Mexico.

Sioux, bands of surly-looking Lakotas. Some from Wounded Knee, they're easy to spot, the men carrying their sliced-off genitals in their hands, the children with crushed heads, the women with breasts removed by bayonet, the pregnant ones neatly eviscerated. And my God, here comes Sundance leading a war party of drunks, their hands clutching broken bottles. Their skin glows from those lovely pink clouds.

Mobs of shoeless Mexicans with machetes and Uzis storm through also—they want special files on some backwater war on drugs.

The dolphins and orcas are here also—scarred of course by their radio-embedded training collars. Horrible to see their teeth flash and grind as they awkwardly thrash down the halls. My God, the marks they leave on the bodies.

I cannot tally the groups, there are too many.

All going different directions as they lunge toward long-dreamed-of files where their lives were buried alive. .

The sound is very unpleasant, endless echoes off the cold walls as people career around corners, the shuffling of their feet, the click of their heels, the strange cries and yells. This sound is not warm, not warm at all. And everywhere on the walls are clocks, the large dials keeping track of something that has ceased to matter.

The random killings cannot be helped.

The coffee always seems bitter in my mouth when I camp out and the metal cup is a monster burning my lips. I have had the same cup now for twenty years, a flat

Sierra-style vessel, and it is caked with the grime of a few million hits of caffeine and it is awkward to hold and use. I cling to it, a dinosaur from my most remote past, from my early days of walking. I've lived in Tucson, Arizona, since a few days after my twelfth birthday and I have stayed in the same neighborhood. All my life, military planes have been flying right over my head—literally, since I live on the flight path. A few years ago, one crashed a couple of blocks away and missed a junior high (my alma mater) by a hair, smashed into a VW bug, and fried two coeds from the nearby university. I stood watching as the black plume of smoke rose into the blue sky.

My city is very ugly and spreads out without a thought in a very beautiful place called the Sonoran desert. I remember first seeing this desert in April 1957 and I have been in love with it ever since. The air is dry, the sun constant, and the cacti get big and arrogant. I want to tell you about the cacti. When I was fourteen, I worked the night shift as a dishwasher at a local hash house (I was a big kid and lied about my age and many other things). We would get off work at two A.M., the cooks and some waitresses would buy some beer and we would go to the park or someone's apartment and drink. One night a cook got mad and beat the busboy unconscious. I still remember the busboy's smug head as the wiry cook slammed it again and again against the linoleum floor in the brightly lit kitchen. The busboy's avocation was working for the local Search and Rescue unit but on this particular night, they did not show up with ropes, stretchers, paramedics, and pitons. Another time, my colleague in the dishroom, a Chicano on parole from prison and his East L.A. gang, stuck a large knife in my gut when he found one of my comments discourteous.

Another night, a cook and a waitress fucked in the fork of a tree in the park while we all sat on the grass and drank cans of beer. It was at this exact moment in my life that I read Thomas De Quincey's *Confessions of an English Opium-Eater.* I can clearly remember the store where I bought it and the shelf on which it stood. The cover was a pale blue.

We were having a party one Friday, it was very late, maybe three or four in the morning, when the cops came banging on the door because a neighbor had complained about our high spirits. I fled out the kitchen door with the Chicano because I was underage and because he could go back to the joint for a single violation. We hid behind some parked cars and when the cops stormed out the back door with flashlights and guns drawn, I took off. I can still hear the click as the cop cocked the hammer on his revolver. I slowly regained consciousness on the ground and felt very strange. I looked up into the cop's face and he didn't seem too happy either. I had collided at full speed with a saguaro and half my body was a pincushion with hundreds of thorns driven deep into the flesh. From the faint tracery of blood weeping down my face, I had just missed impaling one eye. The cop drove me home, and dumped me on my doorstep, mumbling nothing much to my father as he fled back into the night and the safety of straight police work.

I remember my father sitting me at the kitchen table and saying slowly and in a calm voice, "I just want you to remember one thing: I will never pay your bail. If you want to be a man, fine. But don't ever call me."

My mother fussed in the corner near her fine wooden butcher block and said, "Jude, don't you think we'd better take a look at his, his wounds?"

He scowled and said, "No."

I had a long night but at least, thanks to being a human pincushion, I never tossed and turned. The surgeon the next day carved some of the spines out with a scalpel and no anesthesia—I think the old man must have called him before I got there. I worked without a shoe on my swollen foot for a month, the steaming dishwater cascading over it. For six months, thorns would pop out at random moments riding on a surge of pus.

As I said, the cactus are arrogant. But with time I have grown to love them.

I step over a body—the throat has been slashed by either a knife or perhaps a claw. The building seems to reverberate with screams, yells, roars, growls, and howls. This fact does not disturb me. I was born on July 20th, 1945, and every day of my life this pentagon of concrete has run my world and denied that it ran my world.

("If science produces no better fruits than tyranny . . . ," Thomas Jefferson decided in 1812, "I would rather wish our country to be ignorant, honest, and estimable as our neighboring savages are.")

All my natural days, I have choked on this word defense.

I think they used the word to fool us.

I know I prefer to play offense.

I find the file case and open the forbidden drawer.

Ah, the folders for the Cabeza Prieta National Wildlife Refuge, for the gunnery ranges, the bombing ranges, the targets. Reports on the killings of pilots, animals, folks caught on the ground. A slim chapter on the MX test site. So many files.

All in a box labeled WASTE LAND.

I find a special memo for that time in August when I was there illegally. There are cold days when no firing should occur and when visitors are permitted. And then there are hot days when no witnesses are allowed. There it is—the record of the choppers sweeping the desert floor looking for me.

I like it hot.

Even their failure to find and capture me is not enough to heal me.

I step over a dead secretary—her head apparently severed by a now serene one-breasted woman who is resting in an ergonomically designed chair—and walk down the corridor with the file.

I stand in the last steamboat on the Colorado River, one named *Belle*. This boat is on land, hosts a casino, and functions as a hotel. The river is dead, the water rippling past the saloon window an illusion. More human beings have claims on its flow than its flow can ever satisfy. There are tables on these matters—on river flows, on forest production, on soil depletion, on overharvesting of fisheries, on whatever-you-wish-to-examine. We like to deaden ourselves with these tables, forecasts, and studies in two basic ways. One, by constructing scenarios of doom. The other, by denying them and saying something will turn up. Neither response produces any useful ideas or actions, not one concrete thing. I know this to be true because I have pursued both responses.

The only sane response is to say: It is over and now the future must begin, with or without us.

The national debt is huge, the Mississippi never stops rolling. Auto workers leave the plant with dead faces, the mountains brush the clouds. A killing screams in the night, the plains never seem to end. I love the fall because I believe in the spring. We are the richest nation in the world—do not listen to the bankers, they know nothing, absolutely nothing—because we live on the best piece of ground. Then, now, and tomorrow.

We also have the best blood, I suspect, because after the centuries of movement, rape, back-alley loves, and new genetic fusions, we are all the bloods. We can hardly recognize our own faces, they seem so changed by the new noses, the variations in hair, the rich scale of the hues in a half billion eyes, the many colors of our skins. We have all we need—except, ah except, we have no beliefs. Instead we favor one sensation—this fear that eats at us and guides our hand down so many crabbed and narrow lanes. And what we fear is failure and what we fear of failure is that we will have no one to blame but ourselves.

I float across the casino, and scan the rows of machines where people play video poker or the slots. An old woman with black hair, silver earrings, and a rich brown Mediterranean face stares down a machine.

Her husband says, "You've been at that slot machine for four hours."

She says one word: "Longer."

Most of the customers are old women. They sit at the slot machines and the poker machines, cigarettes in their hands, fingers with many rings, silver and gold earrings glowing against their tired skin. Their hair is cropped short and often curled. There is always a drink by their sides—often white wine—and they drop quarters into the machines and I think they are fucking all those men they refused to have in those long ago decades, fucking them at this moment one after another, relentlessly, mercilessly fucking them. These men fall by the sides of the whirling, flashing machines, and weep and moan on the floor and eventually they die there. The bodies are very small, like dolls. The women pay these deaths no mind and play on and they never admit to hearing the cries of the men, not for a single second. And they never look down on the fallen forms where spittle forms on the still lips.

I watch this for hours and it happens again and again just as I have said.

The glass breaks everywhere, smoke begins to bite the air. It cannot be helped. I would prefer a more orderly examination of the files but my colleagues lack my scholarly restraint.

The wolves and grizzlies are not the half of it.

The women, I think, are the fiercest, from Rosie the Riveter, through those Betty Crocker years of sparkling-clean sheets, and on to the women who witness the collapse of the home, the necessity of two incomes per family, the divorce courts, and all the lonely motels where we copulate and watch pornographic movies and shiver from the icy weight of solitude.

The women cannot be controlled.

I walk out into the corridor as a hit squad of one-breasted women storms past. They drop gray folders, little plans for a big world. Ah, those war plans they never revealed to us. I have read about them in articles in obscure magazines. The plans come from pilfered documents, it is said, and no one can verify whether the documents are authentic or frauds. But the odd fact is that I never doubt the documents because their core message is absolutely in agreement with the fierce drive of my country.

JIC 329/1—*Dec., 1945; 20–30 atomic bombs for 20 Soviet cities.*

PINCHER—*June, 1946; 50 big ones for 20 cities.*

BROILER—*March, 1948; 34 bombs.*

SIZZLE—*133 bombs; 20 cities.*

SAC Basic War Plan—1957; 3261 targets.
SIOP-5—1974; 25,000 targets.
SIOP-5D—1980; 40,000 targets.

Small 150-pound atomic bombs would also be back-packed according to the plans, and we would leave little more than our footprints and not even those for long.

I can feel every bone in my feet, my face is swollen and red, the fingers on my hand seem half numb, and I have carried the seventy-pound pack for a hundred miles. I sit in the saddle between the burnt hills and eye the valley. Tucson is more than a hundred miles to the east, Yuma and the Colorado River a hundred miles or more to the west. No one is here. This is the center of my world. At night I can see the glow of the lights of Phoenix in the night sky although the city is at least one hundred miles away.

I walk toward the aluminum forest. Technically, I am on a gunnery range where military aircraft practice hitting targets. Sometimes the targets are inscribed on the ground, and when I stumble across them I find various pieces of arsenal lying about the bull's-eye area. Often the targets have been drones, aluminum gliders pulled by other planes. When these drones break loose from time to time, they often impale themselves in the desert floor: the aluminum forest. For years, nature lovers have fussed and demanded that someone remove the dead drones because they ruin the view of this particular valley, which happens to be in a National Wildlife Refuge. I don't want them taken away. They are a monument to what has happened to this dry ground. Here the Cold War was fought and lost, and by God I want some kind of memorial to this defeat.

Until the Second World War, the Southwest was a failure on all the economic maps drawn up by this nation. No one could make much out of New Mexico, what with those Indians and Mexican Americans. Utah was, well, Mormon, and Nevada was too dry, too high, too cold, and too ugly for normal schemes of development. Arizona had offered promise, first as a mineral warehouse until the mines played out, then as a cattle range till overgrazing killed off all the herds in the 1890s, then as an agricultural paradise until it turned out modern irrigation cost more than it was worth. Nothing really seemed to work until war came back—the earlier booms had been based on either stealing the ground from Mexico or killing Apaches in the following mop-up operation.

My home lives on war, as does the entire American region that begins on the Great Plains when the rains fail and Eastern beliefs about a proper life wither and die. The mistake is to view this war machine as just the military bases—no, no, one must consider the nuclear facilities, the laboratories, test sites, power plants, centers for mining ore and refining ore. The mistake is to stop at the nuclear facilities—what about the poison gas centers, the aircraft factories splashed like acne along the Pacific coast, the huge dams blocking all the rivers to power these enterprises, the butchered forests weeping everywhere, the booming cities that fed off these enterprises? The mistake is to stop anywhere at all—the region is a sacrifice area, a place to bomb, shoot, poison, irradiate, bulldoze, do whatever, to feed the ballistics of projectiles aimed at Russia, at China, at God knows where. Weapons, curiously enough, are seldom used. Except here. And on the people and living things that struggle to cling to this maimed ground. The mistake is stop—do not doubt me, just visit the local campus of your university and there it is again.

The fires burned for days, dark columns of smoke roiled and spread over the capital. Lincoln's memorial grew gray and black from the soot.

The files, alas, proved rather useless.

Too many of us had been involved for any of us to be innocent or capable of claiming to be true victims.

True, many of the files were spirited away, cartons of favored selections, and from time to time they surfaced in badly printed underground publications.

After a while, little of this information was read—though some carefully marked up the maps to indicate sites of massive chemical and radiation pollution.

But even these efforts soon faltered as the maps clotted with dots and became solid masses of disturbing color.

Mainly, it was the fire that was remembered.

It burned for three years.

The trials soon sputtered and ground to a halt.

I walk thirty miles of creosote. I see broken pottery clusters along the arroyo. There are no insect sounds. I move east into the black basalt, avoiding the abandoned villages. I am not a grave robber, I lack the fine degree to disturb the dead for science. A prairie falcon slips past overhead. The aluminum forest is to my west, right where I want it.

It is time to consider the inevitable: the rupture and collapse of the last empire, us. We have been held together by fear and now the big fear has faded. There is no reason for the United States to be united—except a deep passion for suicide. We must remember Blennerhasset Island, that blob in the Ohio where Aaron Burr was accused of plotting the dismemberment of the early republic. It is time to return to Blennerhasset.

I am ready to dream again. She slips up on me without a sound. Her lips are full and brightly lipsticked. The skin smooth and well scented, the eyes very alive. She wears a black bra and black panties. Dreams have their basic needs. I slip them off as she unfastens my pants. We do not speak; perhaps it is the heat. From time to time aircraft roars overhead at anywhere from fifty to five hundred feet off the ground. I spread out my plastic sheet, an emergency blanket I thoughtfully stowed in my pack. She has brought a small dog with her. No problem, we can roast and eat it later.

I realize I am in very dangerous country now. Not the desert with its bones and legends of thirst, no, no, that ground has no particular menace. The woman and I and the dreaming, those things are the menace. Also, perhaps, eating the small dog, that could be very bad form. After fifty years of permanent war, many things still occur but fewer and fewer of these things can be admitted or spoken of. Long ago, we surrendered our politics to the inspection and approval of various agencies. We do not trust the telephones, we do not trust the mails. We do not trust each other. And finally and most importantly, we no longer trust ourselves. So we must operate secretly. Our biology now takes over without the admission that it even exists. We become honest as we become naked and return to our lying ways as soon as we dress again. Truly, this war has been very cold.

We lie down on the sheet and soon my tongue is between her legs and she tastes both mild and sweet. I marvel at her hair—hair always seems a miracle to me, an extra that the body offers as sheer indulgence. Her hands rub against my back as I enter. And then we forget ourselves.

I can see the aluminum forest glistening in the sunlight

across the valley and it will stand with any of the public art of my time. She turns around and I enter from the back and now we both admire the forest. We do not speak—the roar of the jets blocks all other sound.

Finally, the planes leave and quiet returns. She is smiling now. She tells me she once lived in a cave with a man near the sea and then the man left and later he murdered someone. She tells me she is crazy. She tells me she is having an affair with a married man. She tells me she has a serious sexual disease. She tells me she once left her lover's bed and crossed the room and slipped in beside a perfect stranger. (Ah, they are always perfect, we all know this fact—don't deny it. Too late for cheap lies.) She tells me her husband chased her through the house waving a shotgun, then choked her and beat her. She tells me she has a child at her breast and he finds her in a saloon and he sells her to a perfect stranger. She tells me she . . .

There is so much to talk about now that the war is over. We no longer have anyone to blame but ourselves.

It is after midnight in the casino and Sundance must lie down because of the pain. He takes drugs but they do not seem to help and he talks on into the dark night. He runs through his wars, his drinking, the stretches in prison, his life on skid row, his limited world tucked away in the soft belly of Los Angeles, in the dark hideaways that pocket the aerospace empire of blood orchids that cluster that ground. He remembers coming ashore on a Pacific island and the bodies were everywhere—Japanese soldiers and U.S. Marines mingled together—and the lizards who were eating all this carrion. The bones caught his eye also— they seemed to just dissolve in the constant rains. But the lizards—"Jesus, they got fat."

I cannot see him in the dark but this does not matter. He has become nothing more or less than a voice: "That son-of-a-bitch Custer, my grandmothers told me about him. Mad Bear had two wives, you know, and they said—not to me, but to my mother because they were very traditional and talked only Lakota—and they said, it is true that Custer at Little Bighorn had his hair cut short so they could not scalp him easily. When I was a kid, they had these funny-looking knives, like boning knives, and I'd ask my uncle, what are those knives for? And he said, those are scalping knives from Little Bighorn—and Jesus! I was a boy then and that wasn't that long ago—and my grandmothers said, it wasn't his haircut that stopped us from scalping him, no, no. He killed himself. No one can scalp a man who killed himself. Because he gave up."

Ah, but when he died, first graders in his hometown back in Ohio took an oath—to kill Sitting Bull on sight. And General Custer became a first-class beer poster, and the Sioux, well they pretty much became nothing.

There is a bottle of pills on the dresser that cost three hundred dollars—"Yes, they are the newest thing. For three months I could hardly eat, but now I feel better"— and he looks over at me and says, "Ah, I've forgotten your name."

Blood orchids. Everywhere. But no one seems to notice them, or if they notice them, regret them. Perhaps there is no problem. If you can afford the three-hundred-dollar bottle of pills.

"I survived being knifed, being shot," he says (he sounds as if he is raving now), "yeah, I survived the cholera, those years of alcoholism when I was helpless and now I've got this . . . cancer, yeah, and I didn't survive all those other things for this cancer. And I see other guys running around and they've never done anything for anybody and they're healthy and I think it is not fair."

Nothing will grow on this ground.

God has forsaken it.

The forest does not return, the deer can find no grass.

After the fire, the remaining walls soften over time and crumble into dust.

The steel girders rust and vanish into the wind.

The barren ground does sparkle here and there from the melted remnants of millions of computer chips.

But all that really remains in the end is a gigantic outline on the ground—the huge form of a pentagon.

Memories fade—we are only human.

After a while, some think the outline must be a message fabricated by a primitive culture in a fantastic effort to reach beings in outer space.

Others try to link the pentagon with the work of the great mound builders of the Ohio Valley.

Some argue it is the work of a lost tribe—these experts cite passages from obscure and ancient texts as their evidence.

Very few people visit the site.

It is said to possess a feeling of palpable evil.

No one can really explain this sensation.

Still, very few care to venture into the pentagon.

And, of course, the site never enjoys the songs of birds.

They refuse to come here.

They refuse to fly over this five-sided form.

No hawk ever casts its shadow, no falcon cries.

And people, the common people who are, as is to be expected, uneducated and given to crude vernacular terms, well, the common people refer to the pentagon by a name they make up.

They say when you say my country right or wrong—the DZZZZZZs ! ! Or they say when you've had too much to drink and scream it is their fault, that they're out to get

*you—the DZZZZZZZZZZZZZZZZZZZZZZZZZZs ! ! ! !
And when you yell that they are under your bed and
goddammmmmmmmmit better dead than red and recite
your name and serial number and please, urinate into
this cup, and tell us about your drug habits, and have
you slept with people ? ? ? ? and take this simple test
and answer every question FULLY, yeeeeeeeessssss, The
DZZZZZZZZZZZZZZZZZZZZZZZZZZs ! ! ! ! ! !
! ! ! ! ! ! ! ! ! ! ! ! ! ! !*

*They also make up tales of the great fire, or of a great
flood, a great storm such as never happened before or since,
a plague some say, while others claim a rapture with one
and all ascending into the heavens.*

*There is also a dark legend of a day that people and
beasts could speak and acted as one in this place.*

Few believe this tale, it is simply too fantastic.

*Now and then a human bone is found, many strangely
enough bearing the marks of gnawing by serious teeth, and
no one can explain this at all.*

"The DZ," they call it.

The Dead Zone.

The system of the hammer orchid usually fails. How could it be otherwise? If perfect, all the wasps would mate with fake females and soon there might be no real wasps to attract. The fake females, well, they are just not the real thing. No orchid can compete with a real lusty Thynnid female, not at all. Males will hardly visit the flowers when living females are out and about. The scent is just not like a whiff of the real thing. But there is a saving fact, a tiny detail that makes the sex life of hammer orchids possible. Each spring, the males show up a couple of weeks before the females. And the hammer orchid knows this—no! no! that can't be right, these damn things can't really know. During this

interlude, the hammer orchid seduces male Thynn-
nids, and they land, and they fuck the false
female, and the hammer falls. It has been going
on for . . .

They like to drill everywhere. In his head, in odd bones here and there. They tap his spine like a sugar maple. They are young and eager and he is an interesting patient for the freshly minted residents paying off their student loans by doing a few years time in the V.A. hospital. Christ, they now think the thing in his bones has been stalking Robert Sundance's life for maybe eight long years.

The long death of the past two years has not been a good ride. He has fought against entering a hospital until the very twilight days of his life. He will not be a patient. When his ankles hurt, he denies this fact or he says he must have sprained them. Or he refuses to tell anyone they hurt. And by God, he seems for a few weeks to get better—the word whispered is *remission*—and we all pretend. Maybe it is just some thing in his bones. But the problems return. And then he has trouble getting out of a chair. He becomes incontinent. His mind is not always under his command. You call and talk, and then call an hour later and he has no memory of the earlier call. He is taking pills finally—much against his will—but not serious painkillers. Some codeine, that's it. He will not give up control of his mind, you see. All those years he was helpless with the booze, and now for seventeen years he can think clear as a bell. He won't give that up. Been drunk a hundred years, you know.

The pain does not respect his wishes. The thing in his bones keeps eating away. Some nights while he is still clinging to his room on skid row, he can barely take the pain. He starts muttering about suicide, about getting control back. A friend who checks on him is worried so he calls me. Here is the problem as he sees it: Robert Sundance lives in a skid row room on the third floor; if he jumps, can we be sure this is high enough to kill him? Maybe, he rolls on, we should see about getting him moved to, well, how about a fifth-floor room? I listen and I think one simple thought: God, I love this country.

There are other fine moments. A friend of Sundance's is having trouble in his marriage and he forms this plot: he will confront his wife's lover, kill him. And then kill himself. He decides to talk this over with Sundance, who somehow despite his bone-thing-pain manages to pay careful attention to the proposal. When this friend finishes his speech, Sundance weighs in. "Your plan will never work," he counsels. "After you kill this guy, you will feel so good, you won't feel like killing yourself." The man surrenders to his logic.

Then one weekend a man stops by my house to show off a used horse trailer he has bought so that we can haul Sundance's body home when the time comes. And I knew this has been in the cards. An agreement has been made: Sundance can die in Los Angeles, but his body will be taken home for burial with his people. It seems the least one can do. After an hour or so, even the taillights work.

Robert Sundance moves into the spirit world. He has

always traveled such ground at times, his 275 bouts with the dt's have convinced him that there is a separate reality, one invisible to the eyes of most of us most of the time. He knows better after 275 visits to the other place. He leaves the window of his skid row cell open so that the spirits can enter. With their help, he can beat this thing in his bones. That is the only reason he has survived the war, the bars, the prisons, the life. He can reach them and they care what happens to him. Sometimes he conjures up this . . . thing. There is a woman who visits him and he likes her a lot. One night she is sleeping in her bed with her boyfriend when she wakes with a start because she senses someone is sitting on her bed. She can feel this person in the room, sense this person move around the room. She is convinced it is Robert Sundance.

When someone tells Sundance of this event and how it keeps her apprehensive, he says, "I'll let her sleep for a while." So there is no question he believes in his powers. For years he was trapped inside a bottle of booze and now he is trapped inside a body that is committing mutiny. But always he has had belief in his powers and in the existence of such powers, and this has kept him from feeling helpless.

But eventually time on the clock is used up. One Tuesday it all becomes too much, and he finally allows himself to be checked into a V.A. hospital. He has been fighting this bone thing over two years. The doctors with the schedules had him listed as dead and gone long before. He is very weak, and he can't open one eye. He is not good at lifting his arms either. And there is this big blood clot. The doctors think maybe they should cut him open. Of course, he is not a very good surgical risk. Then the clot begins to break up. The clock is running down, but it is like the last three or four minutes of a championship basketball game, a period when a minute takes much longer than usual.

The windows in his room at the V.A. hospital do not open. This is a modern building. Three other people share his room and every one is dying. Within a week, two have died and been replaced with two more highballing toward the charnel house. Sundance cannot see out the window. A visitor comes and he asks, "What's the weather like?"

It is the season for the fires, the time when the grass explodes at the merest suggestion of a spark, when the trees are hungry for the burn, when the chaparral of southern California waits as a warehouse of squat, living bombs. The air is very bad, it is hard to breathe, the kill rate goes up in the barrios, ghettos, sitting rooms, and board meetings as the terrible waiting grows in the parched, incendiary landscape. The arsonists flourish now, they do every year at this time. Americans love the fire, all Americans at all times. The Sioux, like almost all Native Americans, regularly torched the earth. Fire is in the blood. And so Robert Sundance waits, works on dealing with a window that can never be opened, reaches out to the strange creatures he knows and has met in drunk tanks all over the American West. One eye cannot open, yes that is true. Nor can he really lift his arms. The nurses come and go, hauling his dead roommates out on gurneys. And he beckons to the powers. This thing in his bones.

I am in Los Angeles at the end of July. For weeks I have been all business, eating in the fine restaurants, drinking in the best watering holes. I talk to reporters, howl on radio, stare down the dull-witted television cameras. Sign my name again and again. From time to time, I've picked up the phone and checked in on the deathwatch. But the weeks slide by and Robert Sundance keeps living. If he keeps at it this way, he's going to fuck up my schedule— goddamn, doesn't he understand I'm all business now? It is toward evening and I have been at it since four A.M. with a three-hour pit stop in the night for sleep, and I'm sitting in a lounge waiting for the next round of this business. The countertop is black marble, the style Art Deco, the beer Italian with a Mustache Pete glaring off the label. The bartender is a busted dirt peddler from the eighties, his head bald, wallet empty, eyes alert and hungry for the next wave of deals. He'll be back, he lets me know, they always come back. We can't seem to build a tomb solid enough to keep them down and dead. We get to talking and he tells me about one of his wives. "Jesus," he sighs, "she had these big tits implanted out to here and one morning she went out jogging and the bag broke in one—boom! just like that—and she come out of the shower with one huge tit on one side and the other flat as a board. Went to the doctor and he pumped her right back up"—he snaps his fingers—"just like that. Like putting air in a tire." So he'll be back, pump him back up just like that. Just then a woman comes in with huge breasts. She's wearing a tight blue striped dress, a black gaucho hat with a leather chin strap, five-inch high heels, silver bracelets and necklace. She is very slender, has the kind of tan that protects one from a day job, and she does not smile as she clatters past on her way to the ladies' room. She looks about thirty until I stare into her ancient eyes. Her gigantic breasts are firm and round and seem independent of her trim body. She moves like a woman in the park pushing a baby carriage. She never smiles until this balding guy arrives who is about twenty years older than she is. Then I lose track of her as I go to dinner—my end comes to sixty bucks and I only have two glasses of wine. Like I said, this summer I am all business, putting my shabby shoulder to the wheel of the Gross National Product. I remember sipping a Château Lafite Rothschild and thinking of all the doctors scattered around the republic waiting on call with their pumps to keep the body politic shipshape. So while I am in L.A. and my escort (she insists on this term) is hauling me around in her BMW like a suitcase, when I tell her to pull over at this exit, I have things to do that are not on the schedule. She hesitates, then complies with my instructions and pulls in before the huge temple to the killing fields. She has never been here before, she says.

The V.A. hospital skulks by freeway 405 and is big, sterile, and deadly. He has come home to his nation's ultimate skid row. The limbs that once bench-pressed three hundred pounds are thin, the tattoos of naked women have shrunk and their breasts now lie flat on his spindly forearms. Purple stains from the radiation treatment drool down the side of his head. He is on his fifth roommate and has become slightly renowned in the terminal ward—rooming with him is to meet the widow maker. A television drones from a corner shelf but he will not look at it. On the wall are tacked photographs of himself and of friends, battle cries from his endless war ("Columbus, 1492–1992"), and a black hat that shouts, SOVEREIGN INDIAN NATION, CUSTER DIED FOR YOUR SINS. An arrow slashes through the word SINS. I am given the hat, my war bonnet.

He is lucid, remembers my name, introduces me to a friend who is visiting him, a huge man from a Puebloan village on the Río Grande. Robert Sundance is weak and so small I think I can carry him in my arms. His friend carries the conversation as Sundance lies in his bed with an i.v. dripping something into his vein. On the television a daytime program is babbling. Three women face the camera, all are black but two look white. The subject: the trauma of passing in Racist Amerikan Society.

Neither man pays a bit of attention to this program. They are looking for sign. They are reading the wind, listening to the stars, taking down messages from the spirit world. The Puebloan tells me he was at Wounded Knee II in the seventies, came ashore and took part in the seizure of Alcatraz. He seems to have gone straight from Nam to this new one of combat. He says Wounded Knee really got tough after the killing of the FBI agents, after the public thought the siege was really over. "We lost five hundred afterwards," he says matter-of-factly in a soft voice. "Find them in dumpsters . . . the alcohol . . . they picked us off one by one." As he speaks, I can see Sundance nodding.

But that is old business and they are about a new world. Sundance tries to explain this to me. "Do you think this flood raging on the Mississippi and the Missouri is an accident?" he begins. "Do you think the hurricane in Florida just happened? Do you believe this strange disease killing people in the Navajo country is not a message? Goddamn no! It is the Great Spirit, it is the answer for what has happened, for what has been done. A judgment, goddamn right."

I say, what about an earthquake?

He glares up at me from his deathbed and snaps, "It is coming."

The Puebloan picks up his thread, he tells of the Hopi elders and their prophecies, he speaks of the petroglyphs on his home ground, how it is all there scratched in the stone for anyone to read. But the whites will not pay any attention, they will not stop their destructive ways, they will not . . . and so they will perish, the land will revolt, is revolting, lashing back, righting the wrong, settling the score. The high water. The big wind. The plague. The ground shaking and tearing asunder. It is written in stone. It will happen. It is happening.

A pool of silence descends on the room. The thing has been said. Message delivered. I am now warned.

I get up to leave, my new hat screaming SINS and riding square on my honky head.

Sundance looks up from his bed. He tells me he is going to get into therapy, get to walking again—"only I'm so goddamn weak"—and get well so he can go back to his wars. We both know there will be no more visits. He extends his hand, we shake.

He says, "You do a good job."

But he cannot recognize an ending. They forgot to teach him how to give in. I have seen this before. It makes for a hard death, but a good life. He begins pulling people, dragging them toward him as he dwindles in his government bed. Suddenly this woman is leaning over him, blond and very good-looking, her large breasts swinging before his ravaged face. She was walking down the hall, just making her rounds in the federal death house, she is a specialist in internal medicine. Anyway, she is many things but she is not a person who understands what is happening to her, who understands the pulling. So she leans over him, and he looks up and says, "I can feel it. You are part Indian." And she is a sixteenth something, and she wonders how in the hell does he know, and why is she even leaning over his deathbed. He is not her patient. He is in there, pulling, pulling, day after day, night after night. And they all come, like the blond woman, drawn into a room they did not plan to visit, leaning over a patient who is not their patient. His care improves—this thing in his bones!—he is in therapy. He cannot stand, he cannot walk, he cannot lift his arm. But he is pulling, pulling with the power.

Thirteen days after I visit him he leaves just before dawn. It is August 10, one hundred seventeen years and some change after Little Bighorn, when Robert Sundance dies.

("You do a good job.")

I put on my hat, the arrow still slashing through those SINS, and point the truck toward L.A. It is time Sundance went home. The truck is rolling through the night at eighty-five hard on Tuba City, Arizona. This is a stretch of highway where the Navajos are said to believe that all the dead Indian drunks wait by the roadside as ghosts—as the wolves of the Dine—and at say two in the morning when you're tired and loaded, they reach out with their cool bony hands and pull you off into the ditch to join them. Twelve hundred and fourteen miles later, the ignition switch is turned off beside a mortuary in downtown L.A. All the chain-link fences here are topped with concertina wire, and when I crawl out of the cab, a barefoot black wino shuffles by. His eyes have that nice varnish drink can give, his feet are like iron with the untrimmed nails curling, a grizzled gray beard splotches across his face, and he does not see me or much else in this ugly world. The funeral parlor is Japanese—this end of the business has been handled by a Japanese-American friend of Sundance—and a big striped marlin hangs in the lobby. The night before there had been a service with medicine men, the big drum, and a helluva of a lot of noise. The mortician allows he had never heard or seen the like before. Sundance is stretched out in a plain cedar box and we toss him into the fourteen-foot horse trailer for his trip. The body handler gives one parting bit of advice: "When you stop, park in the shade."

We hit the freeway at about eighty riding just ten minutes ahead of the rush. The driver is inspired and slides into the special three-person commuter lane which boasts no traffic and a $270 fine for violators. Hell, he says, with Sundance we got our three. The truck roars right past the motorcyclist lying on the pavement with a busted head and soon we whiz by a sign announcing a new subdivision and "15 MINUTES TO SAFETY." L.A. is a blur of palms, citrus trees, and houses people are fleeing as peace wreaks its havoc and the blood orchids wither and seem to be dying. We gut it through Cajon Pass and into the hot hands of the Mojave. The cruise control is set at eighty-five, as usual, but the damn engine has a governor that kicks in at ninety-two. Well, we have to make the best of it.

At sunset we slip through Baker, the temperature cruising at ninety-seven. Every once in a while, we pop back into the trailer and take a sniff. Then Vegas streams by the windows (rooms ten bucks a throw at the Stardust on the Strip) and we plow up and into the Mormon country, the truck grinding out the grade as we follow the Virgin River and face the moral certainty of St. George, Utah. The land sleeps out of sight in the darkness and the only hint of life in the country is the Wal-Marts feeding off the carcasses of the dying main streets.

The second day we are in Pocatello, Idaho. I am standing in a cell of the abandoned jail. The door is steel, the room about ten by six, the floor busted bottles and piss and shit from countless drunks bunking here. Sundance spent some nights in this closet for misbehavior. He's right outside now resting in the parking lot. Writers have been visiting this gutted jail. The walls host messages— DEATH FOR ALL, FUCK U, DOPE MAN, 666—THE NUMBER OF THE BEAST. The floor is rotted carpet, broken glass from the vanished windows. Sundance spent time here in the late fifties when the nuclear tests boomed away down on Frenchman Lake in Nevada and the hot, pink clouds coursed up here dusting everything in their path. The Air Force secretly monitored the movement of the more than one hundred aboveground detonations and each one gave a dollop of radiation equal to or greater than Chernobyl. Sat here in this basement cell, or was sprawled out on the sidewalk of skid row, his brain spinning from the booze, his face briefly serene from the power of the bottle, a big Lakota, a tough guy with tattoos and muscles and knife scars, just fresh out of the joint in Deer Lodge, Montana, stretched out here and drunk as a skunk, the sun blazing, and up over his head these strange clouds, kind of pink-looking, floating past like a vision of something no one had ever seen before. *This thing in my bones.*

A block away are the bars of skid row, largely gone now, the lots of bulldozed and vacant, the grass green over the remains. Same for the whorehouse. I have a smoke and sit on the lip of the trailer. Sundance lies there taking it all in. Can't trust the weather, goddamn, but who'd a thought a pink cloud could be such a bitch? There is a breeze, the sky is blue today, it seems like the moment for a picnic, light the coals, toss down some hot dogs, hear'm sizzle? Jesus, what a fine day. And what a fine country, so big and inviting. At a gas station back in

Utah a sign behind the cash register announced: TAX
FORM—1. LIST INCOME, 2. SEND ALL. The hard soil of the Mojave, then the sagebrush sea, all blue-green, of the Great
Basin, now Pocatello snoring away in this stone slot just
off the path of the Snake River. We pull out and head
north and then east. The potato fields come in, an endless
stretch of taters and sloughs. The land flat, the houses
huddled against the sky, the whole thing a place where
surely everyone goes mad by January and runs off into
the night praying for a snowdrift to cover them and end
it all. The folks around here are pretty much Mormon,
the women pale, their hair stringy, and their timid eyes
peering through thick glasses. The faces have a look that
suggests some new studs should come into this country.

There is a point where every trip takes on a life of its
own, where the beginning is buried beyond the reach of
the rearview mirror and the destination seems to slip
from consciousness and there is nothing, nothing at all
but the road and its pull, and that is when the road
becomes irresistible and I become the road. There is nothing but the pedal, black coffee, the white line, and this
thing called America stretching forever like the swells of
some ocean. We have escaped something we cannot
name, we are hurling forward at eighty or ninety miles an
hour in a truck with a big trailer snaking behind us.
Country western music drones from the tape player and
we do not have watches. This point is not discussed by
the AAA when they help pick routes and point out the
fine venues. But this take-off when we leave our lives and
break free is why my country is more roads than homes.

A little ways to the north near Big Lost River is the site
of the world's first nuclear power plant—cheek to jowl
with the black lava beds of an earlier fire. The thing went

a little screwy back in the fifties and a rod shot up and impaled one guy on the top of the containment vessel. Very hush hush, they say. There is talk of love—love always seems to be the answer. A triangle, two guys, one woman, and then this nuclear event, as the feds like to call it, and a man pinned to the top of the containment vessel, a new glowing rod sprouting from his body. I swallow some more coffee stale from its hours in the thermos. The potato fields seem endless, then the mountains of Montana loom ahead like flying buttresses. We are careful of the bumps—"Goddamn this highway," shouts the driver as another rupture in our beloved national infrastructure bangs under our wheels, "I hate to be tossing Robert around this way." But he will never slow down. We all have this disease that is outlawed, a thing called speed. Big wheel keep on turning, suck in your gut we're gonna whip it, four carbs poking through the hood. Sometimes I understand that this country has never really been going anywhere but at least it has always been going there in a hell of a hurry. And the hurry, that part of mission impossible, I truly like. I cradle the coffee but it is no use on this insane voyage and the hot fluid slops out on my britches and the calm lights of the speedometer and all those nagging gauges glow in the night and Kitty Wells is singing up a storm and the only goddamn worry we have in the world is the gas gauge because this son-of-a-bitch drinks that petroleum and by God, eventually we'll have to stop—briefly! briefly—and fill its worthless guts and then roll on again. Into the maw of the land.

We roll through Monida Pass, rain splattering the windshield, and head into the serious drinking country. The history books tell of Sacajawea kidnapped near Three Forks, of John Colter making his famous dash downriver from enraged Native Americans. But fuck that stuff, we are on the new Sundance Trail, doubtless bus tours of Japanese and German tourists will soon follow, a scenic route of whores, tokay, and bleak whiskey bars. We pull off and on the road at each and every sacred site, letting Sundance take in one last time the feel of his vision quest—or properly, *banble ceyapi,* crying for a vision. We are guided by old neon signs with martini glasses cunningly outlined by the glowing tubes, by flophouses with the curtains flapping out the open windows. Alas, this part of our national heritage is not being preserved. Sometimes the bars are gone, sometimes they have gone to a peculiar hell where plants hang belligerently in the window and espresso machines look like missile silos behind the bar. Montana is apparently being saved from its grim past by a new breed of chablis-drinking trout fanatics. One fantasy surrenders to the next and no one ever wakes up from the dream. It sure beats the hell out of history.

We roll down the Beaverhead River. The ranch squats in the bottomland hiding from the winds of winter. Sundance would stop here. The rancher is gone up in the hills tending the irrigation on his hay fields. A woman is staying here with her cat. She came six months ago from New York state to . . . well, she tells me she knows ceremonial people at Pine Ridge. It is a very old ranch and buffalo graze on the hills. Inside, the plain wooden house is the center of the universe and I must see it: a huge steel safe worthy of a bank. The door swings open, a light goes on, and before my eyes are a couple of hundred thousand dollars' worth of ancient Winchesters, of big-bore buffalo guns, of old Colts, and case after case of arrowheads. We walk back out to the truck. It is very cool and summer is leaving this place. Over in the shed are buffalo skulls and robes, they're worth a fortune now, pieces of the true cross. The woman from New York climbs up the side of the horse trailer and stares down at the cedar box.

"Nice casket, Sundance," she says. "Goodbye, Sundance."

She wears Levi's and no makeup and is irked at the rancher toiling up in the hills. She will not make it through the winter, this fact is all over her face. She has come for the ceremonies—not the dirty dishes, the grind of moving irrigation units, the dull toil of watching a cow's ass as it moves from one pasture to another, the religion of haystacks.

We move down the two-lane rural road at eighty and the driver turns and announces, "No paranoia." He loves Montana. There are hardly any cops and if one is incredibly diligent and manages to locate one, the fine for speeding is five bucks, paid by the roadside. He is a student of the republic's roads. Once, on one of our many forays, I asked why we were traveling with a .357 magnum under the seat, plus a .22 automatic pistol and an AK-47 with a banana clip. He turned to me with shock and disbelief and asked, "Do you know how many fucking lunatics are out on the American highway?"

Off to the side just across the Beaverhead River is a raised stone butte. The clouds are scudding low, the air sags with damp and cold. We are lancing up toward the three forks of the Missouri, that warehouse of fame for early government types like Jefferson and Madison and of course most importantly, the secretary of the Treasury, Gallatin, all three of whom left their names bobbing on the headwaters because they'd sent their federal employees here to tack names on everything. I brush my fingers against the truck window and feel the cold wet air streaming past us and over Sundance as he rests in his coffin. I suspect he's thinking about fierce broncs at old rodeo grounds and cold mornings in the corrals as he saddled up for a day's work on the ranches that clot these river valleys. Maybe he's savoring one of those women he had out in an alley behind a bar. As the night falls down and blots out the fence lines, everything seems possible. I do not doubt that Sundance is back there dreaming and thinking. I can catch a whiff of long-cold Indian campfires. I can hear the splash of paddles as someone moves steadily westward on the waters. Lewis and Clark are a year out of St. Louis and still working upstream toward the Continental Divide where the waters head off in a new direction and flow toward the Pacific. Their journey marks one of the few happy moments in this place we call the West. They will be out on their own with their men for two years, lose but one soul (to an attack of appendicitis in Iowa), have their great Newfoundland dog, Scannon, kidnapped in the Northwest, but will swiftly effect a recovery of the beast. They will pass through new nations but cause almost no mayhem or violence, face hundreds of days of risk and questions without a single argument between the two captains. After them, it will all be downhill, a spiral of killing and looting and displacement and disease. On the night of Wednesday, May 1, 1805, the wind blows hard and with the dawn comes snow. The party is in Montana, though neither they nor anyone else yet knows this name. The ground goes white, yet the trees are eager for the spring, "flowers had put forth on the plains," and the leaves of the cottonwoods are "as large as a dollar." The camp needs meat and soon the hunters return with two deer, three elk, and several buffalo. There is a peace that stuns them all. "On our way this evening,"

Lewis notes, "we also shot three beaver along the shore; these animals in consequence of not being hunted are extreemly gentle, where they are hunted they never leve their lodges in the day." Permanent night is coming very soon for the beaver. One of the hunters comes upon several yards of scarlet cloth hanging from the limb of a tree hard by an abandoned Indian camp. Lewis speculates it is an offering of some kind: "It being the custom with . . . all the nations inhabiting the waters of the Missouri so far as they are known to us, to offer or sacrifice in this manner to the deity watever they may be possessed of which they think most acceptable to him. . . . This being the most usual method of wershiping the great sperit as they term the deity. . . . The [water] friezed on the oars as they rowed. . . ." Lewis pauses in his jottings, "the wind dying at 5 P.M.," and then notices the land, the endless roll of land, the "wider fertile bottoms and beatifull high level plains." The new American cannot be repressed, the cash register mind dips an oar in the waters of Eden. The air intoxicates the party, the size of the ground overwhelms them, and the struggle begins that has never ended between a love deeper than reason and a reason stronger than love. Lewis scratches on in his journal, trying to pin down both what he sees and what he is: "every thing which is incomprehensible to the indians they call *big medicine,* and is the opperation of the presnts and power of the *great sperit.* This morning, one of the men shot the indian dog that had followed us for several days, he would steal their cooked provision." No one after them could ever be them. They were that first shot out of the cannon, that explosion of our culture into a world that did not yet really understand our kind. They saw the last fresh spring.

Now we sniff and fight over scraps like the lean dogs

following the march of a long-vanished army. A few months before I was in the mountains and it was very late at night and there had been too much drinking. We were driving down an icy road, the driver was holding a big glass of whiskey and snorting a good-sized jolt of cocaine when a cow elk bolted before us and effortlessly cleared a fence. He rolled to a stop, stared where the big animal had vanished into the darkness, and kept saying, "That is a very rare sight, we are privileged, that is a very rare sight." I stared out the windshield at the memory of a thing named the West, now clean tracks in the fresh snow.

We are embedded in this thing called the West but we cannot see it. It is always . . . over the next hill, the far side of that mountain, up the furthest canyon, something that slipped away yesterday, last week, twenty years ago, the last century, no, no, the century before the last. It is the cattle kingdom, or it is the bluecoats picking off braves or it is the buffalo hunters or it is the prospectors or it is the Oregon Trail or it is the Rocky Mountain fur trade or it is Lewis and Clark or it is the buffalo culture or it is the megafauna waning with the end of the Pleistocene, the dire wolves howling on the peaks, the mammoths shuffling toward the water hole, some asshole huddled on the ridge chipping away at his fancy Clovis point. Or it never was at all.

Let's begin again: the West is guns, horses, trout, elk, antelope, bear, Levi's, strange bonnets, boots, pickup trucks, pistols, Indians, beads, rugs, chili, pottery, baskets, steers, blue corn, mountains, chicken-fried steak, forests, streams, hillside lots, log cabins, bronzes by Remington and Russell, turquoise jewelry, buffalo skulls with feathers dangling from the black horns, cliff houses, medicine wheels, sacred pipes, lariats, shirts with snaps, thick steaks bloody on the plate, tepees, ski runs. And your cabin here.

It sure as hell isn't this dead fucking Indian lying in a cedar box flying through the night at eighty or ninety miles an hour in a sixteen-foot horse trailer. Any fool knows that. Sundance spent the last thirty years of his life on skid row of Los Angeles, hardly knew a word of Lakota, loved to bet on the ponies, roll the bones in Nevada, romp with the whores. Spent a quarter century stone-drunk in the whiskey bars. Not authentic, clearly a bogus Sioux (". . . the vilest miscreants of the savage race," according to Meriwether Lewis). This thing in the bones. I pop open one of the skin books from Sundance's three-foot stash. Vaginas flapping open like the Holland Tunnel, huge breasts flooding the pages, asses smiling at the camera. The headlines and text offer vigorous American prose. *"PAGE AFTER PAGE OF WIDE-OPEN SHOTS OF WIVES, MOTHERS & DAUGHTERS."* It's going to be impossible to clean up his act—he seems to have screwed up all of his lines in the script. *"Among other things, Eve dreams of 'doing it' with a dog."* We pull off from time to time at ranches scattered in canyons under the frosty lips of the Rockies. The walls of these houses are plastered with original oil paintings, the coffee fresh ground, the hardwood floors well waxed. Trout streams babble mindlessly just out the door and fine horses blanketed against the cold feed in the corral.

"She's into Greek and French at the same time." We are making one pit stop as part of the endless effort to get Sundance's autobiography published. So far the manuscript has been rejected by everyone in New York with access to a printing press. Pretty damn bleak stuff, seems

to be the consensus. Well, there's no arguing with that. *". . . Would like to leave Indiana, hitchhike to California, and then fuck everyone who gives her a ride."* Things have not been going too well in Montana either. The text has been loaned to a friend of the host's, the head of a Native American Studies program at some university, and I sense that the verdict has not been favorable. Too many hard spirits, not enough Great Spirit (good ol' *Wakan Tanka*, white eyes). *"WHEN MOM CUMS TOO! Under the Covers with Lovers-in-Law!"* It is slipping away, I think, I can feel it slipping away as we talk. When Robert Sundance died, his passing was announced on national network news. Heroic reformer of laws governing alcoholics, selfless toiler in skid row struggling to save the damned, and so forth. Now he's out in the yard by the laurel tree in a cedar box, now his angry words ride across pages of pure white paper. And no one needs any of that. So it goes. *"Oh, dear, is he pointing that big hard thing at us? What does he want, Nell?"* I drain the coffee, listen to happy talk of the crystalline trout streams, and feel a vast peace fill me. He is safe from acceptance, even death, it seems, cannot smother his menace. Of course, he laid his fucking curse—*"You do a good job"*—and I've got his damn CUSTER DIED FOR YOUR SINS bonnet on my head, but this burden rides light on me at the moment. I can't find the West, to be sure, but I can feel the solid ground under my boots. I'm on the Sundance Trail and nobody is likely to frame an elegant map of it and put it on the wall. *"HIGH MOON. How the West Was Fun!"* It's a kind of secret thing, like those fluffy pink clouds that once drifted over this country giving everyone beneath them that special glow, a buried thing unlamented, unseen, unloved. And unwanted. It's the way we lived and that is not the stuff of either memory or art or books, it seems. I'm proud to live in a nation without serious censorship. It is not necessary. We have all been trained. We don't have anything to forget because we have remembered very little. That's how we got to this place under those big pink clouds. *"This thing in my bones."*

I remember when my escort was zipping me around L.A. in her Beamer and she pointed out that I was not wearing a seat belt and this act was against the law—something carved in big stone tablets, The Law—and that there was a hefty fine for this evil behavior and besides 50,000 people died on the highway (where O Lord is the path to the low way?) and I couldn't seriously quarrel with any policy that limited this slaughter, now could I? And I lost it again—this is getting to be a bad habit of mine—and I snapped, "Look out your fucking window at these assholes. There're too many of the motherfuckers. We need more highway death, not less." These episodes must cease. It is unseemly. And besides, the authorities will be alerted. They have the cell ready, the ink pads are fresh, and I will stand over there against the wall chart and they will take my photograph for their wonderful archive. Hell, the president wants to hire a hundred thousand more cops. The pattern is clear. So I've got to shape up, right now. Look, I take it all back. There is no censorship. Just good manners. Stop me before I hate-think again. *"Josie says she would love to have her lover ram a bottle up her cunt as she caresses his nipples."* I love original oil paintings, I believe in trout, I favor the horse, I will only buy Levi's with buttons not zippers. I will brew fine coffee, always have a fireplace, make sure my hounds have sound bloodlines, and scorn all but single malt scotch. I will burn Sundance's fucking book—who needs this depressing shit?—and trust my soul to authentic sand paintings, feathered chief's staff, Two Gray Hills rugs, and silver concho belts. I will buy all my fetishes at Zuñi (goodbye high-heeled shoes) and shoot grouse, then properly marinate. My shotgun will be a side-by-side Parker. My rifle a Weatherby. My boots the finest leather. In town I will favor scuffed Topsiders. I will never drink wine with a screw-top cap. My women will not use eye shadow, at least not so you can notice. And of course, I will love the whales, the dolphins, the bald eagle, black-footed ferret, spotted owl, and yew tree.

And my temper will always be even, like the finest cutlery. I will scorn sugar and lick wild honey. I will take cold showers in canola oil. I will abandon the politics of groping. I will snort corn pollen, neat yellow lines on an obsidian sheet. Ah, I feel better, it will all pass. I know I can pass. I have watched how others do it. But first, I've got to unload this dead Indian.

"You do a good job."

At Billings we take him past more whiskey bars just across the tracks from the banks and real businesses. The whorehouse here has been leveled and fine green grass grows on the lonely lot. Downtown one old bar— "Casey's Golden Pheasant, Firewater"—lingers as a historically restored upscale steak house. The plains are rolling in now, swallowing us in bare hills and knobs of green. The mountains sink behind the horizon line and an ocean of grass smothers us with its fresh raw breath.

The driver is getting a little wacky by now, but how the boy can drive. Keep him somewhere over eighty and he is almost lucid. He's on the CB yammering with the eighteen-wheelers. The guy up ahead of us allows how he's hauling 42,000 pounds of fish out of Seattle and if he doesn't make it home by Wednesday "the old lady will cut my nuts off." The driver counters that he's hauling a dead Sioux in his horse trailer. There is a moment of what in commercial radio they call dead air, and then the trucker replies that he'll stick with his fish. The driver and I have faced this problem before. The reporter from L.A. asked if we didn't think our vacation plans seemed a mite mahcobb. Mahcobb? Who the hell can even spell such a word at eighty-five?

Miles City pulls us over. Indian Town down by the river bottom has vanished. I piss off the shoulder on its remains. The main street is in coitus interruptus—some of its old wino bars still staggering along, the others now gentrified. The whorehouse is now an eight-room motel, though still painted red for the sake of memory. On the edge of town, the rodeo ground lingers, a place where Sundance rode broncs in his prime. The Range Rider has been redone. All the rodeo photographs have been replaced by big portraits of silent-screen stars. The glass case that sold rodeo tapes now displays a model train.

The driver cannot abide progress and tells the barkeep, "It's all been redone. Wished they'd left it the old way."

She looks at him as if he were a bug and says, "That pigsty? Don't think so."

There are four clocks on the wall: Real Time, Bar Time (ten minutes fast), Indian Time (no hands), and Party Time (a starburst of hands). This will be reported to the appropriate authorities, rest assured.

We cross into North Dakota and Lakota ground proper wraps around us. Then down into South Dakota and finally we pull into the long dirt driveway near dusk. The first sign says BEWEAR OF DOG, the second simply MEAN DOG.

Pat, Sundance's brother, is waiting for us. His wife, Virginia, comes out of the house. We are in a bottom close to the dead body of the dammed Missouri River. Our job is almost over, the end is in sight, the light glows at the end of the grave.

Pat calls the undertaker, J.D., and then we drive into town to hand over the corpse. The trip is over but the journey is just starting.

J.D. designed the mortuary and faced it with cold stone. Behind this facing is a sheet-metal building. The driver is busy in the horse trailer untying the ropes from the coffin.

He tells Pat, "We took him through Bozeman, Billings, Miles City."

Pat allows, "Well, you had to really tie him down for that."

J.D. rolls the coffin into the garage and says we'd better take a look at him. He cracks the lid and then leans down and sniffs. "They did a helluva of a job," he offers. "Not a bit of odor." Sundance has been dead five days.

The two honky assholes breathe a sigh of relief. For once, we have not fucked up. We have shaved every morning of the trip—a Sundance obsession, mustn't look like drunks. Our stock is rising, we can sense it. We have brought the warrior home intact, taken him down the holy trail of saloons, flophouses, hot sheet joints, railroad yards, cigar stores, rodeo grounds, and jails.

Pat looks hard at the body and says softly, *"Mi sunka la."*

My younger brother.

The face is tanned (my God, these morticians are artists), filled out, and to my shock, at peace. I've never seen this face before. The anger has been flushed away. A bone choker surrounds his neck, a leather vest with medals encases his big chest. At his side is a roll of sage, various medicine bundles, crow feathers, and a sealed envelope addressed to "To A Beloved Warrior." A quilt with a dolphin rides inexplicably by his side. A child's drawing of a house under a palm tree, "Get Well."

Pat sorts through the bundles and says to himself, "These are medicine. This all goes with him."

I am standing off to the side with Virginia, smoking a cigarette. Goes? Where the hell does he think Sundance is going?

Then there is the matter of the folded American flag. J.D. figures that, like any veteran, Sundance will want it draped over his coffin.

Pat will not abide this idea.

"He doesn't want it unfolded. Sundance said to me, 'They promised us freedom and justice. They never gave us justice.' "

A silence settles. J.D. is white. Pat is Lakota, a Hunkpapa, a great grandson of Mad Bear. And a veteran, 95th Infantry. In April of 1945, he sees a German tank. Three men are hit, two live. Pat falls forward into a puddle, he thinks he is drowning. A big Polish guy throws him over his shoulder. He is in a coma for three days. He took eleven rounds through his body and lived. Twice he's been tribal chairman. The flag stays folded.

(*"You don't know what it was like back then," Pat tells me. "They tried to make us ashamed of being Indians. We couldn't speak the language at school. And those nuns beat hell out of us. I don't think much of this Catholic-ism."*)

For the first time I face the fact that Robert Sundance is dead. And here I thought we'd just been hitting a few old haunts, having one more for the road. But he's dead the way he wanted to be dead. That's what all the fuss has been about. He'd spent years watching winos die—killed in knife fights, hit by cars, done in by mutinous livers—and seen them carted off, cremated, and their ashes pitched like cinders from a coal furnace. And half the time nobody even knew their real names. And all the time nobody cared. By God, he didn't want to be buried as a drunk, tossed out like the garbage. So the horse trailer, so the long ride, so the cedar box. So his seventy-two-year-old brother leaning over and saying, *"Mi sunka la."*

About six weeks before he died, he finally saw the lights, those things the old ones had told him about as a boy, the lights that follow you when death is on your trail. He said, "They are very hard to see, they hide among the car lights at night."

I am standing in front of the Standing Rock swatting mosquitoes. They are so thick I inhale them. The rock is gray black and about three feet high. There was a woman and a child. The tribe moved on, she would not. In Standing Rock, she is frozen forever. The Sioux dragging the damn stone on travois for years—get along goddamn, you're going with us now. Pat nods as he tells me this. We are by the stagnant pond that is now the Missouri River, the Lakota villages of the past buried beneath the waters. It is a sore point with the tribe. They don't give a damn for the impounded lake. They want the ground beneath the waves back. Standing Rock. *("Warriors, women, and children swarmed like bees," Francis Parkman noted in the summer of 1846 when he dropped in on a Sioux camp along the Platte. "Hundreds of dogs, of all sizes and colors, ran restlessly about. . . . The wide shallow stream was alive with boys, girls, and young squaws, splashing, screaming and laughing in the water.")*

Pat is off. So much to see. Get in the car, he says. There in that grove of trees, that's where Sitting Bull used to be buried, that's where Sundance did his heavy drinking after the war. Soon we are going seventy, faster on the straightaways. There, look over there, the tribal buffalo herd. I see things the size of black four-poster beds drifting over the grassy hills.

Did you have them around when you were a kid?

Hell, no, they'd killed them all.

They? Don't ask, I tell myself. Don't ask.

(*"We think," Spotted Tail said in 1866, "we have been much wronged and are entitled to compensation for the damage and distress caused by making so many roads through our country, and driving off and destroying the buffalo and game. My heart is very sad and I cannot talk on business. . . ."*)

I lose myself in the land of Sioux (Lakota? I don't know. Sundance liked the word Sioux—a French corruption of what the Chippewa called the Lakota, and a name that meant snakes—said the name had too much recognition value in it for him to give it up.) There, over there, see it? That's Major McLaughlin's house, Pat says. The white great-grandfather. The . . . what should we say? The Indian agent in the family woodpile? More miles, see that nice house? This Jew, Pat snaps, tricked my grandmother out of that house and we had to move in February, dead of winter, and go live down in the bottoms. See those piles of stone? Guy escaped from prison in Colorado in 1889, came up here, left of trail of dead people behind him. Said to be a member of the James Gang. They finally hunted him down near my place. Supposed to be a lot of money hidden in the woods by the house— damned if I've ever seen it.

Bulldozed bare ground, the site of the future Prairie

Knights, a full-tilt boogie Sioux casino to be managed by the Swiss (global economy, the coming thing). Do you feel lucky, punk? ("*Our design concept is the blending of the old west ambience, with the refined friendly Dakotan hospitality atmosphere to create an up-scale, posh facility. . . .*"—*plan for Prairie Knights Casino.*) Right over the front door there'll be an Indian in a war bonnet on his pony. Inside there'll be murals of buffalo, mountain streams, tepees, bucks on horseback. The chandelier in the Hunter's Club Steakhouse will be festooned with antlers. Roll those bones, sucker. Is this table warm?

Tantanka Iyotake, 1831–1890. Sitting Bull, catch him in the Wild West Show? The monument has a dark granite base and on top is a bust of the old boy with a feather, pigtails, and a peace pipe—well, it's a pipe, anyway. He is staring off at Lake Oahe, the name given to this snakelike pond that once was the Missouri River. (Maybe we should chew on a few numbers. When the lake came up and covered the Sioux ground in 1960, it took 220,000 acres, which translates into forty percent of the winter shelter for stock on the reservations, ninety percent of the timber land, and caused twenty percent of the Sioux to resettle. Among other details, Mad Bear's camp went under the water.) Originally, Sitting Bull was buried north of here at Fort Yates, back in the wonder days when Major McLaughlin's cops whacked him in the process of arrest. But Mobridge (Missouri Bridge, get it?) dug him up and hauled him south, hoping for those fabled tourists. Then the big dam came, the waters rose, and by 1960 the town was severed from the grave by the pond. The slab sketches the white details of a red life: 1876, Little Bighorn; 1877, Asylum in Canada; 1881, Returned to United States; 1885, Toured Buffalo Bill's Wild West Show. And 1890, shot dead in the foolishness of the

Ghost Dance fad. He was born a few miles south of here before the lake came into being and pike became the local sensation. Scattered around the base of the monument are various medicine bundles. The plaque does not explain these.

(What is it the Bull said? Oh, yes, one more time: "Look at me and see if I am poor, or my people either. . . . You are fools to make yourselves slaves to a piece of bacon fat, some hardtack, and a little sugar and coffee.")

Who the hell handed out these names anyway? They're worse than "Prairie Knight": Sitting Bull, Crazy Horse, Rain-in-the-Face, Young-Man-Afraid-of-His-Horses, Little Big Man, Touch-the-Clouds (a seven-footer), and Gall.

Time to visit Gall. He's resting on a bluff overlooking Lake Oahe a few miles north of Sitting Bull. Gall, called Pizi by the Sioux, was a key player at Little Bighorn. Some think his acts that hot June afternoon were the crucial ones in propelling General Custer into a better world. The stone is simple: GALL–PIZI, DIED DECEMBER 5, 1894, AGED 55 YEARS. Then it says, WICASA OWOTANNA KIN OHINNYAN KIKSUYAPI KTACE: an honest man should always be remembered. The grave is overgrown with weeds and two- to three-foot sunflowers dance around the burying ground. No matter, the Sioux were never keen on being gardeners. Gall's planted in the midst of a mob of strange-sounding Lakota families: Swift Cloud, Brown Elk, Loves War, Standing Bear, Running Hawk, White Eagle, Walking Shield, Bone Club, Eagle On High, No Heart, Two Hearts. The sun is out, a light breeze, the river below is a still puddle. It took a while to find Gall's grave, it seems it is not on the official tour. Just a little ways to the north is yet one more burying ground, the one where Mad Bear sleeps, the place where Rita Ann—Sundance's sister—rests (Miss Indian America in 1953; the tribe then gave her the name Shining Water Woman). I am in Pat's house again and he is showing me a photograph of Rita Ann. She is a beautiful woman all decked out in beaded buckskin, and a beaded headband with a single feather. Cancer got her. Pat thinks cancer kills more Indians on Standing Rock than the booze. Those strange pink clouds, floating like dreams overhead. You still doubt that God is Lenny Bruce? Here're the names of some of the nuclear shots: Annie, Baneberry, Climax, Diablo, Dirty Harry (aka Harry), Dog, Hood, Met, Mighty Oak, Moth, Nancy, Priscilla, Simon, Smoky, Turk. . . .*

Well, hell, let the dead bury the dead, as our Lord once said. I remember my dad once pointing this passage out to me—he was a veritable fiend on his scripture—and noting that Christ wasn't always much of a Christian. But then when I was in L.A. being escorted around in that Beamer a comedian on late-night television asked, "If Jesus was a Jew, how come he has a Mexican name?" And damned if I wasn't stumped.

The past, we've got to let go of it. It gets in the way of the future. Pick up a newspaper, Tonto, everyone knows that. So I decide to taste some progress and we pull in to the Chief Gall Inn. The place was built in the seventies with federal money when Pat was chairman in the hope that some tourists could be snared for the Lakota side of Lake Oahe. There are over fifty units clumped in buildings shaped like tepees. I enter through an open door, carefully stepping on the rotted carpet and avoiding the sea of broken glass. Messages greet me near the pool area.

---

*Anyone truly hungry to know what atmospheric testing of nuclear weapons did to this country should read Carole Gallagher's *American Ground Zero: The Secret Nuclear War.* Then read it again.

B l o o d   O r c h i d

I HAD LEON IN THE BUTT.

JESUS LOVES ME. HOW ABOUT YOU?

GREENPEACE WAS HERE! SAVE THE WHALE. (AND SUCK MY DICK.)

The pool is nine feet deep and filled with broken light fixtures, lumber, twisted metal vents, shattered toilets, doors, bottles and cans, and rainwater. Above, the sun shines through the shattered skylight. On the bottom of the pool, the tribal seal (with Sitting Bull's memorial in the center) stares up bleary eyed. Pink tongues of insulation lap down from the destroyed ceiling. I move on to the restaurant and lounge area, a delightful room with excellent views of Lake Oahe. The big range is bent and bashed in and what looks to be serious salt and mineral deposits grow on the grill. The two refrigerated lockers are empty, the deep fat fryer empty of oil and hope. The whole set of buildings is faced with pumice. I look out the busted windows at the gentle lake that entombs the Sioux lands and feel the hot breath of rage in the summer air. At my feet is a large plywood board with row after row of keys for those guests who were going to savor the local hospitality.

Back at the motel (run by subcontinent Indians) I gather my spirits. I pull on the dark brown tooled cowboy boots (10½ D) that were Sundance's, shave once again (Shave every morning, don't want to look like a common drunk), and step out into the hall. The child is . . . short, dark-skinned, Lakota, and bent under a huge plastic sack of trash. The smile reveals a mouth with few teeth and almost no lips. Most of the face is burned also, and half the top of the head is nothing but scar tissue, a hank of black hair pulled over the bald area. The ears are gone and one leg and one arm are mass of white burn marks. The child smiles and laughs, and hobbles down the corridors as if nothing, nothing really, had happened.

I walk to the mortuary. The driver is there taking photographs of Robert Sundance all decked out in his coffin. The chapel is cedar paneled, plastic simulations of stained glass glowing with reds, oranges, greens, yellows, and here and there a clear fragment. A stone bas-relief of Jesus Christ dominates the front of the room—I Am the Resurrection and the Life. The casket is surrounded by floral displays (one studded with eagle feathers) with red ribbons announcing Cousin, Uncle, Brother, Nephew, Brother-in-Law. Off to the left is a small table covered with a Mexican serape and displaying snapshots: there's Sundance with Los Angeles Mayor Tom Bradley, with Connie Stevens, with Iron Eyes Cody, with various wild men from AIM. Or he stares out at me from an Air Force base in Fairbanks, Alaska (that second hitch during Korea), a faint smile on his handsome mug, skis leaning behind him, and images of women tacked to the wall. Two quilts, one of a sunburst, the other of an eagle, drape the coffin, and a single feather dangles from each quilt.

The small blue program has a band of buffalo on the cover, a prayer to the Great Spirit inside, and the basic numbers of a life: Robert Sundance aka Rupert S. McLaughlin, February 27, 1927, Mad Bear Camp–August 10, 1993, Los Angeles, California. Pat is in fine fettle, dressed in clean Levi's, a cowboy shirt, boots, and wearing his VFW cap with a row of battle stars. So are a lot of the other men. The battle shifted after Little Bighorn but apparently not the modus operandi. A woman comes up to view Sundance, and Pat says, "My golly, Thelma." She went to school with Sundance.

Pat peers down into the coffin and offers, "He lost a lot of weight out there in California." Lloyd Thompson ("raised sixty miles west of here, way out in no-man's-land") sits on a chair in the back of the big room and strums a guitar. Sundance has requested a song, "Cowboy at Heart." As the mourners file in slowly, Lloyd lets loose:

Campfire and coffee, clean cup in my hand,
Sure can warm the fingers when it's cold.
Sleeping in the moonlight, a blanket for a bed,
Sure can ease the wrinkles in my soul.
Waking in the morning with an eagle overhead,
Can make me fly away before my time.

The men wear the costumes of the cattle industry—big hats, boots, snap shirts, Levi's. Steers may not be buffalo but they'll have to do for the moment. This is a place where the plow pretty much gives up to the grass. A poster in town announces a horse sale: "We've used these horses to: sort cattle, earmark calves, drag calves to fire, cut studs, arena rope." There are no suits, no ties. I am not a disgrace, it turns out. A nephew enters with his son, walks to the front of the room, doffs his black cowboy hat, and drops a single feather in beside Sundance. It goes on like that for about an hour.

Ricky is here, one of Pat's sons. He's driven up from Phoenix, arrived broke after his battery gave out on the road. He's wearing a lavender and black shirt with long ribbons trailing and a blanket vest. A black ponytail snakes down his back, a carved buffalo skull bolo tie grabs at his throat and in his hands he clutches a bundle of woven sweet grass and a Bic lighter. He moves slowly about the room gently waving his smoking bundle and soon the chapel is infused with the scent. He doses the coffin real good (a group of ancient women with canes pays him no mind) and patiently freshens every nook and cranny of the funeral parlor. After a while the air takes on that blue quality pool halls are renowned for. Ricky is set up pretty solid, has had a few rounds with the law, a rough tour in Nam, and is now following the powwow trail. Uncle Sundance is part of the coursework he studies to find the way home.

At precisely ten A.M. Pat stands and goes to a small wooden podium. *Mi sunka la.* "Sundance," he tells the crowd of about one hundred, "was a prompt person, a proud person, and a person of his word. He told me he didn't want anyone coming here this morning who was drinking because he fought drinking all his life. He always had his reasons. And he didn't want anyone coming here who had to work 'cause he didn't want anyone losing their job over this."

Then he pauses for a few seconds and adds, "He said each ending can be a new beginning." He returns to the family benches in front: a sister has come in from Montana, there are nieces and nephews.

The Reverend Wilbur Bear's Heart takes over, a schoolmate of Sundance's.

"We called him Rup," the Reverend notes. "When he visited back in 1985, he put his arm around me and said, 'I'm proud someone made it from our school.' Rup and I got together in grade school because we both liked to smoke behind the schoolhouse. . . ."

A woman with the last name of Iron Cloud Two Dogs stands and speaks as an emissary of the Oglalas. A tribal proclamation is read. Clearly, Sundance is a big man on this ground. Because he fought the booze and won. Because he fought the government and won. And fought, and fought and fought.

Pat steps up to the podium again. He is a short man—

his boxing weight in high school was 118 pounds—but he never seems small. He says that he talked with Sundance at length those last few weeks about how he wanted his burial handled, and how Sundance wanted his old drinking buddies to speak at the ceremony but this proved difficult: they were almost all dead from the bottle. Two did survive and now they come before the gathering.

The man is in his sixties, gray haired, soft spoken, his VFW cap perched on his head. Like many Sioux, he is a tall man and takes up space. He entered the military during World War II as a minor, as did Sundance, he notes. Mary Mad Bear, Sundance's mother, fed him when he was orphaned. The hunger of the 1930s blows through the room like a cold wind. "We had things in common," he continues, "a drinking problem. But he went to battle." The man's words are as soft as summer clouds floating silently over the plains.

Another drinking buddy walks to the front of the room. He is also tall, but heavier. He met Rup when they were boys and he was visiting. He remembers how all the other boys talked a lot about the local priest and what a special guy he was. And then he discovered the priest was giving the boys "sacrificial wine." He too joined the military during the war as a boy. "We did our share of drinking," he explains, "Rup and I. We fought over the last drink in the bottle, we fought over women." You have to understand, he continues, what it was like coming back to Standing Rock after the big war. Everyone was poor. We had been away, we had seen the world, it had been very exciting. The reservation was boring. "So," he adds so very softly, "the drinking life."

(Erik Erikson, the psychoanalyst, is out among the

Lakota just before the Big Show and he catches a whiff of the boredom as the old dudes "sit in a semi-circle under a shade and discuss old times and the deeds of men now dead, while from mouth to mouth passe[d] the inevitable red stone pipe filled with 'red willow' tobacco." Seen through the lens of mondo-Freudo, all this looks pretty damn weary, "empty except for those vivid bits of the present in which he [could] be his old self, exchanging memories, gossiping, joking or dancing, and in which he again [felt] connected with the boundless past wherein there was no one but himself, the game, and the enemy.")

But the man insists on an honesty this morning in the cedar-paneled room with Sundance listening in his wooden box. "He found a purpose," the man confesses, "and I never have."

He pauses now, he has been speaking off the cuff, his voice low and very conversational. He is not an orator nor does he seek to be such a creature. "You know," he trails off, "there are no words in the Lakota language to say goodbye."

The talking is done now. Lloyd from the back of the room strums into "The Great Speckled Bird."

> What a beautiful thought I am thinking
> Concerning a Great Speckled Bird
> Remember her name is recorded
> On the pages of God's Holy Word.

Everyone slowly files out. Many stand out front smoking. The sky is blue, the temperature about seventy, the wind is down. It is a good day for a burying. A color guard of veterans is forming, all Sioux, and they stand with rifles at the ready and two chiefs' staffs with feathers arching over the doorway.

I'll be joyful if scared to meet Him
On the back of the Great Speckled Bird.

The sounds are very low now, a flutter of words like a breeze faintly playing across the front of the funeral parlor. Pat announces there'll be a lunch at the meeting hall after the burial. Rev. Bear's Heart nods and takes a deep drag on his smoke. Iron Cloud Two Dogs look on, her chiseled brown face serene. The pickups and cars form a line, the coffin is loaded into the hearse, and we lurch forward and cross the bridges over Lake Oahe into Lakota ground.

> *I have forsaken mine house,*
> *I have left mine heritage;*
> *I have given the dearly beloved of my soul*
> *into the hand of her enemies.*
> *Mine heritage is unto to me*
> *as a lion in the forest;*
> *It crieth out against me:*
> *therefore have I hated it.*
> *Mine heritage is unto me as a speckled bird . . .*
> *Come ye, assemble all the beasts of the field,*
> *come to devour.*
> *—Jeremiah 12:7–9, King James Version*

We are standing on a grassy knoll in St. Bede's Cemetery. A short ways off is Rattlesnake Butte, a holy place of visions. Below it snakes Oak Creek, and along Oak Creek Robert Sundance had his first taste of delirium tremens. The honor guard fires its salvo. A huge pile of dirt is heaped by the hole, the coffin rides on props over the void. All the flowers have been tossed on a dirt mound, Flower Mountain. The big drum is beating, four men circle it, feathers trail from its sides. Christ hangs nearby. He is white plaster on a dark wooden cross. The thump of the drum pounds against Him. *("Sundance was a prompt person.")*

Joe Walker, a traditional man, stands by the grave with a fist full of big feathers. He faces each of the four directions—boom! boom! boom! boom!

(The magic numbers are nine and four. He cannot say why this is so.)

"Watch over and guide him," Joe Walker says, "in his journey to the Third World, Grandfather."

(Hot, cold, nine, four, buffalo. It is the way of power. He is a Lakota and these are the things he says as the red dice tumble down the green table in the tired casino.)

"And," Joe Walker continues, "Grandmother the Earth, forgive him." And then he breaks into the Lord's Prayer. You want authentic? I have a hundred blooded witnesses to authentic. It has been a long road since Little Bighorn and Wounded Knee I and Wounded Knee II and the survivors have a right to their say and they are saying it now on a bluff above Lake Oahe in a light summer breeze as I scratch words down on a notepad and they watch me make my marks.

The drums fall still. It is over.

Except for the buffalo man. He steps forward, brings greeting from the bands at Cheyenne River. He says the first time he met Robert Sundance "I knew he was a great man."

That's it.

The coffin sinks into the ground, the mourners file past the mountain of flowers, pluck blossoms, and toss them down. Patty Ann, Sundance's niece, picks the last bloom, a long-stemmed red rose. It flutters from her hand and

lands silently on the center of the box. The driver and I
end it. We each clutch a fistful of dirt, the sods thumping
as Robert Sundance's final drumbeat.

(The way to place a wager is very simple.

*"You must see the number in your mind before the dice
are rolled," Robert Sundance explains.)*

I am eating lunch next to the buffalo man from Cheyenne River. The food is simple—a ham sandwich, potato
chips, a Coke, some berries for dessert. The man speaks
softly. Like many Sioux, there has been a past to deal
with—he has done time in the joint. One man at the
funeral had a warrant out on him for manslaughter,
he killed someone with his bare hands.

I ask, "How many buffalo do you have now?"

"Seven hundred."

"How many do you figure you'll need to have the
proper-sized herd?"

"Fifty million."

(The numbers today are nine and four.

The buffalo are coming back.

The table is.)

He does not manage this herd, he refuses to let them be
dehorned, castrated, artificially inseminated. He wants
them to have their culture, to work out their way of
doing and being.

"You know Indian culture was based on buffalo culture. The families organizing into bands, the bands in
tribes or herds. They taught us."

For the moment, he wants 5,000 buffalo on one hundred thousand acres. After that he wants 100,000 buffalo. After that . . .

"There are people trying to make this a business. The
whites want to organize it, to put buffalo in feedlots so

they'll be more tender. That will lead us right back where we started."

"Are they dangerous to work with?" I ask.

"Not unless you are in a place you should not be. They are very smart, they get to know you. They watch you. And they remember what you do."

"Have they ever broken out?"

"All the time." And then he pauses and smiles. "On one side they are only contained by the river. They swam the river. It is a mile wide."

He is alert to the virtues of buffalo, to the fact that they can take the winters, can eat almost anything, can handle thirst. That their meat has less fat, that they thrive on this ground. He is building something bigger than a herd, bigger than a tribal business peddling meat, hides, skulls, and bones. He is building a biological bomb out on the Great Plains. The buffalo will keep breeding and growing and growing, they will teach the people, they will show them how to organize, they will lead them back into the country.

"You know, I was going to say something at the burial but I did not. I was going to say that when a storm hits this country, the cattle all turn their asses toward. The buffalo stand with their faces into the wind."

He is a very soft-spoken man. He tells me it is a grassroots kind of thing. He says if the grassroots don't go along with him it doesn't matter. And if they do go along with him and they are opposed by somebody or something or some force, well then, the opposition won't matter. He says you have to let it play out, be loose, be determined. But be loose.

(He once told me, "If I leave with money, then when I get home I think I could have bet that money and have been

rich. I could have stayed and played and won big. So the money does not feel good if you take it home because you always think of what could have been if you had acted.")

Nine.

Four.

Buffalo.

N O T E S

on the

S e x u a l   L i f e

o f   O r c h i d s

Monsieur A. Pouyanne studied the orchids for twenty years. But he told no one what he suspected, "pseudo-copulation." He worried what people would think if he published the fact that insects are fucking flowers. Beating their meat, as it were, pointlessly. The whole thing smacked of those sex dolls advertised in certain magazines, the inflatable dummies that men buy and fornicate with as a substitute for actual women. He tested and tested and tested. If the labellum, the sexual dummy, were held upside down, the males came near but did not land. If he placed a bunch of the sexual dummies under, say, a newspaper, and the scent, that sexual scent, wafted off, male wasps began to appear and seemed to search for their lovers. But eventually, he nailed down the evidence, published it, and now the whole world knows of this, well, bizarre circumstance, this *phony fucking, this unseemly thing. Not that anyone seems to pay much notice. It is almost as if the hammer orchids do not exist, and the sexual dummies do not exist. It is as if it were all invisible, a fact, an act, a history, that everyone pretends never really happened.*

exit interview

The spiders remain motionless on the wall as I sprawl on the sofa across from the smoldering mesquite fire. Winter is ending here and soon the Sierra Madre will cease to be merely warm and become hot again. Last night everyone got drunk, it was the end of the five-and-a-half-day workweek, and no man will be sober until Monday morning. I could hear singing in the calle, the sound of horses' hooves on the cobbles. I have not budged.

What have I learned? That the land is good, bad, and indifferent but this never matters because it is all we have or ever can have. That people vary except in one fact—they are all coming out of an illness now, a fevered delirium that almost killed us and everything around us. That I am a coward and must learn to be brave. That I am cold and diminished and must learn to warm and larger. That we have lost the war and for this fact should be grateful. That we have been drunk so long we think the orchids are a native species. That my faith must be like a mustard seed, that no great speckled bird of prey can win if I have faith. That I can never be forgiven and should not look for such cheap salves, that the coffee still is black, bitter, and stabs me awake with the dawn. That she was right, she just didn't see the point of arguing. That Robert Sundance is dead and I am alive and . . .

You do a good job.

Cradled in my lap is a tattered volume I bought on impulse in a used-book store: Harrison Salisbury's *The 900 Days: The Siege of Leningrad.* I am on page 512 when I slam to a halt. An empty wine bottle lies beside me on the floor—I can sense Sundance's disapproval as he rides the wind.

In the book it is almost spring in 1942 and more than a half million people have been evacuated from Leningrad and a helluva lot more have starved to death—about ten times the slaughter engineered by Americans at Hiroshima. In Hiroshima charred bodies of one sex floated down the river on their backs and the other on their stomachs but I can never remember which sex floated in which position. The Germans wait patiently outside the city in the snows and let weather, Joseph Stalin, and those schedules no doubt monitored by fine Teutonic cuckoo clocks slowly strangle the city of Peter to death. B. I. Zagursky has an idea. He is stuck in bed, as are a lot of his fellow citizens, too weakened by hunger to move. But he realizes that no one has held a concert in the city since December and he thinks that the cultural capital of Russia must make this gesture. Rounding up the orchestra is a bit of a problem: twenty-seven members have died from hunger in the past few months. Just about everyone else is like him—too weak to get out of bed.

But eight people can still play, after a fashion. Volunteers are recruited and by the end of March thirty-odd musicians begin to rehearse. At seven P.M. on April 5, the performance starts—Glazunov's *Triumphal Overture,* dribs and drabs from *Swan Lake,* the overture to *Ruslan and Ludmilla.* It does not go on long. The musicians lack the strength. The concert is not a wall of sound, but more a defiant whisper against the long night.

In an hour or two it will be dawn and I will open the shutters and watch the fingers of light stroke the Sierra Madre. Sundance, where in the hell are you? *Mi sunka la.* I've got one of the burial quilts—the family insisted, honest—the one with a big fucking eagle soaring above a field of patchwork.

What do you think of your blue-eyed boy now Mr. Death?

The spiders probably will remain motionless. They can sit in one place hour after hour, day after day, and then an insect will crawl nearby and they . . . I have never been able to really see them cross the distance between their waiting place and their prey. It is just a blur ending in the kill.

I think of the musicians tottering with their instruments as they struggle to make that vital concert in a city where human flesh is being sold in the black markets and where the war will go on and on for three more hard years. The music always matters and that is what must never be forgotten. Only the siege has taken far longer than 900 days. But who could know that grim fact until now when it may be finally ending?

I'm sure the cannons mattered, and the canons, and the trenches, and the five-year plans and the bureaus and the headquarters staff and the leaders and The Leader. But not as much as the music, not ever. In one more year in the dead of winter the Soviet Army will be moving on Stalingrad and seem eager to slaughter a trapped German Army. And as the breath of death laps out hungrily that

December, a German soldier will sit at a grand piano that has been hauled out into the street and he will play and play as his last hours lurch toward him.

It always seems to be the music that drives us on to any hope of our better selves.

They're floating by, some on their backs, some on their bellies. They're closing in with curved scalping knives, General. They're drinking tokay, they're begging for money for their friend Pinky, who, you know, is in the can. And they say they can't change the tune, or they say they never listen to music, or they say . . .

And she is saying in Spanish, "Do you think this is a dream?"

(The old man says that when a horse is gentle broke the horse works with you but when you simply break a horse, you work the horse. The old man sits in front of his trailer at dusk shooting coyotes that have foolishly forgotten their fear.)

"If destruction be our lot, we must ourselves be its author and finisher. As a nation of freemen, we must live through all time, or die by suicide."

It is time for some killing in the orchid garden.

"I've often wondered what became of that Swede woman. She was something. I mean to tell you she was the best piece of ass I ever had."

And then he shuts up and there were these beads of spittle on his old lips.

"Grandmother the Earth, forgive him."

Ink Man, put this down straight on your paper.

Two cops ride by on horses. Their badges shine on their blue uniforms and they wear blue cowboy hats. They have no medicine.

"When I take a stand," he snorts as he leans into my face, "I do not back down."

I have visited the future. She lives a mile or two away in a cheap cathouse.

"I survived being knifed, being shot," he says (he sounds as if he is raving), "yeah, I survived the cholera, those years of alcoholism when I was helpless and now I've got this . . . cancer, yeah, and I didn't survive all those other things for this cancer. And I see other guys running around and they've never done anything for anybody and they're healthy and I think it is not fair."

"What would you like me to do?"

And I say, yes.

Just that.

Yes.

Imagine the problem has never been physical.

I sinned in a way I never knew before was possible.

She will be gentle with me the first few times and then I will remember who I am . . .

She travels in a litter protected by shades made of fine linen, crosses a river by canoe . . .

Blue teeth glowing in the dark.

Yes.

Jeremiah was a bullfrog
He was a good friend of mine.
Never understood a single word he said
But I helped him drink his wine
And he always had some mighty fine wine.
Singing joy to the world
All the boys and girls now.
Joy to the fishes in the deep blue sea
Joy to you and me.

—Hoyt Axton, "Joy to the World"

trail guides

Sherwood Anderson, *Poor White,* New Directions, New York, 1993 [1920].

John Baker, *The Peregrine,* University of Idaho Press, Moscow, Idaho, 1967.

Geoffrey Barraclough, editor, *The Times Atlas of World History,* Hammond, Inc., Maplewood, New Jersey, 1978.

Fyodor Dostoevsky, *Notes from Underground,* (translated by Richard Pevear and Larissa Volokhonsky), Alfred A. Knopf, New York, 1993.

Carole Gallagher, *American Ground Zero: The Secret Nuclear War,* Random House, New York, 1994.

Richard Harris, *Freedom Spent: Tales of Tyranny in America,* Little, Brown & Co., New York, 1976.

Humphrey Jennings, *Pandaemonium: The Coming of the Machine as Seen by Contemporary Observers, 1660–1886,* Free Press, New York, 1985.

Edward Lazarus, *Black Hills White Justice: The Sioux Nation Versus the United States, 1775 to the Present,* HarperCollins, New York, 1991.

Nunca Más: The Report of the Argentine National Commission on the Disappeared, Farrar, Straus & Giroux, New York, in association with the Index on Censorship, London, 1986.

Clyde Edwin Petit, *The Experts,* Lyle Stuart, Inc., Secaucus, New Jersey, 1975.

John Reed, *Insurgent Mexico,* International Publishers, New York, 1969 [July 3, 1914].

Tina Rosenberg, *Children of Cain: Violence and the Violent in Latin America,* Penguin Books, New York, 1991.

Frederick W. Turner, *Beyond Geography,* Rutgers University Press, New Brunswick, New Jersey, 1983.

Thorstein Veblen, *The Instinct of Workmanship,* Augustus M. Kelley Publishers, 1964 [1918].

Ronald Wright, *Stolen Continents: The "New World" Through Indian Eyes,* Houghton Mifflin Company, Boston, 1992.

past-due bills

Let me say that no one works alone who does real work. Despite the increasing barbarism of our society, most people are still kind, and a host of friends have nurtured and shaped this book even though they have never read a word of it. A lot of the people who have helped me and comforted me would prefer, for reasons of taste or police files, not to be mentioned in any association with my name or my work. I can understand this desire.

I could not have done this book without Ruth Fecych, though I suspect the experience has made her legally clinical (don't worry, Ruth, I'll send a postcard to your ward from time to time when my cruise ship docks). It's a great comfort to have an editor who tells you that you are full of shit and then is kindly enough to suggest possible remedies. Naturally, it is not her fault if I have failed to take my medicine in a timely and responsible fashion.

I'd also like to thank Tim Schaffner, my agent, who woke up one day and decided to find a different line of work. He never complained about the unseemly manuscripts I would leave at his door like scat. And we never had a contract. Or a disagreement. If you think this is a common experience, ask around. I wish him well in his new life. Also, I would like to extend my apologies to his assistant, Jennifer Powers, who (I believe after dealing with me) decided to seek honest work and is now in the music business.

The matter of refuge must be addressed. Chris and Meg Clarke took me in when I was on the run and about out of gas (leaded), planted me in a house in a deserted valley, and gave me the keys. Naturally, the doors can't be locked but the thought is what counts. I wrote most of this book there and if they had not taken me in, I don't think I'd be here at all.

Finally, there is the matter of a dead woman who is in this book under the name of Ofelia. She has been underground one year and sixteen days now, and I think of her often and never forget that all she wanted was a taste and she never got it from me or anyone else. They tell me she was of the Third World but I know she is of my world and until things are changed so her life really is a life, she will not rest easy, nor will I.

A B O U T T H E A U T H O R

CHARLES BOWDEN gets his mail in Tucson, Arizona, and lives wherever it is dry. He has dabbled in television and radio, written for newspapers and magazines, and published ten books. He watches with alarm and delight the growing keenness in the eyes of his eight-year-old son. He has been very lucky, with the wind usually at his back and the sun warm on his face. His desert is not godforsaken.

A B O U T   T H E   T Y P E

This book was set in Sabon, a typeface designed by the well-known German typographer Jan Tschichold (1902–74). Sabon's design is based upon the original letter forms of Claude Garamond and was created specifically to be used for three sources: foundry type for hand composition, Linotype, and Monotype. Tschichold named his typeface for the famous Frankfurt typefounder Jacques Sabon, who died in 1580.